Legal Approaches and Corporate Social Responsibility: Towards a Llewellyn's Law-Jobs Approach

From the late 20th Century, a catalogue of high profile disasters and controversies has drawn attention to the changing relationship between corporations and society. This is taking place against the context of globalisation and this change has become the driving force for demands that corporations become socially responsible. Corporate social responsibility (CSR) has therefore emerged as a concept which attempts to encapsulate these demands for social responsibility. Yet at the heart of CSR is the debate about the role and relevance of law.

This book will explore the proposition that CSR is a valid legal enquiry and will suggest a law-jobs approach which offers a potential general analytical perspective for examining such fluid concepts such as CSR in law. This approach is innovative because of the insistence of some users of CSR on placing law outside the parameters of CSR or giving it a very limited role; however, Okoye argues here that the very nature of CSR as seeking legitimacy for corporate power pushes to the fore the question of what role law can play. Law is an essential and important aspect of legitimacy and thus this work explores a legal theoretical approach that holds potential for a legal framework of CSR.

This interdisciplinary book will be of great interest to students and scholars of corporate law and business studies in general.

Adaeze Okoye is a Senior Lecturer at Canterbury Christ Church University, UK.

Routledge Research in Corporate Law

Available titles in this series include:

The Changing Nature of Corporate Social Responsibility
CSR and Development – The Case of Mauritius
Renginee Pillay

Rethinking Corporate Governance in Financial Institutions
Demetra Arsalidou

Board Accountability in Corporate Governance
Andrew Keay

Piercing the Corporate Veil in Latin American Jurisprudence
A comparison with the Anglo-American method
Jose Maria Lezcano

Disqualification of Company Directors
A Comparative Analysis of the Law in the UK, Australia, South Africa, the US and Germany
Jean Jacques du Plessis and Jeanne Nel de Koker

Forthcoming titles in this series include:

Behavioural Risks in Corporate Governance
Regulatory Intervention as a Risk Management Mechanism
Ngozi Vivian Okoye

Revisiting the Corporate Objective
Shareholder Wealth Maximisation vs Stakeholder Model and Its Relevance for China
Min Yan

Legal Approaches and Corporate Social Responsibility

Towards a Llewellyn's Law-Jobs Approach

Adaeze Okoye

Routledge
Taylor & Francis Group
LONDON AND NEW YORK

First published 2017 by Routledge

2 Park Square, Milton Park, Abingdon, Oxfordshire OX14 4RN
52 Vanderbilt Avenue, New York, NY 10017

Routledge is an imprint of the Taylor & Francis Group, an informa business

First issued in paperback 2018

British Library Cataloguing in Publication Data
A catalogue record for this book is available from the British Library

Library of Congress Cataloging in Publication Data
Names: Okoye, Adaeze, author.
Title: Legal approaches and corporate social responsibility : towards a Llewellyn's law-jobs approach / Adaeze Okoye.
Description: Abingdon, Oxon [UK]; New York : Routledge, 2017. |
Series: Routledge research in corporate law | Includes bibliographical references and index.
Identifiers: LCCN 2016029642 | ISBN 9781138838499 (hbk) |
ISBN 9781315734293 (ebk)
Subjects: LCSH: Social responsibility of business—Law and legislation. |
Business enterprises—Law and legislation.
Classification: LCC K1329.5 .O36 2017 | DDC 346/.0664—dc23
LC record available at https://lccn.loc.gov/2016029642

ISBN: 978-1-138-83849-9 (hbk)
ISBN: 978-0-367-07547-7 (pbk)

Typeset in ITC Galliard
by Keystroke, Neville Lodge, Tettenhall, Wolverhampton

Contents

Acknowledgements

This book is partly based on my PhD thesis and refers to some of my previous work including:

'Exploring corporate social responsibility (CSR) from a law jobs perspective' (2012) 12(1) *Contemporary Issues in Law* 20–45

'Theorising CSR as an essentially contested concept, is a definition necessary?' (2009) 89(4) *Journal of Business Ethics* 613–627

'Corporations and corporate governance: what do these concepts mean for multinational corporate power and social responsibility?' (2007) 1(1/2) *International Journal of Liability and Scientific Enquiry* 29–49 (Special Issue on Transparency, Accountability and Liability)

My initial thanks go to the team at Routledge: Katie Carpenter, Mark Sapwell and Olivia Manley.

I am also very grateful for the support and advice received from Professor Charlotte Villiers, Dr Lisa Whitehouse, Dr Mike Varney and Dr Rhuks Ako.

I must also thank Professor Robin Bryant and the Canterbury Christ Church University's School of Law's research and knowledge exchange committee for their research support.

I have had the great opportunity to share my ideas at different fora and I have benefitted immensely from this.

In 2010, I had the opportunity to attend the Harvard Law School, IGLP Workshop. This gave me an excellent platform to exchange ideas at an international level.

I also benefitted from a visiting fellowship at the Institute of Advanced Legal Studies in 2015 and I am very grateful for that opportunity.

I have presented at a number of Society of Legal Scholars conferences as well as conferences on business in society and business ethics. This has given me the opportunity to expose parts of my work to multidisciplinary audiences.

Thanks to friends and colleagues for all their support and advice.

Academic life can be so arduous at times and then it's wonderful to have the support and encouragement of the family. I would like to thank my husband: Obi and my children: Samuel, Andrew and Adaobi. Immense gratitude is also owed to my mum and dad who started me on this path. Not forgetting my darling sisters and brothers: Unoma, Chilota, Nonye, Ifeduba, Ugochukwu and Chijioke. I have indeed benefitted from having a big loving family.

My final thank you is one of faith: To God who makes all things bright and beautiful.

1 Introduction – viewing corporate social responsibility through a legal lens?

> What kind of institutional or legal arrangements will best promote the assumption by businessmen of their social responsibilities? . . . On one thing we can be definite. The unrivalled freedom of economic decision-making for millions of private businessmen which characterizes our free enterprise system, can be justified not if it is good merely for the owners and managers of enterprises, but only if it is good for our entire society.[1]

1.1 Introduction

In the late twentieth and early twenty-first century, a catalogue of high-profile disasters and controversies has drawn attention to the problematic nature of the relationship between large corporations and society. The list would include: the Shell Brent, Spar incident.[2] the Shell crisis in Nigeria,[3] the Bhopal chemical spill,[4] the Exxon Valdez oil spill,[5] the use of slave labour in Burma and the controversial

1 H R Bowen, *Social Responsibilities of the Businessman* (University of Iowa Press, Iowa 2013 (originally published 1953)) 5

2 In 1995 Greenpeace controversially stopped the dumping of the Brent Spar (North Sea) oil storage facility in the ocean. See G Jordan, *Shell, Greenpeace and the Brent Spar* (Palgrave, Basingstoke 2001)

3 Shell's alleged complicity in the deaths of Ogoni human rights activists in 1995 and other human rights violations. See D Wheeler, H Fabig and R Boele, 'Paradoxes and Dilemmas for Stakeholder Responsive Firms in the Extractive Sector: Lessons from the case of Shell and the Ogoni' (2002) 39(3) *Journal of Business Ethics* 297–318 and B Manby, *Shell in Nigeria: Corporate Social Responsibility and the Ogoni Crisis* (Carnegie Council on Ethics and International Affairs, Case 267 published by Institute for the Study of diplomacy, Georgetown University, Washington, DC 2000)

4 In 1984, there was a chemical leak from a storage facility in Bhopal, India that resulted in the death of thousands of people. See R A G Monks and N Minow, *Corporate Governance* (3rd ed., Blackwell, Oxford 2004) 18–19. See also J Woodroffe, 'Regulating Multinational Corporations in a World of Nation States' in M K Addo (ed.), *Human Rights Standards and the Responsibility of Transnationals* (Kluwer International, The Hague 1999) 131–140

5 In 1989 there was an oil tanker accident resulting in one of the largest oil spills ever. This occurred in a region of Alaska which is a habitat for many different species of sea creatures and

working conditions in Asian factories,[6] the baby milk scandals,[7] the conflicts between indigenous peoples, mining communities and mining companies in South American countries, Papua New Guinea and other areas,[8] the pharmaceutical industry and the anti-retroviral drugs crisis,[9] the Enron collapse,[10] the banking crisis of 2008,[11] the BP-Gulf of Mexico oil spill[12], the Rana-Plaza building collapse in Bangladesh[13] and the VW emissions scandal[14] to mention but a few. These incidents and crises have thrown open questions about the impact of corporations, especially multinational corporations, on various aspects and actors within society. Freeland observes that:

fish. The livelihood of the local fishing population was also adversely affected. J A Wiens, *Oil in the Environment: Legacies and Lessons of the Exxon Valdez Oil Spill* (Cambridge University Press, New York 2013)

6 A Ramasastry, 'Corporate Complicity: From Nuremburg to Rangoon, an Examination of Forced Labour Cases and Their Impact on the Liability of MNC' (2002) 20 *Berkeley Journal of International Law* 91–137

7 Most of the controversies and scandals have taken place in developing countries, see the 1970s Nestlé SA scandals and the 2008 China baby milk scandal– C Boyd, 'The Nestlé Infant Formula Controversy and a Strange Web of Business Scandals' (2012) 106 (3) *Journal of Business Ethics* 283–293; 'China's Baby-milk Scandal: Formula for Disaster' *The Economist* 20 September 2008, 57

8 N Yakovleva, *CSR in the Mining Industries* (Ashgate, Aldershot 2005); T E Downing, J Moles, I McIntosh and C Garcia-Downing, *Indigenous Peoples and Mining Encounters: Strategies and Tactics* April 2002 Report No. 57 Mining, Minerals and Sustainable Development (MMSD), Institute for Environment and Development (IIED) and World Business Council for Sustainable Development (WBCSD), 2002 http://pubs.iied.org/pdfs/G00548.pdf

9 World Bank Development Report 2006, *Equity and Development* (International Bank for Reconstruction and Development)), World Bank and Oxford University Press, Washington, DC 2005) 215, E Cloatre, *Pills for the Poorest: An Exploration of TRIPS and Access to Medication in Sub-Saharan Africa* (Palgrave Macmillan, Basingstoke, 2013)

10 The sudden collapse of a large energy corporation, Enron, opened up questions on the ethical aspect of such corporations. Buhr and Grafstrom remark that 'the collapse of ENRON in the autumn of 2001 marked a watershed in the discussion of CSR'. See H Buhr and M Grafstrom, 'The Making of Meaning in the Media, the Case of CSR in the FT' in F Den Hond, F G A De Bakker and P Neergaard, *Managing CSR in Action: Talking, Doing and Measuring* (Ashgate, Aldershot 2007) 15–32, 26

11 R A Posner *A Failure of Capitalism: The Crisis of '08 and the Descent into Depression* (Harvard University Press, Cambridge, MA 2009)

12 C Freeland, 'What's BP's Social Responsibility?' 19 July 2010 Reuters online <http://blogs.reuters.com/chrystia-freeland/2010/07/19/whats-bps-social-responsibility> accessed 3 February 2016

13 This tragedy involving garment factory workers resulted in the death of 1,100 people. For an analysis of the implications in English private law, see A Ruhmkorf, *Corporate Social Responsibility, Private Law and Global Supply Chains* (Edward Elgar, Cheltenham 2015) 213–233

14 The Volkswagen diesel emissions scandal which was revealed in September 2015. VW admitted installing sophisticated software to cheat emissions tests in at least 11 million vehicles. <http://www.theguardian.com/business/2015/dec/10/volkswagen-emissions-scandal-timeline-events> accessed 3 February 2015. See also C M Elson, C K Ferrere and N J Goossen, 'The Bug At Volkswagen: Lessons in Co-Determination, Ownership, and Board Structure' (2015) 27(4) *Journal of Applied Corporate Finance* 36–43

> the Gulf oil spill and the financial crisis have taught us, rather brutally, that the heart of the relationship between business and society doesn't lie with the charitable deeds companies do in their off-hours but whether they are doing in their day jobs in ways that help – or hurt – the rest of us.[15]

Therefore the changing nature of the relationship between large corporations and society in this period has become the driving force for renewed demands that corporations become 'socially responsible'. These demands have come from several sectors of society including non-governmental organisations (NGOs), local communities and academics amongst others.[16] This is because of perceptions of a sustained shift towards private corporate interests through privatisation and the consequential involvement of these private corporate interests in many aspects of public societal life.[17]

Yet corporate social responsibility (CSR) has a longer history, one that can be traced back to the United States where there were debates in the late 1920s and early 1930s about the nature and role of the corporation in the aftermath of the Great Depression. These debates, which took place in various academic and business settings, is exemplified in the writings of Dean Donham of the Harvard Business School in 1927,[18] the seminal debate between Berle and Dodd in the *Harvard Law Review* in 1931 and the Berle and Means publication of the *Modern Corporation and Private Property* in 1932.[19] The Berle-Dodd debate raised fundamental questions about the nature of corporations and whether the business managers could be trustees for a wider group of stakeholders. Dodd's

15 Freeland (n,12)

16 M Haigh and M T Jones, 'The Drivers of CSR: A Critical Review' (2006) 5(2) *The Business Review* 245–251; J Moon and D Vogel, 'CSR, Government and Civil Society' in A Crane, A McWilliams, D Matten, J Moon and D Siegel (eds), *Oxford Handbook on CSR* (Oxford University Press, Oxford 2008) 303–326; G Eweje, 'Multinational Oil Company Initiatives in Nigeria: The Scepticism of Stakeholders in Host Communities' (2007) 49(5/6) *International Journal of Law and Management* 218–235; W Visser, 'CSR in Developing Countries' in A Crane, A McWilliams, D Matten, J Moon and D Siegel (eds), *Oxford Handbook on CSR* (Oxford University Press, Oxford 2008) 473–502

17 This shift is new and recreated rather than a direct transfer: Ruggie asserts that there has been no actual shift, instead firms have created new transnational world of transnational flows that did not exist previously. The key issue on which there is consensus is the significant impact this is having on the lives of individuals in society. J G Ruggie, 'Reconstituting the Global Public Domain – Issues, Actors and Practices' 10(4) *European Journal of International Relations* 499–531, 503

18 W B Donham, 'The Social Significance of the Businessman' (1927) 5(4) *Harvard Business Review* 406–419, 410

19 The debate between Berle and Dodd was published in a series of articles between 1931 and 1932. See A A Berle Jr, 'Corporate Powers as Powers in Trust' (1931) 44 *Harvard Law Review* 1049–1074 ; E M Dodd, 'For Whom are Corporate Managers Trustees?' (1932) 45 *Harvard Law Review* 1145–1163; A A Berle Jr, 'For Whom Corporate Managers are Trustees: A Note' (1932) 45 *Harvard Law Review* 1365–1372. A A Berle and G C Means, *Modern Corporation and Private Property* (Macmillan Co, New York 1933)

point that business had a wider social responsibility, which it already assumed, is also echoed in quotes credited to business leaders of the time.[20]

This view is also echoed in Bowen's on *Social Responsibilities of the Businessman*. Often remembered for its widely cited definition of social responsibility, this book was driven by contextual observations in the United States on the choices facing the businessman in the face of wider questions prompting the re-evaluation of the role of business in society following various failures in the economic system.

Bowen observed that:

> it was of course, a serious delusion to believe that in a laissez-faire system no rules for the individual would be required except those of following one's self-interest ardently and competing vigorously . . . in practice, however, many conflicts arose between individuals and social interests. Some of these conflicts developed because the inability or failure of people to accept moral responsibilities necessary if the system were to achieve acceptable social results. Examples were tendencies of businessmen towards deceptive behaviour . . . failure of the businessman to provide for protection of life, limb and health; the frequent failure of competition and the lack of restraint in imperfectly competitive situations and the frequent failure to recognise the human rights of workers. The earliest tendencies toward social and governmental control of business arose from these failures.[21]

That this observation could still so easily encapsulate the challenge faced in 2015 is quite telling of the progress (or lack thereof) made in this area. Nevertheless Bowen perceptively captures the essence of the problem, which is that corporate 'failures' hint at the many conflicts in the relationship between large corporations and society and thereby trigger demands for CSR. This is reinforced by the dominance of the corporate form of business in the commercial world, with commerce as the mainstay of varied capitalist economies.[22] With the fall of the Soviet Union and the spread of varieties of capitalism, these concerns are now global concerns in ways hitherto unrecognised.[23] CSR thus arose as an attempt

20 A A Berle Jr, 'Corporate Powers as Powers in Trust' (1931) 44(7) *Harvard Law Review* 1049–1074; E M Dodd, 'For Whom are Corporate Managers Trustees?' (1932) 45 *(7) Harvard Law Review* 1145–1163; A A Berle Jr, 'For Whom Corporate Managers are Trustees: A Note' (1932) 45(8) *Harvard Law Review* 1365–1372. Bowen (n. 1) at p. 49 gives quotes from as early as 1929

21 Bowen (n. 1) 17, 21

22 A Keay, *The Corporate Objective* (Edward Elgar, Cheltenham 2011) 2. The lasisez-faire form of capitalism would ideally have the following characteristics – 'private property, free labour, free enterprise, free consumer choice and . . . competition' Bowen (n. 1) 15 The company also allows for easier pooling together of capital, a vital ingredient of capitalism

23 W Elsner and H Hanapi, *Varieties of Capitalism and New Institutional Deals: Regulation, Welfare and the New Economy* (Edward Elgar, Cheltenham 2008)

to encapsulate these demands for social responsibility. It is therefore a concept which could have significant implications for corporations and society.

At the heart of CSR is the debate about its meaning and contestations about the role and relevance of law. The emphasis of several proponents in defining CSR as 'beyond law' may have its roots in reluctance both within law and business to portray CSR as a legal issue. Company law in the main privileges company interests and externalises social interests, within business there is a push for an exclusively 'voluntary' assumption of responsibilities. As early as 1927, Dean Donham observed that lawyers appear to have abdicated their responsibility to society in favour of serving the businessman's interests and thus losing their relevance in solving the complex social problems which face the wider community.[24] He observed that:

> when the lawyer ceased to be advisory leader and sound counsellor and . . . went to work as a servant of the businessman, mainly doing his will, he lost something and the community lost a great deal . . . these conditions exist in the law because the men of real imagination and ability in the legal profession have not, on the whole, retained their social point of view or used their talents to solve the increasingly complex problems of our organised community.[25]

He then proposed that this left the businessman by default in a position where he had to voluntarily assume these social responsibilities as a result of his position 'in control of the mechanisms of production, distribution and finance'.[26]

Nevertheless when one examines the relationship between corporations and society, law is a fundamental aspect of such a relationship. Law is important in structuring and enabling the corporate objective, it is an important tool of government and social control and law is also more sophisticated than the voluntary-mandatory dialogue which pervades CSR.[27] Law can be examined from contemporary social perspectives that will allow it flexibility to achieve certain stated or contextual social functions. The recurring nature of problems which drive for more CSR mean that it is also important to recapture the vital questions about the role of law and legal arrangements in ensuring social responsibilities.

24 W B Donham, 'The Social Significance of the Businessman' (1927) 5(4) *Harvard Business Review* 406–419, 410. Donham was a lawyer himself

25 Ibid.

26 Donham (n. 24) 411

27 Significant writing on the complexity of law and its relationship with CSR is beginning to emerge and this book hopes to contribute to that field. Some other works include: D McBarnet, A. Voiculescu and T Campbell (eds), *The New Corporate Accountability – Corporate Social Responsibility and Law* (Cambridge University Press, Cambridge 2007); N Boeger, R Murray and C Villiers (eds), *Perspectives on Corporate Social Responsibility* (Edward Elgar, Cheltenham 2008); A Beckers, *Enforcing Corporate Social Responsibility Codes: On Global Self-Regulation and National Private Law* (Hart Publishing, Oxford 2015)

Bowen, who is widely viewed as 'the father of modern CSR',[28] considered one of the key CSR questions to be that of institutional and legal arrangements which enable the assumption of social responsibilities.[29] In many ways, it is vital that law recaptures its ability to suggest solutions to complex social problems and proffering legal approaches to CSR could be a good start.

The objective of this book is to reveal that although the meaning of CSR is contested, it has a common reference point which permits the examination of legal approaches and perspectives. This common reference point or central theme can be found in complex social problems arising from questions about the legitimacy of corporate power and this permits the exploration of chosen legal approaches with the potential to structure and influence the external use of power in the relationship between corporations and society. The book then proposes a functional legal approach (the law-jobs approach) which can examine, shape and structure some of the embryonic CSR rules that are developing.

1.2 Context

The changing relationship between corporations and society that has been introduced in this chapter must be placed against the context of globalisation.[30] Globalisation places emphasis on a world without borders, with the aim of achieving record levels of global 'interconnectedness'.[31] The emphasis has been on persuading more states to pursue 'good'[32] economic governance, 'based on the precepts of macroeconomic stability, liberalization of markets and privatization

28 A B Carroll, 'Corporate Social Responsibility: Evolution of a Definitional Construct'(1999) 38(3) *Business and Society* 268–295

29 Bowen (n. 1) 5

30 I have chosen to refer to these business organisations as corporations but this term is used interchangeably with companies. For more on the globalised context, see A G Scherer and G Palazzo, 'Globalisation and Corporate Social Responsibility' in A Crane, A McWilliams, D Matten, J Moon and D Siegel (eds), *The Oxford Handbook of CSR* (Oxford University Press, New York 2008) 413–431, where they point out that with globalisation there should be a paradigm shift in the CSR debate as a different scenario applies. A global framework that is fragile and incomplete

31 Gidden supplies a good definition of globalisation, describing it as 'the intensification of worldwide social relations, which link distant localities in such a way that local happenings are shaped by events occurring many miles away and vice- versa', A Giddens, *The Consequences of Modernity* (Stanford University Press, Stanford, CT 1991) 64. There is a dialectic nature to globalisation that involves both simultaneous and contradictory effects. An indicative list on the topic includes: D Held and A McGrew (eds), *The Global Transformations Reader* (2nd ed., Polity Press, Cambridge 2003); D Held and A McGrew, *Governing Globalization: Power, Authority and Global Governance* (Polity Press, Cambridge 2002); J A Scholte, *Globalization: A Critical Introduction* (2nd ed., Palgrave Macmillan, Basingstoke 2005); J H Dunning (ed.), Government, Globalisation and International Business (Oxford University Press, Oxford 1997); A M Taylor and J G Williamson (eds), *Globalisation in Historical Perspective* (University of Chicago Press, Chicago 2003)

32 'Good' refers to the successful adoption of market economy as an economic model

of economic activity'.[33] This represents a capitalist approach and has resulted in the expansion of markets and the private sector. The focus has been on the protection of foreign investment through principles such as the principle of national treatment. This principle makes it possible for corporations to establish business in almost any state without hindrance, unless the host country imposes similar restrictions on its own corporations.[34] Cutler points out that 'forces of globalisation and the privatisation and deregulation of industries, sectors, commodities and services are transforming authority relations locally and globally'.[35]

This trend of global integration has been intense, with 'the intensification of world-wide global relations'[36] and events, but also varied, with uneven benefits, significant tensions and contradictions.[37] The opening up of markets has been of immense benefit to multinational corporations (MNCs).[38] It has resulted in 'globalisation of the production of goods and services as well as of financial markets'[39] thereby projecting MNCs onto the global stage as international actors. MNCs can be defined as large corporations which control operations or income-generating assets in more than one country.[40] This control and the resulting revenues for the corporate group have led to claims that corporations possess more economic power than certain states.[41] This has also meant that the private decisions of business regarding questions of investment can affect whole communities as well as states. This 'ability to affect' has resulted in countervailing demands for corporations to take on social responsibility. Lydenberg proposes the current dilemma as follows

> Assets and power around the world have shifted from governments to private sector on a tremendous scale, with this shift has come expectations of great benefits to society. But simultaneously business scandals, financial meltdowns, global environmental and health care crises and persistent poverty casts doubt on business ability to deliver on its promises in meaningful ways. It can be

33 United Nations Development Programme (UNDP) Human Development Report (HDR) *Millennium Development Goals, a Compact to End World Poverty* (Oxford University Press, Oxford 2003) 16

34 *Corporate Social Responsibility and Development: Towards a New Agenda?* Report of the United Nations Research Institute for Social Development (UNRISD) Conference 17–18 November 2003, Geneva at 19

35 A C Cutler, *Private Power and Global Authority- Transnational Merchant Law in the Global Political Economy* (Cambridge University Press, Cambridge 2003) 19–20

36 A Giddens, *Sociology* (Polity Press, Cambridge 1990) 64

37 B D Santos, *Towards a New Legal Common Sense* (2nd ed., Butterworth, Cambridge 2002) 177

38 Jones, a leading business historian, points out that multinationals became the leading driver of the integration of the global economy. See G Jones, *Multinationals and Global Capitalism-from the Nineteenth to the Twenty-first Century* (Oxford University Press, Oxford 2005) at 38

39 Santos (n. 37) 178

40 Jones (n. 38) 5

41 The UNDP HDR 1999, *Globalisation with a Human Face* (Oxford University Press, Oxford 1999)

legitimately asked: are corporations really serving a public good, or are they robbing the public blind?[42]

Santos points to a major dichotomy within globalisation: on the one hand, the '*globalized localism*' which is when a local phenomenon is globalised, for example the worldwide spread of the MNC and, on the other hand, '*localized globalism*' which involves the altering of local conditions to respond to transnational imperatives, for example depletion of resources to pay for debt.[43] This can also be characterised by the '*home*' versus '*host*' state dichotomy in the global economy which creates tensions, regulatory gaps and different interests.[44]

The dissatisfaction with the unevenness of globalisation and the inability of the global spread of capitalism to present an adequate social response to effects of misuse of corporate power continue to drive questions about the social responsibility of corporations. This view is reflected in Dean Donham's telling statement that 'the only way to defend capitalism is through leadership that accepts social responsibility and meets the sound needs of the great majority of our people'.[45]

While Donham's concern was for the American people, it is now a global concern with the spread of capitalism. This is captured in global terms by Kofi Annan's call at Davos for business leaders to give 'a human face to global markets'.[46] Annan cited the lessons learnt from the Great Depression and challenged corporations globally specifically asking for 'a set of core values in the areas of human rights, labour standards and environmental practices'.[47]

The changing nature of the relationship hinges on increasing corporate power and its ability to significantly affect society. The disasters and incidents also draw attention to the inter-linkages that exist in modern society, inter-linkages fostered by globalisation. While some writers argue that corporate power is perceived rather than real and that the measurement of revenues of MNCs against gross domestic product (GDP) of states are inadequate,[48] it is rather difficult to deny that states are, at worst, unable and, at best, unwilling to strictly regulate the large

42 S Lydenberg, *Corporations and the Public Interest: Guiding the Invisible Hand* (Berrett-Koehler Publishers, San Francisco 2005) 9

43 Santos (n. 37) 179

44 S Picciotto, 'Rights, Responsibilities and Regulation of International Business' in F Beveridge (ed.) *Globalisation and International Investment* (Ashgate, Aldershot 2005) 177–198

45 This was reported in the Dodd article (n. 18) 1155–1156

46 'Globalisation is a fact of life. But I believe we have underestimated its fragility. The problem is this. The spread of markets outpaces the ability of societies and their political systems to adjust to them . . . History teaches us that such an imbalance between the economic, social and political realms can never be sustained for very long.' The address of the UN Secretary-General Kofi Annan to the World Economic Forum in Davos 31 January 1999 <http://www.un.org/press/en/1999/19990201.sgsm6881.html> accessed 2 February 2016

47 Ibid.

48 J Tullberg, 'Illusions of Corporate Power: Revisiting the Relative Power of Corporations and Governments' (2004) 52 *Journal of Business Ethics* 325–333, 325

MNCs.[49] This leaves the responsibility of corporations for their impact or negative effect on society in a vacuum.

Bowen defined the social responsibilities of the businessman as 'the obligations of businessmen . . . to pursue those policies, to make those decisions or to follow those lines of action which are desirable in terms of the objectives and values of our society'.[50] This definition instigates the shift of focus to 'what' business can do.[51] This also partially explains how CSR has come to symbolise an all-encompassing term for *all* questions about the nature of the relationship between corporations and society as business points out various lines of action of their own accord which they propose are desirable for society. Yet through this CSR has provided fertile ground for debates on the nature of the relationship between corporations and society and all issues that have arisen from this.[52] This relationship between corporations and society is a multifaceted one, with several dimensions and the potential to change over time.

The relative nature of the relationships within CSR has resulted in other attempts to define CSR so as to satisfy the various objectives of a particular viewpoint within distinct fields in society such as management studies, economics, political science and law. Along these lines, Windsor defines CSR as 'any concept concerning how managers should handle public policy and social issues',[53] while Werther Jr and Chandler contend that the significance of CSR is directly related to the value of the firm's global brand,[54] therefore making it a marketing issue. Marrewijk indicates that CSR has been adapted to management studies, marketing, reporting and accounting; each aligning CSR to its specific situations and challenges.[55]

49 This has been exemplified more recently in the failure in 2004 of the UN Human Rights Commission to pass the Norms on the Responsibilities of Transnational Corporations and other Business Enterprise with regard to Human Rights (The Draft Norms). This would have been a unique instrument because it would have extended international regulation to non-state actors and framed the responsibilities in mandatory terms with mechanisms for implementation and enforcement. E/CN.4/SUB.2/2003/12 (2003) See also A De Jonge, *Transnational Corporations and International Law: Accountability in the Global Business Environment* (Edward Elgar, Cheltenham 2011) 34–37

50 Bowen (n. 1) 6: he further states that 'This definition does not imply that businessmen as members of society lack the right to criticise the values accepted in society and to work to their improvement. Indeed in view of their great power and influence, they may well have an obligation to do so'

51 Bowen points out that 'the term doctrine of social responsibility refers to the idea now widely expressed, that the voluntary assumption of social responsibility by businessmen is, or might be, a practicable means towards ameliorating economic problems and attaining more fully the economic goals we seek', Bowen (n. 1) 6

52 This is also because there were no direct channels of communication between corporations and their contextual society except through the state, its laws and regulation

53 D Windsor, 'Corporate Social Responsibility – Three Key Approaches' (2006) 43(1) *Journal of Management Studies* 93–114, 93

54 W B Werther Jr and D Chandler, 'Strategic CSR as a Global Brand Insurance' (2005) 48(4) *Business Horizons* 317–324

55 M V Marrewijk 'Concepts and Definitions of CSR and Corporate Sustainability: Between Agency and Communion' (2003) 44 *Journal of Business Ethics* 95–105,96

The popularity of CSR is also driven to a large extent by the changes in the dynamics of societal relations, through globalisation of markets, globalisation of communications technology, mobile communication and the internet and global exchange of knowledge, information and ideology.[56] In spite of this flexibility within CSR, it has resulted in a situation where CSR is quickly becoming all things to all men. While the flexibility within CSR is necessary because it addresses the relationship between two dynamic groups (society and corporations), nonetheless the lack of a common reference point hampers progress.

Progress in this sense refers to the difficulty in identifying and achieving purposes that triggered CSR in the first place. MNCs that claim to have adopted CSR practice are nevertheless accused of abuses of human rights, environmental rights, labour rights or complicity in corruption.[57] It has been identified that the lack of a settled definition and the 'subsequent diversity and overlap in terminology, definitions and conceptual models hampers academic debate and on-going research'.[58] In another sense this prolonged battle to find expression for several viewpoints and issues within one concept has resulted in a contested concept with doubtful practical value. CSR may not be amenable to a 'fixed universal definition'[59] as it has been asserted that the notion of what is socially responsible is driven by contemporary needs and concerns which cannot be pinned down in precise unchanging terms.[60]

What is important is to identify a common reference point within CSR. This is because CSR attempts to grapple with many important and crucial issues in today's society. Frederick points to some ideas seeking recognition through the CSR doctrine. They include questions about the corporate manager's role in society, the challenge of balancing competing claims to corporate resources and philanthropy.[61] In addition to this are calls for social justice represented in appeals

56 M McIntosh, R Thomas, D Leipziger and G Coleman, *Living Corporate Citizenship* (Pearson Education Ltd, Harlow 2003) 15

57 C Villiers, 'Corporate law, corporate power and corporate social responsibility' in N Boeger, R Murray and C Villiers (eds), *Perspectives on Corporate Social Responsibility* (Edward Elgar, Cheltenham 2008) 85–112, 86; N Klien, *No Logo* (Knopf, Toronto 2000); D Korten, *When Corporations Rule the World* (Berret-Koehler Publishers Inc, San Francisco 2000); J Bakan, *The Pathological Pursuit of Profit and Power* (Constable, London 2005); N Hertz, *The Silent Takeover: Global Capitalism and the Death of Democracy* (Arrow Books, London 2001); Lydenberg (n. 27). Even in terms of the proactive use of MNC capacity in the area of development, the utility of CSR is doubtful: see J G Frynas, 'The False Developmental Promise of CSR: Evidence of Multinational Oil Companies' (2005) 81(3) *International Affairs* 581–598

58 Marrewijk (n. 55)

59 M Kerr, R Janda and C Pitts, *Corporate Social Responsibility – A Legal Analysis* (LexisNexis, Ontario 2009) 5

60 Ibid.

61 W C Frederick, *Corporation, Be Good! The Story of Corporate Social Responsibility* (Dog Ear Publishing, Indianapolis 2006)

for a human face to global markets[62] and the re-examination of the business role in the face of sustainable development as well as the problems of 'financial scandals, human rights violations, environmental side-effects, collaboration with repressive regimes . . .'.[63]

It is in view of the fundamental nature of the issues which CSR is attempting to grapple with, that it is important to establish a common reference point or central theme around which these debates centre. As Horrigan points out:

> deep divisions amongst CSR advocates and critics combined with multiple competing theories and models of corporate social responsibility and governance, sometimes distract attention away from the remarkable degree of common ground that exist on most sides of the CSR debate.[64]

On initial examination, it can be deduced at a general level that the central reference point is that of questions regarding the relationship between business (corporations) and society. However, a further underlying theme has been the demands for the legitimacy of this enhanced corporate power and impact. Legitimacy as a concept can be defined in a number of ways, but a crucial element is the accountability of the exercise of corporate power based on accepted normative standards.[65]

This common reference point of CSR is also important because of the insistence of some users of CSR on placing law outside the parameters of CSR or giving it a very limited role. The nature of CSR as examining questions of the corporation's role in society and thereby seeking legitimacy for corporate power pushes to the fore the question of what role law can play. Law is an essential and important aspect of legitimacy and it also frames and empowers corporations but it is capable of being utilised as an instrument for societal organisation and expression. Law can be pluralistic embracing more contemporary global concepts such as CSR. The exploration of other conceptions of law applied to CSR will reveal more of law's ability to drive progress towards CSR's legitimacy core.

62 Annan (n. 46)

63 G Palazzo and A G Scherer, 'Corporate Legitimacy as Deliberation: A Communicative Framework' (2006) 66 *Journal of Business Ethics* 71–88, 71

64 B. Horrigan, *Corporate Social Responsibility in the 21st Century: Debates, Models and Practices Across Government, Law and Business* (Edward Elgar, Cheltenham 2010) 7

65 Debates about legitimacy abound in politics, constitutional law and international law, often linked to other debates about constitutions, democracy, governance and authority. For example, see: M C Suchman, 'Managing Legitimacy: Strategic and Institutional Approaches' (1995) 20(3) *Academy of Management Review* 571–610, 574; R H Fallon, 'Legitimacy and the Constitution' (2005) 118(6) *Harvard Law Review* 1787–1853. With regard to the corporation, legitimacy debates are often found in the debates about corporate governance, see: P Ireland, 'Company Law and the Myth of Shareholder Ownership' 62(1) *The Modern Law Review* 32–57; E W Orts, 'The Complexity and Legitimacy of Corporate Law' (1993) 50 *Washington and Lee Law Review* 1565–1623

Yet, for the most part, the role of law within CSR is at worst contested[66] and, at best, minimal,[67] therefore it is important to explore law and legal theory to re-emphasise the role of law as expressive (regulatory), facilitative and stimulative.[68] Law can be used as the framework that governs the relationship between groups within society and makes it possible to create frameworks that may facilitate and stimulate the achievement of certain objectives. The contribution of law and legal perspectives within CSR literature has been limited by the lack of a definition of CSR and the obvious attempt to exclude law from the purview of CSR through a plethora of definitions that define CSR actions as actions beyond law.[69]

This limitation may also be self-imposed as law has been slow to develop general jurisprudence applicable to concepts such as CSR driven by globalisation. This is why Kerr points out that although law may first appear uncomfortable within the CSR sphere, it increasingly has to deal with other flexible legal concepts which may not have fixed definitions.[70] Therefore in examining legal approaches to CSR which deal with CSR's common reference point, it is important to examine law itself from both a traditional and non-traditional approach.

Twinning suggests that one of the primary tasks of such analytical general jurisprudence arising from globalisation is the elucidation and construction of concepts that can be used to transcend legal traditions and cultures.[71] When applied to CSR this approach will not focus on prescribing substantive targets to be achieved by CSR in a specific manner, rather it will ensure that procedures and mechanisms are installed addressing vital jobs or functions focused towards the central CSR objective.[72] These mechanisms can then utilise a number of traditional and non-traditional law tools and also be responsive to the changing societal needs and claims.

It is in this vein that Krause suggests that:

> There is reason to believe that the principle of social responsibility operates effectively mainly by providing for principles and mechanisms of social

66 S B Banerjee, *Corporate Social Responsibility: The Good, the Bad and the Ugly* (Cheltenham: Edward Elgar 2007) 16–18

67 One of the best examples of definitions that include law is that of A B Carroll but this identifies law only in its traditional state. law form as one of the factors relevant to CSR, see A B Carroll 'Corporate Social Responsibility – Evolution of a Definitional Construct' (1999) 38(3) *Business and Society* 268–295

68 G Teubner, 'Corporate Fiduciary Duties and Their Beneficiaries: A Functional Approach to the Legal Institutionalisation of Corporate Responsibility' in K J Hopt and G Teubner (eds), *Corporate Governance and Directors Liabilities: Legal, Economic and Sociological Analyses of Corporate Social Responsibility* (De Gruyter, Berlin 1984)149–177, 165

69 Banerjee (n. 66)

70 Kerr *et al.* (n. 59) – this will include sustainable development, precautionary principle, corporate governance, 'best interests of the child'

71 W Twining, *General Jurisprudence: Understanding Law from a Global Perspective* (Cambridge University Press, Cambridge 2009) xix

72 Problems are visible in corporate law, international law and other substantive law analysis for several reasons

> exchange or more generally of social regulation or guidance . . . in short social responsibility proves to be substantially a problem of principles and means, i.e. mechanisms and institutions required to build up and to guide social interactions within society.[73]

The context reveals the lack of an accepted definition of CSR and contestations about the role of law.

1.3 Focus

The main focus of the book is therefore to ascertain to what extent law and the law-jobs theory can contribute to the concept of CSR, where it is redefined as a legitimising force for corporate power? Therefore in order to effectively examine this question, the book will focus on two sub-questions. First can CSR be redefined to reveal a central theme or common reference point? Second what can chosen legal approaches contribute to this identified common reference point?

For the first aspect, expressions of how to tackle the question of the definition of CSR have taken many forms within the literature.[74] Various definitions of CSR from subjective viewpoints abound.[75] Yet it is apparent that the drivers for CSR stem from the discontent with the status quo in the relationship between

73 D Krause, 'Corporate Social Responsibility: Interests and Goals' in K J Hopt and G Teubner, *Corporate Governance and Directors Liabilities: Legal, Economic and Sociological Analyses of Corporate Social Responsibility* (De Gruyter, Berlin, 1984) 95–121, 96

74 For an overview of several approaches E Garriga and D Mêlé, 'Corporate Social Responsibility Theories: Mapping the Territory' (2004) 53(1–2) *Journal of Business Ethics* 51–71

75 For some CSR is synonymous with virtue. *The Economist* cites CSR as 'the tribute that capitalism everywhere pays to virtue'. 'The Good Company' *The Economist* 22 January 2005, 3 and D Vogel, *The Market for Virtue: The Potential and Limits of Corporate Social Responsibility* (Brookings Institution, Washington, DC 2005) 3. These tie in with a philanthropic view of CSR which endorses the voluntary adoption of good business practice. It is in this sense that it appears to be the push for adoption of best practice or morally acceptable behaviour and advocates for a voluntary aspirational adoption of CSR beyond the law. This is a critique raised by C Villiers, 'Corporate law, corporate power and corporate social responsibility' in N Boeger, R Murray and C Villiers (eds), *Perspectives on Corporate Social Responsibility* (Edward Elgar, Cheltenham 2008) 85–112, 86. These practitioners define CSR as 'the continuing commitment by business to behave ethically and contribute to economic development, while improving the quality of life of the work force and their families as well as of the local community and society at large', World Business Council for Sustainable Development 'Corporate Social Responsibility: Meeting Changing Expectations' (March 1999) cited in A Crane, D Matten and L J Spence (eds), *Readings and Cases in a Global Context* (Routledge-Cavendish, Oxford 2008) 6; 'a concept whereby companies integrate social and environmental concerns in their business operations and their interaction with stakeholders on a voluntary basis', Commission of the European Communities, *Green Paper: Promoting a European Framework for Corporate Social Responsibility* Brussels 18 July 2001 COM(2001) 366 Final (now updated and redefined in 2011 – the EU now defines CSR as 'the responsibility of enterprises for their impact on society'), *A Renewed EU Strategy for CSR COM/2011/0681 final*

corporation and society.[76] This contention over definitions of CSR and the consequential insistence of many users on the exclusion of law and binding principles has detracted from progress on the issue of CSR.[77]

Therefore the book in its initial analysis acknowledges this contested nature of CSR, by treating CSR as an essentially contested concept (ECC)[78] and then applies Gallie's ECC thesis to derive an 'exemplar' or common reference point for CSR as a concept. Gallie proposed the foremost thesis on contested concepts. He points out that there are concepts '*the proper use of which inevitably involves endless disputes about their proper uses on the parts of their users*'.[79] These concepts are referred to as essentially contested concepts (ECCs). Nevertheless they derive from an exemplar or common reference point which allows an acknowledgement that contestation proceeds on the same subject. The necessity within CSR is to address the crucial challenges in the relationship between business and society that prompted its emergence in the first instance. This book proposes that this can be done by reconnecting to its central discourse which is about power and its accountability and that this is an area where law has significant relevance.

The aim of this analysis is to establish that although the meaning of CSR is contested, there is a central theme which triggers the demands for social responsibility. The analysis will suggest that this theme can be found in the impact of corporate power and questions about the legitimacy of such power in society. The examination of power and its legitimacy as a central theme for CSR forms the basis to which the chosen legal approaches can then be applied. This question is

76 A situation where some of the corporations with strong CSR claims are nonetheless accused of committing abuses in areas of human rights, environment, labour rights, issues of corruption and other social issues. See: Villiers (n. 75); N Klien, *No Logo* (Knopf, Toronto 2000); D Korten, *When Corporations Rule the World* (Berret-Koehler Publishers Inc, San Francisco 2000); J Bakan, *The Pathological Pursuit of Profit and Power* (Constable, London 2005); N Hertz, *The Silent Takeover: Global Capitalism and the Death of Democracy* (Arrow Books, London 2001); S Lydenberg, *Corporations and the Public Interest: Guiding the Invisible Hand* (Berret-Koehler Publishers Inc, San Francisco 2005)

77 Campbell notes that 'assessing the legitimacy of CSR is seriously hampered by the tangle of overlapping and conflicting terminology within the literature and the many different understanding of the concept among practitioners', T Campbell, 'The Normative Grounding of Corporate Social Responsibility: A Human Rights Approach' in D McBarnet A Voiculescu and T Campbell (eds), *The New Corporate Accountability: Corporate Social Responsibility and the Law* (Cambridge University Press, Cambridge 2007) 529–564, 534. Whitehouse also proposes that 'the apparent failure of CSR to fulfil its potential in remedying the adverse impact of corporate activity is due in part to the failure on the part of its advocates to establish a universally accepted definition of the term and the normative grounding necessary for effective regulation . . .', see L Whitehouse, 'Corporate Social Responsibility, Corporate Citizenship and the Global Compact: A New Approach to Regulating Corporate Social Power' (2003) 3 *Global Social Policy* 299–318, 300

78 See W B Gallie, 'Essentially Contested Concepts' (1958) 56 *Proceedings of the Aristotelian Society* 167–198, reprinted in M. Black (ed.), *The Importance of Language* (Prentice-Hall, Englewood Cliffs, NJ 1962) 121–146

79 Ibid. (emphasis added)

especially important as achieving the desired socially responsible corporate behaviour has been described as one of the greatest global challenges of the twenty-first century.[80] This is because it raises questions about the role of corporations in society at a time when corporate power has a significant impact on global issues. Even corporate failures (collapses) in themselves have been shown to trigger substantial social impact.[81]

For the second aspect, the book proposes that this central theme of legitimacy of corporate power will serve as an ideal basis for re-examining law's role within CSR. This is because law not only frames the corporation and its powers internally but can also structure and influence its external use of power as well. The book focuses on two key legal perspectives to examine how law approaches concepts of this nature. It identifies that law can be approached from a traditional state law centralist approach or from a more flexible pluralistic approach. The work then exemplifies these contrasting approaches by examining the traditional corporate law perspective and the non-traditional pluralistic law-jobs perspective.

By doing this, the book seeks to reveal the potential and limitations of law to structure, influence and legitimise the external use of power in the interactive relationship between corporation and society under the CSR theme. The corporation is a creation of law and its limitations as a corporation are set out in corporate laws. The corporate form is now common to most legal systems of the world.[82] It is seen as 'the most important institution for social wealth creation in capitalist economies'.[83] There are long-standing debates about corporate law's tackling of issues relating to large corporations and their role in society.[84] This would

80 B. Horrigan, *Corporate Social Responsibility in the 21st Century: Debates, Models and Practices Across Government, Law and Business* (Edward Elgar, Cheltenham 2010) 3. CSR is a concept but in line with such emerging concepts from the social sciences it is also a field of study and can be spoken of, in terms of value achievements as well. Banerjee (n. 66) points to it as a field of study in management (p. 5) and as a mini-industry in academia and the business world (p. 1). Jones also agrees when he states that 'the field of corporate responsibility has come a long way in a few years. (in D Leipziger, *The Corporate Responsibility Code Book* (Greenleaf, Sheffield 2003) 13. This is also demonstrated when examining issues of achieving CSR objectives. See J Peloza L Falkenberg, 'The Role of Collaboration in Achieving CSR Objectives' (2009) 51(3) *California Management Review* 95–114

81 Keay (n, 21) 7

82 'The comparative analysis of the domestic law of states belonging to different legal systems shows that individuals may combine their efforts by establishing entities enjoying rights and duties of their own and that such entities may have a separate legal personality', I Seidl-Hohenveldern, *Corporations In and Under International Law* (Grotius Publications Limited, Cambridge 1987) 1

83 Keay (n. 22) 2

84 'A corporate enterprise does not exist simply as a self-serving and self –realizing institution for the unique benefits of its shareholders and workers but rather exists above all, to fulfil a broader role in society.' G Teubner 'Corporate Fiduciary Duties and their beneficiaries: A Functional Approach to the Legal Institutionalisation of Corporate Responsibility in K J Hopt and G Teubner (eds) *Corporate Governance and Directors Liabilities: Legal, Economic and Sociological Analyses of Corporate Social Responsibility* (De Gruyter, Berlin 1984)149–177, 157

include questions linked to debates on corporate theory and which influence its engagement with CSR. Corporate law covers the inward aspects of corporate power through governance of the managers/directors who run the company.[85] The pressure on corporate law is also to formulate an external facing aspect which deals with other affected constituencies. [86]

This is not simply a case of identifying mechanisms for allocating decision-making to more constituencies as this is self-limiting because of the indefinite nature of affected constituencies that may arise in society but law can facilitate and stimulate procedures that allow for meaningful social relationship and utility between corporations and society. Teubner highlights this functional approach, when pointing out that in corporate law 'all three questions – the identification of beneficiaries, the available mechanisms, the role of law – led to the same need for identifying the social functions of CSR in a broader context'.[87] He makes the essential point that CSR serves as a 'decentralised integrative device'[88] and therefore it should draw on the stimulative role of law to design legal structures which strengthen reflexive or responsive mechanisms.[89]

Therefore, these external aspects of law will not only necessarily be prescriptive or definitive substantive rules, rather it could also be functional: highlighting jobs/roles which law can stimulate.[90] Yet as corporate law has inherent limitations in its format, especially its attachment in most Anglo-American and Commonwealth countries to the fundamental objective of profit for the success of the company (shareholders) through strong adherence to utilitarian principles of corporate personality and limited liability,[91] this may mean that external mechanisms will need to be developed outside corporate law. Furthermore while several authors have also explored the utility of various 'add-on' areas of responsibility within international law, contract law and competition law to CSR,[92] they face similar limitations in applying prescriptive substantive laws within CSR because of the fluidity of the concept.

85 J E Parkinson, *Corporate Power and Responsibility: Issues in the Theory of Company Law* (Clarendon Press, Oxford 1995)
86 H Ward 'Corporate Social Responsibility in Law and Policy' in N Boeger, R Murray and C Villiers, *Perspectives on Corporate Social Responsibility* (Edward Elgar, Cheltenham 2008) 8–38
87 Teubner stresses that 'to be sure, this functional conception of CSR needs no a-priori-definition of the substantive goals to be achieved', Teubner (n. 84) 166
88 Ibid. at 162
89 Teubner (n. 84) 165
90 Teubner stresses that 'to be sure, this functional conception of CSR needs no a-priori-definition of the substantive goals to be achieved', Teubner (n. 84) 166
91 P Ireland, 'Limited Liability, Shareholder Rights and the Problem of Corporate Irresponsibility' (2010) 34 *Cambridge Journal of Economics* 837–856, 838–839
92 These include: J A Zerk, *Multinationals and Corporate Social Responsibility – Limitations and Opportunities in International Law* (Cambridge University Press, Cambridge 2006); D McBarnet, A. Voiculescu and T Campbell (eds), *The New Corporate Accountability – Corporate Social Responsibility and Law* (Cambridge University Press, Cambridge 2007)

Therefore this book proposes another legal approach that will be an effective way of analysing and capturing the potential role of law. This involves re-examining a conceptual legal theoretical approach that can then be applied in context. Each context could then build into this approach its own choice of substantive rules. For that reason the work will draw on an effective way of spelling out the relevant role of law in this (corporate-society) relationship highlighted through the legal approach of law-jobs and applies this to CSR. This represents a non-traditional analytical view of law's potential role in CSR. It also represents a shift from questions of 'form' to questions of 'role'.

This approach is drawn from Karl Llewellyn's law-jobs theory.[93] This theory identifies law from a functional perspective and perceives roles for law around the doing of five law-jobs. These are: the disposition of trouble cases; the preventative channelling and the re-orientation of conduct and expectations so as to avoid trouble; the allocation of authority and the arrangement of procedures which legitimise action as authoritative; the net organisation of the group or society as a whole so as to provide direction and incentive; and the use of the juristic method.[94] Twining argues for the possibility of transforming the law-jobs theory into a general jurisprudence.[95] It, in turn, will have possible application to fluid contemporary concepts such as CSR arising in an era of increasing globalisation.

This approach proposes the framing of the external aspect of law and CSR through the analysis of key issues such as dispute resolution, allocation of authority, orientation and channelling of conduct, net organisation and juristic method. The book suggests that such frameworks geared towards the doing of the law-jobs between corporations and society will have the potential to increase accountability and legitimacy within CSR. Overall the aim is to explore the potential of law not yet utilised by corporate law to legitimise corporate power through framing jobs for law within CSR. The rest of this introductory chapter will outline the scope and overview of further chapters.

1.4 Scope

The scope of the book covers some of the significant CSR debates that will be tackled within this work. One of the first issues is that of the meaning of CSR. The problem is encapsulated in Votaw's statement that '*CSR means something*

93 K Llewellyn, 'The Normative, the Legal and the Law Jobs: The Problem of the Juristic Method' (1940) 49 *Yale Law Journal* 1355–1400

94 Ibid. at 1392. It must be noted that the juristic method is not a law-job *per se* but an advocated method for the evaluation, reform and upkeep of the law-jobs. It therefore in essence goes to the doing of the law-jobs

95 Twining (n. 71). I am also grateful to have received from Twining a draft copy of his 2005 paper on 'general jurisprudence' which was published in M Escamilla and M Saavedra, *Law and Justice in a Global Society* (International Association for Philosophy of Law and Social Philosophy, Universidad de Granada, Granada 2005).

but not always the same thing to everybody'.[96] This means that establishing a common reference point of CSR is a precursor to any significant CSR analysis. Establishing such a core is also necessary for the concept and the achieving of any CSR objectives as these contestations have hampered significant results in the context of a concern which has become a global challenge.[97] There is a fundamental reassessment of the way in which society relates to corporations taking place in the difficult context of unprecedented global relations.[98] The complexity of analysis within CSR extends throughout the social sciences and occurs at international, cross-national, national and local levels. The practical drivers of the debate are real-world problems and critical incidents which fuel the questioning of the role of corporations in society.[99] These questions come from various sectors of society, civil society, consumers, investors, governments and academia, and occur at various levels, international, national and local.[100]

This breadth also prompts the second debate which will be addressed, the relevance of legal approaches. This is because one of the common denominators of defining CSR has been to exclude or limit the relevance of law within such an important context.[101] Ward emphasises her frustration at the definitional insistence that CSR is only about voluntary action over and above legally defined minimum standards and points out that this 'consequent separation of "CSR" and corporate accountability serves no one well'.[102] This is also ironic in view of the historical academic roots of CSR as found in a debate between two corporate law professors.[103]

However the problem may also be that law has so far been slow to show its relevance to concepts emerging from globalisation. A major reason for this has been the form of law emerging within such contemporary global concepts as CSR. CSR is dominated by emerging rules which often occur in loose and 'soft' forms and law, at least in its traditional sense, is seen as defined, precise and linked to the state. In light of this, Kerr and others point out that, at first glance, CSR does not appear to fit comfortably within the traditional legal setting because of its constant state of evolution as it tries to remain responsive to contemporary needs and concerns.[104]

96 D Votaw, 'Genius Becomes Rare: A Comment on the Doctrine of Social Responsibility Pt.1' (1972) 15(2) *California Management Review* 25–31, 25 (emphasis in original)
97 Horrigan (n. 80) ix
98 Ibid.
99 I Vaaland and M Heide, 'Managing Corporate Social Responsibility: Lessons from the Oil Industry' (2008) 13(2) *Corporate Communications: An International Journal* 212–225. They point out that the role of critical incidents is crucial to corporations' response to CSR. Yet these incidents are symptomatic of corporations' power to affect and impact lives
100 The complexity of analysis is seen as CSR's capability to be discussed from any angle
101 Banerjee (n. 66)
102 H Ward 'Corporate Social Responsibility in Law and Policy' in N Boeger, R Murray and C Villiers, *Perspectives on Corporate Social Responsibility* (Edward Elgar, Cheltenham, 2008) 8–38
103 Berle-Dodd debate (n. 19)
104 Kerr *et al.* (n. 59)

Nonetheless law, even in its most traditional form, still has an impact on CSR. For example, Ward remarks that company law will necessarily have a very basic impact on CSR as it is law that frames and forms a corporation.[105] There is also a significant range of traditional legal aspects which have implications for CSR, this includes torts, contract, criminal international law, human rights, trade law, tax, accounting, environmental law and so on.[106] Yet law itself embraces more than its traditional form, especially when related to cosmopolitan concepts arising as a result of globalisation, the way in which law is defined captures its role. What is required is a conception of law which is responsive and dynamic and manifests in pluralistic forms. This wider conception may allow for the construction of a legal framework more relevant to CSR action in context. Therefore a key contention in this book is that the way in which law is defined will dictate its role and relevance to important concepts such as CSR. Twining proposes that:

> A reasonably inclusive cosmopolitan discipline of law needs to encompass all levels of relations and of ordering relations, relations between these levels and all important forms of law including supra-state (e.g. international, regional) and non-state law (e.g. religious law, transnational law, chthonic i.e. tradition/custom) and various forms of 'soft law'.[107]

This is one of the key areas which will be explored in seeking insights into the concept of CSR and its relationship with law: the possibility of extending the role of law so that it projects a broader perspective of law as it governs social relations. Selznick points out that:

> To extend the rule of law is to build firmly into the life of society, to make the master ideal of legality a true governor of official conduct. *If this is to come about political and legal theory must lend a hand. It can do so by fashioning concepts and doctrines to bridge the gap between the new social realities and the received legal tradition.*[108]

So when exploring law's role within CSR, some exploration and use of legal theory is relevant if the aim is to gain insights into newer concepts which may help achieve the objective. The chosen conception of law is that of Llewellyn's law-jobs theory which defines law in given relationship such as that between business and society from the viewpoint of its role or jobs. It identifies five jobs law can do in group relationships. These jobs are: dispute resolution and grievance handling; channelling and rechannelling of conduct; allocating authority; net organisation;

105 N Boeger, R Murray and C Villiers (eds), *Perspectives on Corporate Social Responsibility* (Edward Elgar, Cheltenham 2008) 2. This was cited in the Introduction

106 D McBarnet A Voiculescu and T Campbell (eds), *The New Corporate Accountability: Corporate Social Responsibility and the Law* (Cambridge University Press, Cambridge 2007) 2

107 Twining (n. 71) 362 (emphasis added)

108 P Selznick, *Law, Society and Industrial Justice* (Russell Sage Foundation, New York 1969) 35

and the use of the juristic method.[109] This theory is already applied in some analytical public law literature[110] but is not uniquely public law oriented. It can be applied to any legal analysis because it adopts a generalist perspective on the role of law for collective activity in societies. This may be why it has been referred to as 'one of the most comprehensive and rational considerations of the role of law'.[111]

A perceived advantage of this type of analytical application is the ability to move beyond a traditional definition of law to a broader definition that takes cognisance of the changing terrain such as that necessitated by globalisation. Feintuck and Varney point out that 'law-jobs move beyond a narrow technical definition of law into a broader, socially grounded model'[112] The kinds of powers and function envisaged by law-jobs can be found outside the scope of hard law encompassing practices identifying themselves as legal '*despite the absence of the trappings of formal legal form*'.[113]

The transferability of the law-jobs is also a major advantage as it emphasises the 'legal quality' on the basis of role and not form, therefore diversity of regimes is still possible. McCoubrey highlights this perspective by pointing out that:

> granted the diversity of municipal societies, such a functional criterion seems far more soundly based than a demand for institutional convergence with particular forms of Western Urban Industrial societies . . .[114]

There may be pitfalls in pursuing a somewhat functionalist approach because questions of function are relative.[115] This application of the law-jobs does not assert that only law can do these jobs or that law does them best. It just crucially identifies that law can do this in society and opens up room for analytical debate and re-evaluation. This is essential when examining the law and CSR relationship in the current global context.

Nevertheless some suggest that CSR itself is just a corporate response and therefore corporations by design have dominated the discourse of CSR and by choice excluded law. This is the sense in which Shamir speaks of the 'de-radicalisation

109 Llewellyn (n. 93)

110 For example, I Harden and N Lewis, *The Noble Lie: The British Constitution and the Rule of Law* (Routledge, London 1988); M Feintuck and M Varney, *Media Regulation: Public Interest and the Law* (Edinburgh University Press, Edinburgh 2006) N D Lewis, *Law and Governance: The Old Meets New* (Routledge-Cavendish, Oxford 2001)

111 D Longley, *Health Care Constitutions* (Cavendish Publishing, London 1996) 12

112 Feintuck and Varney (n. 110) 33

113 Ibid. at 34 (emphasis added)

114 H McCoubrey, 'Natural Law, Religion and the Development of International Law' in M W Janis and C Evans (eds), *Religion and International Law* (Kluwer/Martinus Nijhoff, Netherlands 1999) 177–190, 178

115 For aspects of this debate, see L Green, 'The Functions of Law' (1998) 12 *Cogito* 117–124, compare K M Ehrenberg, 'Defending the Possibility of a Neutral Functional Theory of Law' 29(1) *Oxford Journal of Legal Studies* 91–113

of CSR'.[116] He analyses various strategic moves of corporations towards shaping the meaning of social responsibility in ways that do not threaten entrenched commercial interests and invest the term with voluntary and self-regulatory meaning.[117] However it is important that law as part of CSR is re-emphasised in a way that allows for space, structure, contestation and limitations. This is why, in response, Rajagopal points out the inability to avoid the use of law in a counter-position because it also provides 'space for resistance'.[118]

He points out that 'there is an increasing sensibility that law is a terrain of contestation between different actors including social movements and states and that a theory of law or adjudication that ignores this fact is inadequate'.[119] It is therefore important to project the conception of law that is capable of being used in counter-position. This conception must involve a broader pluralistic perspective.[120] Therefore law remains essential in this contested arena of CSR as, on the one hand, it can frame and empower corporations and yet, on the other hand, it is also important when seeking to constrain or render such power accountable or legitimate. These arguments provide reasons for a demand of the literature to examine such legal aspects of CSR. This is an area where there is still limited literature, although there has been some notable CSR legal literature in recent years.[121] There are still insufficient books and articles that directly address the aspect of CSR and law.

116 R Shamir 'Corporate Social Responsibility: A Case of Hegemony and Counter-Hegemony' in B De Sousa Santos and C A Rodriguez-Garavito (eds), *Law and Globalisation from Below – Towards a Cosmopolitan Legality* (Cambridge University Press, Cambridge 2005) 92–117, 95

117 R Shamir, 'The De-radicalization of Corporate Social Responsibility' (2004) 30(3) *Critical Sociology* 669–689

118 B Rajagopal, 'Limits of Law in Counter-hegemonic Globalisation: The Indian Supreme Court and the Narmada Valley Struggle' in B De Sousa Santos and C A Rodriguez-Garavito (eds), *Law and Globalisation from Below – Towards a Cosmopolitan Legality* (Cambridge University Press, Cambridge 2005) 183–217, 183. He points out that popular struggles may see law as a force for status quo and domination . . . yet it also provides space for resistance

119 Ibid. This echoes Santos's study on counter-hegemonic social movements, B De Sousa Santos, *Towards a New Legal Common Sense: Law, Globalization and Emancipation* (Butterworths, London 2002)

120 Santos ibid. demonstrates that several forms of law exist in transnationalised or globalised legal relations. In Chapter 5 where he discusses the globalisation of legal relations, he depicts the contrary tensions that all work the legal field: *lex mecatoria*, law of regional integration, transnational factors causing changes in state law, migration laws, laws of groups within the state (indigenous peoples, grass-root movements, NGOs and so on), cosmopolitan law

121 Some of the most notable views have emerged from D McBarnet, A Voiculescu and T Campbell (eds), *The New Corporate Accountability- Corporate Social Responsibility and Law* (Cambridge University Press, Cambridge 2007); N Boeger, R Murray and C Villiers (eds), *Perspectives on Corporate Social Responsibility* (Edward Elgar, Cheltenham 2008); J O'Brien (ed.), *Governing the Corporation* (Wiley, Chichester 2005); I Demirag (ed.), *Corporate Social Responsibility, Accountability and Governance* (Greenleaf, Sheffield 2005); J A Zerk, *Multinationals and Corporate Social Responsibility – Limitations and Opportunities in International Law* (Cambridge University Press, Cambridge 2006); S Tully (ed.), *Research Handbook on Corporate Legal Responsibility* (Edward Elgar, Cheltenham 2005); 20 (n. 58), Horrigan (n. 80)

This suggested law-jobs approach is important because it will recognise the relevance, flexibility and dynamism which is now required of law. It will indicate the possibility of a universal CSR legal theoretical framework that can be adapted in a localised context making it possible to give a tailored response. The book concludes with the basis of this suggestion. The desired outcome is that this analysis will give new insights into this fundamental area that will augment progress on the agenda of achieving greater social responsibility.

The emphasis of this work is on large corporations, specifically MNCs. They are also occasionally referred to as transnational corporations (TNCs) or multinational enterprises (MNEs).[122] CSR analysis can be applied to corporations of all sizes but the demands for responsibility have been mainly directed at MNCs because of their size, structure and globalised nature. MNCs are the largest corporations and they account for 70 per cent of the world's trade and trillions of dollars of foreign direct investment.[123] In this vein, Hopkins points out that:

> because of the often immense size of transnational corporations, decisions about the location of their investments, production and technology not only influence the distribution of factor endowments – notably capital, skilled labour and knowledge – between countries in which they run activities, but they also assume a critical importance for their political and social consequences.[124]

The MNCs or TNCs have been described by the Draft UN Code of Conduct for Transnational Corporations as:

> an enterprise comprising entities in two or more countries regardless of legal form and field of activities of these entities, which operates under a system of decision-making permitting coherent policies and a common strategy through one or more decision-making centres, in which the entities are so linked by ownership or otherwise that one or more may be able to exercise significant influence over the activities of others and in particular share knowledge, resources and responsibility with others.[125]

The MNC is a unique business construct which is fairly modern in origin. However it shares common characteristics with earlier forerunners, the chartered

122 In UN documents, they are often referred to as transnational corporations (TNCs). In this work they will be called MNCs and used interchangeably.

123 M Hopkins, *The Planetary Bargain: Corporate Social Responsibility Matters* (Earthscan, London 2003) 3

124 Ibid.

125 Section 1(a) Draft UN Code of Conduct for Transnational Corporations 23 ILM 626 (1984); G Jones, *Multinationals and Global Capitalism: From the Nineteenth to the Twenty-first Century* (Oxford University Press, Oxford, 2005) 5 – 'A multinational is a firm that controls operations or income-generating assets in more than one country'

trading companies of the sixteenth–eighteenth centuries.[126] The factors common to most definition of MNCs are association and control. This implies that MNCs contain entities which are associated by ownership, often evidenced through direct investment, but in addition the main investing entity (that is, the parent corporation) should be able to exert a significant amount of influence or control on the management of the subsidiary corporation.

Wilkins in her work on MNCs specifies that operations often involve cross-border control, potential for control or at least influence.[127] The World Investment Report defines the parent MNC as an enterprise that controls the assets of other entities in countries other than the home country, usually owning a certain percentage of equity capital stake.[128] The uniqueness of MNCs partially derives from their problematic nature in law. Although they are legal entities, they are not recognised in law as an 'MNC' rather, in a strict legal sense, they are groups of corporations or companies.

Muchlinski indicates the nature of this problem, when he points out that:

> Indeed if one were to look at legal sources alone the multinational enterprises would not exist: all one would find is a series of national companies whose principal shareholder happens to be a foreign company and/or a network of interlocking contracts between entities of different nationalities. No hint of the complex systems of international managerial control, through which the operations of the multinational group are conducted, would be discovered.[129]

This is because corporations are often formed within a single legal system. Once formed and incorporated they gain separate legal personality, a legal feature common to most legal systems.[130] This allows for groups of corporations incorporated in different states, linked together by ownership and control, to retain

126 P Hertner and G Jones, *Multinationals: Theory and History* (Gower Publishing Company, Aldershot 1986) 1

127 M Wilkins, 'European and North American Multinationals 1870–1914: Comparisons and Contrasts' in M Casson (ed.), *Multinational Corporations* (Edward Elgar, Cheltenham 1990) 541

128 UNCTAD World Investment Report (WIR) 2005 *Transnational Corporations and the Internationalization of Research and Development* (United Nations, New York and Geneva 2005) 297. See also J H Dunning, *Multinational Enterprises and the Global Economy* (Addison-Wesley Publishing Ltd, Massachusetts 1993) 3 where he points out that there is no international consensus – he states that the Organisation for Economic Co-operation and Development (OECD) recommends 10 per cent minimum. This is used by the United States, Canada and Australia while Germany and France use 20 per cent and New Zealand 25 per cent. However international usage as evidenced from data used by UNCTAD WIR 2005 at p. 297 shows that 10 per cent is acceptable

129 P T Muchlinski, *Multinational Enterprises and the Law* (Blackwell Publishing, Oxford 1999) lv-lvi

130 I Seidl-Hohenveldern, *Corporations In and Under International Law* (Grotius Publications Ltd, Cambridge 1987) 1

distinct personality under legal rules. This legal *invisibility* has not prevented the corporations from exercising significant influence on society, rather it may have aided the rise and influence of the MNC.[131] This is because of the absence of an international legal framework for MNCs.

Cioffi points out that 'given the absence of a global regulatory framework, the relation of corporate governance to globalisation must be sought at the level of the national political economy and the degree and nature of change viewed cross-nationally'.[132] This cross-national perspective is endorsed within this work because it is also the universality of the corporate vehicle that enables the existence of MNCs.

In his book *Corporations In and Under International Law* Seidl-Hohenveldern states that:

> the comparative analysis of the domestic law of states belonging to different legal systems shows that individuals may combine their efforts by establishing entities enjoying rights and duties of their own and that such entities may have a separate legal personality.[133]

The notion of separate legal personality has become integral to laws around the world and therefore the relationship between MNCs, CSR and law is a vital one for analysis. Indeed these blind spots of law and the insistence on national jurisdictions can be seen as a source of corporate irresponsibility as MNCs exploit the gaps perpetuated by this legal fiction. This forces the issue of alternative flexible legal approaches that may be effective cross-nationally.

A further choice is made in this book, when giving specific examples from MNCs. The choice is to use specific examples from the oil industry in a small portion of the work. This selection is made in view of the MNC sample size under study and the variety of sectors.[134] This choice of the oil MNC examples is also influenced by the assertion that the large oil corporations have been judged as leaders in championing CSR.[135] Utting and Ives, CSR scholars, point out that this

131 Cutler (n. 35) 196

132 J W Cioffi, 'Governing Globalisation: The State, Law and Structural Change in Corporate Governance' (2000) 27(4) *Journal of Law and Society* 572–600, 573

133 Nevertheless there are several types of MNCs. Muchlinski (n. 128) points to structures with contractual linkages, informal alliances, joint ventures and state-owned corporations. Yet the equity-based multi-corporation structure is still the most common. These may be composed in different ways, some examples of which include the Anglo-American pyramid groups, the European transnational mergers and the Japanese *kereitsu*

134 This is also is because there are over 63,000 MNCs with more than 800,000 subsidiaries and numerous linkages of suppliers and distributors across the global value chain. See J G Ruggie, 'Reconstituting the Global Public Domain – Issues, Actors and Practices' (2004) 10(4) *European Journal of International Relations* 499–531, 510

135 P Utting and K Ives, 'The Politics of Corporate Responsibility and the Oil Industry' (2006) 2(1) *St Anthony's International Review* 11–34, 12

overt engagement of large oil corporations with CSR can be judged by their adoption of codes of conduct, reporting practice and interactions with leading CSR institutions.[136] Yet it is an industry that continues to attract new demands, for example, an influential former oil industry CEO recently declared that CSR has failed.[137] Therefore the emphasis is on these corporations as a valid example for ascertaining reactions to the conceptions of CSR in a useful format. This serves the practical purpose of providing a focused group of MNCs to draw examples from.

This choice is also underscored by the significance of this industry. The UNCTAD World Investment Report (WIR) points out oil's critical role for most world economies. It still is the industry which provides basic essential raw materials which are essential to all modern economies.[138] Yet it is an industry which best demonstrates some of the existing global inequalities. This is because there are a significant number of major producers in developing countries and transition economies while the major consumers are mainly in developed countries which rely on imports.[139] Therefore issues of ineffective management of social, environmental and other responsibilities are very vividly demonstrated in the oil industry. The juxtaposition of the capacity of oil corporations and their responsibilities has triggered significant CSR debate.[140]

1.5 Overview of chapters

The book is arranged in eight chapters with Chapter 1 being the introduction.

Chapter 2 examines the meaning of CSR. This is because it is the crucial starting point for this book on CSR and it provides essential analysis through which a central theme or core of CSR is revealed. This chapter begins with the premise that CSR has been defined in a number of ways and with varied emphasis on

136 Ibid.

137 J Browne, *Connect: How Companies Can Succeed by Radically Engaging with Society* (W H Allen, London 2015). Browne is former CEO of BP who championed the notion of BP becoming a 'force for good'. He now appears disillusioned with CSR in its current form. He asserts quite strongly that 'CSR is dead'. He states that 'the connection between business and the world can only thrive if companies integrate societal and environmental issues deeply into their core business strategy and operations'. This view termed radical, illustrates in itself the issues with CSR's meaning as this 'radical view' is remarkably similar to existing CSR definitions – for example, 'a concept whereby companies integrate social and environmental concerns in their business operations and their interaction with stakeholders on a voluntary basis', Commission of the European Communities, *Green Paper: Promoting a European Framework for Corporate Social Responsibility,* Brussels 18 July 2001 COM(2001) 366 Final (now updated and redefined as 'the responsibility of enterprises for their impact on society', *A Renewed EU Strategy for CSR* COM/2011/0681 final)

138 UNCTAD World Investment Report (WIR) 2007 *Transnational Corporation, Extractive Industries and Development* (United Nations, New York and Geneva, 2007) 83

139 Ibid. at 85

140 See Frynas (n. 56)

various issues. The chapter offers a historical overview of the development of CSR as well as an overview of current multiple interpretations of CSR. Then the chapter uses the essentially contested concepts (ECC) theory set out by Gallie and applies this to CSR in order to discover an exemplar or a core which the analysis within the book will address. The core is proposed as the relationship between business and society predicated on questions of legitimacy for corporate power.

Chapter 3 follows on from this discovery of the core of CSR contestation and examines corporate power. The aim of the analysis in this chapter is twofold: first to reveal the varied meanings of power as a concept in this context and then to link this to legitimacy. The analysis illustrates the meaning of corporate power from the perspective of the MNC and identifies crucial areas of capacity and influence. It introduces the issue of legitimacy as a requirement for the exercise of significant corporate power which affects society.

The fourth chapter focuses on the second aspect of the book by examining law, structure and legitimacy. It examines law as a key aspect of legitimacy, especially in view of a conception of legitimacy which accepts accountability as a key aspect. As a result this chapter examines law and regulation as key aspects of legitimacy. The chapter analyses law in its wider pluralistic sense. It examines the interrelationship between law and regulation. It proposes that law's role as legitimiser can be examined from two key approaches, that is, the traditional and the non-traditional. From the traditional approach, it can be based on state-centred laws within a legal system and in a non-traditional approach, it shifts the focus from 'form' to a role-based perspective (as this allows for pluralistic forms of law towards identified roles) which would allow legal scholars to propose new roles and new law-tools for law when fulfilling the legitimacy role within CSR.

Chapters 5 and 6 explore these two legal approaches further. Chapter 5 examines the issue of the legitimacy of corporate power from a traditional legal approach of corporate (company) law.[141] This is law that frames and forms the corporation. It is common to most legal systems of the world. It has become the main vehicle for enabling business enterprise. This chapter identifies that legitimacy of corporate power should be a core concern for corporate law. Yet corporate law manifests a utility and responsibility division within legitimacy and the focus on the utility aspect of legitimacy to the detriment of the responsibility aspect has left little room in corporate law for issues of legitimacy of corporate power.[142] Chapter 5 begins by examining existing corporate law theories to discover what dominant perspectives influence and shape corporate law. Then it examines the notion of corporate governance within corporate law which directly addresses the issue of the legitimacy of corporate power. The focus of corporate governance on the internal perspectives of the corporation are addressed as a

141 This does not undermine the fact that several state laws have significant relevance for corporations

142 This view is expounded in more detail in J W Hurst, *The Legitimacy of Business in the Law of the United States 1780–1970* (University of Virginia Press, Charlottesville, VA 1970)

limiting factor when addressing debates on constraints and limitations to the exercise of corporate power. The chapter outlines the two main models of corporate governance in use globally and points to a potential convergence. It then uses the recent example of the UK company law reform to indicate the difficulties of trying to reconcile the 'utility' and 'responsibility' elements of the legitimacy debate within corporate law. The notion of directors running the company successfully while taking into account internal and external factors has not been fully worked out even in this reform legislation heralded as a best example.

This chapter highlights that there are significant limitations to the types of control and legitimating that may arise from such corporate law and governance theories because of the primarily internal focus. The focus of corporate law seems tilted to the internal utility question which centres on the success of the corporation and not the external question of legitimacy and accountability to society. It also displays the classic limitation of traditional law in being reactionary and limited in scope and jurisdiction. This also underlies the mismatch between MNC structure and state law in general.

Yet novel ways of looking at law in global contexts are emerging. This is what recommends a non-traditional pluralist law perspective for CSR. Therefore Chapter 6 proposes a move to such a non-traditional approach. It has also been singled out by some notable legal scholars as a legal theoretical concept capable of being adapted to address phenomena arising out of globalisation and its implication for law.[143] The skeletal nature of the theory lends it a flexibility and utility to most current phenomena arising out of inter-relationships in society.[144]

Twining in this regards, points out that:

> The law-jobs theory is a valuable and underused tool . . . it can easily accommodate notions of normative and legal pluralism, non-state law and different levels of global, transnational and local relations and so can provide a basis for dealing with issues raised by globalisation and interdependence.[145]

It proposes a more holistic way of addressing social responsibility through law that imbibes and addresses more aspects of the dynamic relationship between society and corporations existing within globalisation. This will come from a role-based perspective of law which addresses the role that law in its pluralistic forms can play within CSR.

The focus will be on reinterpreting Llewellyn's law-jobs as applicable to CSR. This allows for the contemplation of various forms of law and regulation (hard, soft, state-centred and private law) within CSR focused towards the doing of the

143 Twining (n. 71)

144 Llewellyn (n. 93)

145 Twining (n. 71) 115. However Twining also points out that this interdependence is a relative matter. See also W Twining, *Globalisation and Legal Scholarship* (Montesquieu Lecture, Tilburg University 2009)

law-jobs, which are: dispute resolution and grievance handling, channelling and rechannelling of conduct, allocating authority, net organisation and the use of the juristic method. The chapter addresses the 'capacity' which law in the non-traditional sense affords corporate power not only to be restricted from doing wrong but also to stimulate doing right and to help with society's social agenda.

The aim here is to demonstrate that such a legal framework can be used to address the CSR relationship. It will permit the contextual flexibility necessary within CSR while addressing distinct jobs.[146] It gives new insights to the role of law as legitimacy of corporate power and suggests the foundational framework for a legal perspective for CSR which can be further analysed in future research in diverse contexts. Chapter 7 delves further into the proposed law-jobs framework exemplifying the proposed legal approach.

Finally Chapter 8 forms the conclusion. This chapter summarises the findings of the book from the above examination. It gives an overview of this exploration of CSR from the chosen legal approaches and proposes that new insights can be gained by the extension of law-jobs theory to CSR. These insights might prompt others to examine the range of law tools applicable in their given context. Furthermore it could prompt a re-evaluation of the centrality of law to the question of CSR.

146 It could be seen as neither endorsing universal substantive law, which is open to criticisms of imposing the dominant power structures, or relativism, which is open to criticism of inequality of treatment, rather it proposes, in line with Santos 'Cosmopolitanism', that there can be dialogue structured by procedural ideals which cultures and societies aspire to: for example, dispute resolution, channelling conduct, allocation of authority and net organisation. See Santos (n. 36) 272

2 Defining corporate social responsibility

> Corporate social responsibility means something, but not always the same thing to everybody. To some it conveys the idea of legal responsibility or liability; to others, it means social responsible behaviour in the ethical sense; to still others, the meaning transmitted is that of 'responsible for' in a causal mode; many simply equate it with a charitable contribution; some take it to mean socially conscious; many of those who embrace it most fervently see it as a mere synonym for legitimacy in the context of belonging or being proper or valid; a few see a sort of fiduciary duty imposing higher standards of behaviour on businessmen than on citizens at large.[1]

2.1 Introduction

Establishing what CSR means within this book requires a larger enquiry about the definition of CSR. It will involve examining the main issues and debates on the meanings of CSR. In other words, the nature of CSR as meaning 'something' but not always the same thing to different people. This is because CSR has been defined in a variety of ways, with regard and focus given to diverse aspects of the concept.

These contestations infer that CSR can be seen as an essentially contested concept in the 'Gallie' sense, because it can be described as '*a concept the proper use of which inevitably involves endless disputes about their proper uses on the parts of their user*' (emphasis added).[2] Within CSR a significant amount of the contestation goes to the core of the concept and this is why there is no universally accepted definition of CSR. Nevertheless, in expounding essentially contested concepts Gallie pointed out that even those concepts must have a common basis (an exemplar), if only to ensure that contestants refer to the same subject-matter.[3]

1 D Votaw, 'Genius Becomes Rare: A Comment on the Doctrine of Social Responsibility Pt. 1' (1972) 15(2) *California Management Review* 25–31, 25

2 W B Gallie, 'Essentially Contested Concepts' (1958) 56 *Proceedings of the Aristotelian Society* 167–198, reprinted in M. Black (ed.), *The Importance of Language* (Prentice-Hall, Englewood Cliffs, NJ 1962) 121–146, 121

3 Ibid.

Gray supports this position by stating that 'definitional contests have a point only if there is something not treated as contestable'.[4] Therefore the aim in this chapter is to identify the common basis or common reference point which unifies CSR issues.

Within CSR contestation about its meaning is having a significant impact on the progress being made on the CSR agenda. This is because a fuzzy concept does not lend itself easily to defined agendas. Boeger and colleagues point out that 'where definitions are not settled, identifying aims and expectations also becomes difficult'.[5] The identification of the exemplar will also justify putting forward another approach to CSR that will be of relevance and enhance or advance the debate. Therefore the identification of the common basis will underscore the relevance of law and legal theory to CSR debates.

In order to identify what CSR means and the complexity of approaches within CSR, the next section will examine the history of the CSR movement and the competing ideologies that have sought to express themselves through the CSR banner over the years. The following section then analyses more specifically the problems of defining CSR and these include the various theories and approaches adopted to explain CSR action.

However the problem of defining CSR is not exclusive as defining concepts in the social sciences is often subject to contest. It is for this reason that the fourth section draws on the foremost theory on such contested concepts. This section proposes the extension of the essentially contested concept (ECC) theoretical framework to CSR to enable the discovery of a common basis or 'original exemplar' which can be utilised by this work.

The seven criteria framework based upon Gallie's ECCs forms the analytical tool for contextualising the CSR debate and locating inherent conflicting positions. The fifth section outlines the proposed exemplar of CSR and this forms the basis of our exploration of CSR within this work. Definitions of CSR cannot be incontrovertibly settled, as it is an EEC, however the chapter will indicate an exemplar that underpins CSR analysis and this also forms the basis of analysis which is to follow.

2.2 Historical background of CSR

Corporate social responsibility is a product of the twentieth century.[6] It differed in substance from nineteenth-century corporate philanthropy because it was

4 J N Gray, 'On the Contestability of Social and Political Concepts' (1977) 5(3) *Political Theory* 331–348, 342

5 N Boeger, R Murray and C Villiers (eds), *Perspectives on Corporate Social Responsibility* (Edward Elgar, Cheltenham 2008) 1

6 Although in his work Heald points to nineteenth-century corporate philanthropy there are essential differences between philanthropy and corporate social responsibility. The latter is not entirely self-willed and is a reaction to the 'external', where the 'external' takes many forms. M Heald, The *Social Responsibilities of Business Company and Community* (Transaction Publishers, New Brunswick, NJ 1970)

not driven merely by individual religious and ethical charity but by a bigger rationale: 'a concept of relationship of business to the community in which social responsibility was clearly seen as a charge not merely upon individual conscience and concern but upon corporate resources as well'.[7]

The 1920s began a period of enquiry in the United States into the responsibility of large corporations.[8] Some of this earlier normative strand is articulated in the early 1930s academic debates between Berle and Dodd in the *Harvard Law Review* on the role of corporate managers. These debates occurred in the aftermath of the economic collapse of 1929 and in the period of the Great Depression.[9]

They focused on the question of responsibility and accountability for corporate power. In his essay in 1931 'Corporate Powers as Powers in Trust' Berle proposed the traditional view of the corporate objective which is that corporate managers exercise powers, held in trust on behalf of the shareholders. This assertion adopts a traditional legal position which endorses the governance structure within the corporation, of managers (directors) owing responsibility to its shareholders.[10] However, Dodd responded by re-examining the issue from an essentially different perspective, he emphasised that 'business is permitted and encouraged by law because it is of service to the community rather than because it is a source of profit to its owners'.[11] This was a perspective indicating the ultimate responsibility of the corporation to society. He also pointed out that business leaders and students of business were not only expressing a growing feeling that business had a responsibility to the community but also voluntarily assuming such responsibility.[12]

In this response Dodd broadened the scope by examining the role of the corporation in society. He pointed out that substantial strides were being made in 'the direction of a view of the business corporation as an economic institution which has a social service as well as a profit-making function'.[13] He asserted that business in the 1930s in the United States was already contemplating and assuming some forms of social responsibility but, more importantly, affirmed that the law was a facilitator of such action and concluded that such action does not run

7 Ibid. at 19

8 Heald (n. 6) 83–84

9 M Hopkins, *The Planetary Bargain: Corporate Social Responsibility Matters* (Earthscan, London 2003) 2; L Whitehouse, 'Corporate Social Responsibility, Corporate Citizenship and the Global Compact: A New Approach to Regulating Corporate Social Power' (2003) 3 *Global Social Policy* 299–318, 301; A A Berle Jr, 'Corporate Powers as Powers in Trust' (1931) 44(7) *Harvard Law Review* 1049–1074; E M Dodd, 'For Whom are Corporate Managers Trustees?' (1932) 45(7) *Harvard Law Review* 1145–1163; A A Berle Jr, 'For Whom Corporate Managers are Trustees: A Note' (1932) 45(8) *Harvard Law Review* 1365–1372. This is sometimes referred to as the start of corporate governance debates yet this is only because the resulting answer entrenched the internal focus of the corporate governance structure on what is 'practicable', that is responsibility to 'the company'. This is an internal focus

10 Berle 1931 (n. 9)

11 Dodd (n. 9)

12 Ibid.; Heald refers to this as the 'managerial' version of capitalism, see p. 55

13 Dodd (n. 9)

counter to law, as the law will treat the directors as fiduciaries for the institution (not merely shareholders). This, he felt, should allow for flexibility and modifications of legal views on the role of the corporation in future.[14] His work is an early indication of the fact that the voluntary assumption of social responsibilities is not an end in itself and can be facilitated by law. He suggests that the 'principal object of legal compulsion might then be to keep those who failed to catch the new spirit up to standards which their more enlightened competitors would desire to adopt voluntarily'.[15]

Berle in later research acceded to Dodd's position but did so from a different point of view.[16] In Berle's final reply within this debate he stated that:

> Most students of corporation finance dream of a time when corporate administration will be held to a higher degree of required responsibility – a responsibility conceived not merely in terms of stockholders rights, but in terms of economic government satisfying the respective needs of investors, workers, customers and the aggregated community. Indications, indeed are not wanting that without such readjustment the corporate system will involve itself in successive cataclysms perhaps leading to its ultimate downfall.[17]

In his research with Means,[18] he analysed the internal position of the large corporations and found the managers/directors devoid of control from the owners (shareholders). This was termed the separation of ***ownership from control*** and on that basis Berle concluded that corporations could be called to account by society where such separation resulted in a lack of accountability.[19]

Yet this work showed a tension between those who required society (through government reform of corporate law) to call corporations to account. and make them responsible to other constituents within society versus others who insisted on redressing the relationship between the directors and the corporation (that is, its shareholders). Branson characterises this as a battle between 'CSR' and

14 Dodd (n. 9) 1163. This is evidenced in the modification of UK company law making it the duty of directors not only to promote the success of the company but also to include broader social and environmental considerations

15 Dodd (n. 9) 1153

16 Berle stated that 'the argument has been settled (at least for the time being) in favour of Professor Dodd's contention'. A Berle cited in Lord Wedderburn of Charlton, 'The Legal Development of Corporate Managers: For Whom will Corporate Managers be Trustees? K J Hopt and G Teubner, *Corporate Governance and Directors Liabilities: Legal, Economic and Sociological Analyses of Corporate Social Responsibility* (De Gruyter, Berlin 1984) 3–54, 3

17 Berle 1932 (n. 9) 1372

18 A A Berle and G C Means, *The Modern Corporation and Private Property* (with a new introduction by M. Weidenbaum and M. Jensen) (Transaction Publishers, New Brunswick, NJ 1991 (originally published 1932))

19 Ibid. Berle's position remained essentially a contractarian one, as distinct from a concessionary or communitarian perspective

'law and economics'.[20] Nonetheless these debates placed corporate theories and corporate governance and regulation at the heart of the CSR debate either as causation or consequence. [21]

As law has remained slow to react to these primary debates, the more prolific strand of CSR, which emanated from the practitioner businessman's point of view, now dominates CSR literature.[22] This second strand is a follow up to some of the issues highlighted in Dodd's article which pointed out that business executives were already expressing the notion of a social service function for large corporations.[23] This assertion is also evidenced in journal articles written by business executives in the 1920s.[24]

However in the 1950s, there was an increase in the volume of writing on the issue of a social role for business. This emerged from within the field of management but also included a diverse range of authors including 'theologians, philosophers, economists, business leaders and historians'.[25] This was because of an increasing consciousness of the growth of corporate power and its need for justification. Frederick writing in 1960 pointed out that:

> The collapse of laissez faire posed a giant intellectual conundrum for social theorists: How could a society with democratic traditions and democratic aspirations rationalise the growing amount of power accruing to businessmen? And how could that power be channelled into socially useful functions without driving the populace into some Orwellian nightmare of 1984 proportions?[26]

20 D M Branson 'Corporate Governance "Reform" and the New Corporate Social Responsibility' (2001) 62(4) *University of Pittsburgh Law Review* 605–648, 605

21 Branson comments that 'Seldom in the annals of jurisprudence has one jurisprudence ascended so quickly'; ibid. Yet the battle between both strands (of jurisprudence) can be traced to the tentative conclusion in Berle and Means (n. 18) 312

22 A good account of the history of CSR from this perspective can be found in A B Carroll, 'A History of Corporate Social Responsibility: Concept and Practice' in A Crane, A McWilliams, D Matten, J Moon and D Siegel (eds), *The Oxford Handbook of Corporate Social Responsibility* (Oxford University Press, Oxford 2008) 19–46

23 Dodd cites Mr Young, a business executive, President Swope of the General Electric Company and Dean Donham of the Harvard Graduate School of Business Administration as business persons who had in different ways expressed this notion of a social service role for large business. Dodd (n. 9)

24 Most notably Dean Donham had written in the *Harvard Business Review* of the necessity for responsibility of businessmen towards other groups in the community as early as 1927 and 1929. W B Donham, 'Business Ethics – A General Survey' (1929) 7(4) *Harvard Business Review* 385–394; 'The Social Significance of Business' (1927) 5(4) *Harvard Business Review* 406–419

25 S B Banerjee, *Corporate Social Responsibility: The Good, the Bad and the Ugly* (Edward Elgar, Cheltenham 2007) 7

26 W C Frederick, 'The Growing Problem of Business Responsibility' (1960) 2(4) *California Management Review* 54–61

From the 1950s onwards writers had begun to address this task. Abrams, the President of Standard Oil of Jersey (now Exxon), pointed out that business management in the United States is increasingly acquiring the characteristics of a profession and as such the new job for professional management 'is to conduct the affairs of the enterprise in its charge in such a way as to maintain an equitable and workable balance among the claims of various directly interested groups'.[27] He defines these various interested groups to as including 'the stockholders, employees, customers and the public at large'. His statement is very similar to the modern notion of 'stakeholders'.[28]

Bowen pointed out in 1953 that 'social responsibility refers to the obligations of businessmen to pursue those policies, to make those decisions, or to follow those lines of action which are desirable in terms of the objectives and values of our society'.[29] Bowen is largely credited in CSR literature as being 'the father of CSR'.[30] His book is acknowledged in most CSR literature as a poignant point in CSR history and is perhaps responsible for the business focus of CSR.[31] Yet Carroll points out that Bowen's work emerged from a belief that these large businesses were vital centres of power and decision-making and that their actions affected the lives of citizens at many points.[32] This is a fundamental observation that underlies CSR as a concept.

From the 1950s to the 1970s, the debate for the assumption of social obligations to society was significantly explored. Some of the notable debates can be found in the writings of Johnson,[33] Davis[34] and Carroll.[35] This represented a strengthening of this management perspective of CSR and a shift of focus from normative legal debates. Even so, this perspective did address some other normative and ethical aspects of CSR that have emerged in current analysis.

Johnson in his 1957 article 'Can the Businessman Apply Christianity?' used an analogy from the Christian doctrine to analyse the nature of the businessman, highlighting man the angel and man the devil. Within his analysis two relevant points stand out. First that

27 F W Abrams, 'Management's Responsibilities in a Complex World' (1951) 29(3) *Harvard Business Review* 29–34, 29

28 Ibid. at 30. Although the modern notion of stakeholder theory is accredited to Freeman

29 H R Bowen, *Social Responsibilities of the Businessman* (University of Iowa Press, Iowa City 2013)

30 A B Carroll, 'Corporate Social Responsibility: Evolution of a Definitional Construct' (1999) 38(3) *Business and Society* 268–295, 270

31 That is, examining CSR from the perspective of the businessman

32 Carroll 1999 (n. 30), 269

33 H L Johnson, 'Can the Businessman Apply Christianity?' (1957) 35(5) *Harvard Business Review* 68–76

34 K Davis, 'The Case For and Against the Assumption of Social Responsibilities' (1973) 16(2) *Academy of Management Journal* 312–322; K Davis, W C Frederick and R L Blomstrom, *Business and Society: Concepts and Policy Issues* (4th ed., McGraw-Hill, New York 1980) 50–57

35 A Carroll, 'A Three-dimensional Conceptual Model of Corporate Social Performance' (1979) 4(4) *Academy of Management Review* 497–505

> company executives may stress that their socially responsible philosophy works to the general benefit; yet basically such a philosophy may be a subtle device to maintain economic power in their own hands by extending their influence and decision-making power into so many non-business areas that they become benevolent dictators.[36]

Second that 'corporations may give funds to charitable or educational institutions and may argue for them as great humanitarian deeds, when in fact they are simply trying to buy community good will'.[37] These issues are still echoed by sceptics of CSR today. In 2005 Shamir pointed to the continung fuzzy nature of the concept as in part precipitated by corporate power and business desire to dictate the agenda on this issue.[38] Examining CSR in the development context in 2008 Esclava concluded that most of its benefits are illusory. He proposes that 'CSR is a major component of the "anti-politics machine" which works primarily to consolidate its own power and neutralise its critics'.[39]

In 1973, Davis wrote an important article examining the case for and against the business assumption of social responsibilities. His focus was not wholly on the businessman but on business as a whole. The first important element within his article is his definition of social responsibility as 'the firm's consideration of, and response to, issues beyond the narrow economic, technical and legal requirements of the firm'. In giving this definition, he can be credited with the introduction of the notion of CSR as 'beyond the law'. He even specifically mentions that 'it is a firm's acceptance of a social obligation beyond the requirements of the law'.[40]

There are several problems with such a narrow definition but it suffices to mention at this point that in 1979 Carroll improved upon Davis's definition and crucially pointed out that 'for a definition of social responsibility to fully address the entire range of obligations business has to society, it must embody the economic, legal, ethical and discretionary categories of business performance'.[41] He thus reinstated law as a category and allowed for the possibility of legal considerations as a substantial part of CSR. Nevertheless the Davis article makes other substantial contribution to CSR history by including a concise summary of most of the contemporary arguments for and against social responsibility.

In the first category, *arguments for*, he points to several cogent points. First the pursuit of the long-run self-interest of the corporation, which can best be

36 Johnson (n. 33)

37 Johnson (n. 33)

38 R Shamir, 'Corporate Social Responsibility: A Case of Hegemony and Counter-hegemony' in B De Sousa Santos and C A Rodriguez-Garavito (eds), *Law and Globalisation from Below – Towards a Cosmopolitan Legality* (Cambridge University Press, Cambridge 2005) 92–117, 95

39 This view is contained in his article: L Esclava 'Corporate Social Responsibility & Development: A Knot of Disempowerment' (2008) 2 *Sortuz: Oñati Journal of Emergent Socio-Legal Studies* 43–71, 44

40 Davis 1973 (n. 34) 312

41 Carroll 1979 (n. 35) 499

understood as carrying out social activity compatible with and beneficial to, the long-term interest of the company.[42] In light of this argument, several studies have attempted to examine the question whether CSR activities pay in the long term, but this is a question which has so far failed to elicit incontrovertible answers.[43] In 2005 Vogel examined the evidence analysing the business case for CSR and found this inconclusive.[44]

Davis also raises the possibility that CSR enhances the corporation's public image and it is therefore closely associated with notions of corporate vulnerability to questions of reputation and image. This follows up on the notion that the popularisation of CSR is closely associated to the bad image of certain large corporations being brought to the attention of society through public campaigns and scandals; public campaigns by NGOs against large MNCs for human rights, environmental and labour rights violations in various parts of the world. A modern example would be the Brent Spar & Ogoni campaigns against Shell.[45] Publicity of wrongful corporate actions and threats to corporate reputation have been a potent force in the adoption of CSR;[46] however, the vulnerability of corporations to reputational risk differs from sector to sector. Therefore it may only result in limited social responsibility geared towards good public relations. It is also possible that CSR as response lasts only as long as publicity focuses on it.

Next, Davis points out two original ideas on the issue of CSR's relevance to the viability of business; first that 'society gave business its charter to exist, and that charter could be amended or revoked at any time that business fails to live up to society's expectations',[47] an idea which ties in with the social contract theory[48] and the concession corporate theory[49] and second that 'if business wishes to retain its

42 Such an enlightened self-interest model is more eloquently advocated in Jensen's article, where he proposes that maximisation of the long-term value of the corporation should be the objective and criteria for any trade-offs to be made among stakeholders or decisions about which CSR actions the corporation should pursue. M Jensen, 'Value Maximisation, Stakeholder Theory and the Corporate Objective Function' (2002) *Business Ethics Quarterly* 12(2) 235–256

43 P L Cochran and R A Wood, 'Corporate Social Responsibility and Financial Performance' (1984) 27 *Academy of Management Journal* 42–56; K E Aupperle, A B Carroll and J D Hartfield, 'An Empirical Examination of the Relationship Between Corporate Social Responsibility and Profitability?' (1985) 28 *Academy of Management Journal* 446–463; J D Margolis and J P Walsh, 'Misery Loves Companies: Rethinking Social Initiatives by Business' (2003) 48 *Administrative Science Quarterly* 268–305

44 D Vogel, *The Market for Virtue: The Potential and Limits of Corporate Social Responsibility* (Brookings Institution, Washington, DC 2005)

45 S Liversey, 'Eco Identity as Discursive Struggle: Royal Dutch/Shell, Brent Spar and Nigeria' (2001) 38(1) *Journal of Business Communications* 58–91

46 J V Mitchell, *Companies in a World of Conflict* (Earthscan/RIIA, London 1998)

47 Davis 1973 (n. 34) 314

48 T Donaldson and T Dunfee, *Ties that Bind: A Social Contract Approach to Business Ethics* (Harvard Business School Press, Boston, MA 1999)

49 K Iwai, 'Persons, Things and Corporations, the Corporate Personality Controversy and Comparative Corporate Governance'(1999) 47 *American Journal of Comparative Law* 538–632

present social role and social power, it must respond to society's needs and give society what it wants'.[50] This is referred to in CSR literature as the Davis iron law of responsibility asserting that, 'in the long run those who do not use power in a manner which society considers responsible will tend to lose it'.[51] This is another crucial observation on the centrality to CSR of notions of corporate power within the corporation and society relationship. The role of corporate power will be examined in further detail in Chapter 3.

Within the article, Davis points to further interesting arguments such as that CSR can be used as a tool in avoidance of governmental regulation and as such regulation is often costly to business and restricts its flexibility in decision-making it may be best to take proactive action. This argument can be termed, 'rational' or 'strategic' CSR. In current CSR literature, Werther and Chandler suggest it may be more cost-effective to address issues voluntarily rather than wait for the legally mandated requirements and react to them.[52]

In this vein, the Confederation of British Industry (CBI) also points out that 'many companies prefer to be one step ahead of governmental legislation or intervention, to anticipate social pressures themselves and hence be able to develop their own policies in response to them'.[53] Such pre-emptive action may, however, be motivated by self-interest as the main objective may simply be to dictate the agenda on the relevant issue in a manner compatible or conducive to their business, economic or personal interests. It is also important to add that the avoidance of litigation is also a possible motive for CSR practice as demonstrated by class action suits filed in the United States under the Aliens Torts Statutes (preceding the Kiobel decision).[54] Aggrieved parties are often prepared to seek out an available forum for redress even in foreign countries.[55]

To appreciate the scale of this threat, analysts point out that:

> Firms such as Citibank, Coca-Cola, IBM, JC Penny, Levi-Strauss, Pfizer, Gap, Limited, Texaco and Unocal have all faced possible suits under this same law, which may extend to hundreds of other national and international firms.[56]

50 Davis 1973 (n. 34) 314

51 This idea is further developed in Davis 1980 (n. 34) 50–57

52 W B Werther Jr and D Chandler, *Strategic Corporate Social Responsibility* (Sage Publications, Thousand Oaks, CA 2006) 17

53 J Moon and D Vogel, 'Corporate Social Responsibility, Government and Civil Society' in A Crane, A McWilliams, D Matten, J Moon and D Siegel (eds), *The Oxford Handbook of CSR* (Oxford University Press, New York 2008) 308

54 *Kiobel v. Royal Dutch Petroleum Co.*, 133 S.Ct. 1659 (2013), which severely limited the scope of the ATS (Alien Torts Statute 28 U.S.C. § 1350) application extraterritorially

55 The UK is now a possible option following the Court of Appeal case of *Chandler v Cape plc* (2012) EWCA Civ. 525

56 Werther and Chandler (n. 52) 12

In spite of the lack of complete success of these suits, these types of litigation still remain a powerful motive for the adoption of CSR.[57] Where corporations or business set the agenda or, as the CBI argues, define CSR, this may result in a lack of clarity over what CSR means and to whom. For CSR to fulfil this potential it must have objectives that are clearly identifiable and address the relevant issues in context but it cannot be fuzzy or woolly or restricted to public relations alone.

In the article Davis also highlights other issues in support of CSR including: socio-cultural norms which reflect that businessmen as individuals operate from a set of cultural norms derived from society; the possibility that CSR could be in stockholders' interest, indicating that such activities could open up new opportunities for profit and the option of allowing business an attempt to deal with social issues, where the government may have failed.

This latter argument reflects the notion that people may be frustrated with the failure of other social institutions. This is an action that could be validated by the privatisation of public utilities and the new sense of business provision of 'public goods'. He acknowledges that business may have relevant resources: money, management talent, functional expertise and capital resources. This is also the reasoning behind the adoption of business ideology and management strategy in public institutions, as demonstrated by the recommended use of 'best value' strategy by local authorities in assessing, contracting and other activities.[58]

Davis also points to the argument that CSR may be capable of turning problems into profits as many social problems can be handled profitably according to traditional business concepts. Although this can be linked to the earlier business case for CSR argument, it is more closely echoed by Prahalad and Hammond in their notable article 'Serving the World's Poor, Profitably'[59] where they posit that:

> by stimulating commerce and development at the bottom of the economic pyramid, MNCs could radically improve the lives of billions of people and help bring into being a more stable, less dangerous world.[60]

This position is, however, countered by other literature citing the limitations of pursuing a strictly economic or profitable strand of CSR within development.[61]

57 The threat of legal action can be seen in the £55 million pay-out agreed in an out of court settlement between Bodo community, Nigeria and Shell in the UK. <https://www.leighday.co.uk/News/2015/January-2015/Shell-agrees-55m-compensation-deal-for-Nigeria-Del> accessed 2 February 2016

58 Best value with the central principle that local authorities are to secure continuous improvement of functions having regard to a combination of 'economy, efficiency and effectiveness' in M Elliot (ed.), *Beatson, Matthew and Elliot's Administrative Law – Text and Materials* (3rd ed., Oxford University Press, Oxford 2005) 28

59 (2002) 80(9) *Harvard Business Review* 48–57

60 Ibid. at 48

61 J G Frynas, *Beyond Corporate Social Responsibility: Oil Multinationals and Social Challenges* (Cambridge University Press, Cambridge 2009)

The business profit driven strand may be unable to fully comprehend the inherent nature of development as a concept whose content must be dictated by the developing societies themselves.

Finally, Davis applies the adage that 'prevention is better than curing' as he points out the possibility that 'if business delays dealing with a social problem now, it may find itself constantly occupied with putting out social fires so that it has no time to accomplish its primary goal of producing goods and services'.[62] This is reminiscent of issues arising from the adoption of CSR policies by oil industries in Nigeria as a delayed response to social and environmental issues of oil pollution and degradation of the delta region.[63]

The Davis article presents an excellent synopsis of the arguments for the second strand of CSR but it also examines significant arguments against. As a counterpoint, he raises the traditional notion of 'profit maximisation' as the main responsibility of the corporation. This is encapsulated by Friedman who states that:

> In a free enterprise, private property system, a corporate executive is an employee of the owners of the business . . . and his responsibility is to conduct the business in accordance with their desires, which generally will be to make as much money as possible . . . [64]

He therefore observes that social involvement incurs costs which may not necessarily make economic sense, 'many social goals do not pay their own way in an economic sense'.[65] This is similar to Vogel's findings which point out an end result where several empirical studies 'report a positive relationship between ethics (CSR) and profits, some find a negative relationship and still others find the relationship to be either neutral or mixed'.[66] This is also the sense in which some CSR advocates propose a shift from a simple economic bottom line to a triple bottom line of people, planet and profits because this will permit more than an economic justification for socially responsible action by corporations.[67]

Davis also adds that businessmen may lack the necessary skills to deal with social problems and this could lead to the dilution of business's primary purpose, which may lead to business performing poorly both in its economic and its social roles.[68]

62 Davis 1973 (n. 34) 317

63 B Manby *The Price of Oil* (Human Rights Watch, New York 1999)

64 M Friedman, *Capitalism and Freedom* (University of Chicago Press, Chicago 1962) 12–16; M Friedman, 'The Social Responsibility of Business is to Increase Its Profits' *The New York Magazine*, 13 September 1970, 32

65 Davis (n. 34) 318

66 Vogel (n. 44) 16–45

67 J Elkington, *Cannibals with Forks: Triple Bottom Line of the 21st Century Business* (Capstone Publishing, Oxford 1997)

68 He points out a more localised argument that where US firms adopt CSR as against other firms it may create a disadvantage, which could lead to a weakened international balance of payments. This is no longer valid as CSR in one form or another is a global phenomenon both for developed and developing country business

Furthermore he points out that business may already have enough power and therefore the adoption of social responsibility may threaten the pluralistic division of power and reduce the viability of our free society, thus indicating a lack of accountability because accountability should always go with responsibility.

Davis suggests the possibility that 'until society can develop mechanisms which would establish direct lines of social accountability from business to public, business should stand clear of social activities'.[69] The fear is that this could become a subversive doctrine where businessmen become 'benevolent paternalistic rulers'. This was an issue Leitt had addressed earlier in 1958, when he pointed out:

> the frightening spectacle of a powerful economic functional group whose future and perception are shaped in a tight materialistic context of money and things that impose its narrow ideas about a broad spectrum of unrelated non-economic subjects on the mass of man and society. [70]

This comment underlines the integral nature of accountability to the CSR agenda. It is a fundamental observation that goes to the heart of CSR, the question of legitimacy and accountability. The Davis article is pivotal in CSR history as it highlights several significant debates within CSR.

Unwittingly it highlights the arguments that lend credence to the calls for development of the normative legal aspects of CSR and attempts to reconnect CSR with its normative strand. A normative strand geared towards accountability with significant relevance for law. For, as Lord Wedderburn affirmed in 1986, the celebrated exchange between Professors Adolf Berle and E Merrick Dodd is central to the modern problem of corporate responsibility.[71] Therefore,

> the need is for mechanisms both internal and external to the enterprise through which social responsibility can emerge – procedures which will inevitably modify the objective of maximising profits without attempting to replace it at a stroke by some other substantive formula.[72]

In addition, in examining the lessons learnt from the Berle-Dodd debate in the intervening years, Teubner points out that the central issue remains that 'a corporate enterprise does not exist simply as a self-serving and self-realising

69 Davis 1973 (n. 34) 320

70 T Levitt, 'The Dangers of Corporate Social Responsibility' (1958) 36(5) *Harvard Business Review* 41–50

71 Lord Wedderburn, 'Legal Development of Corporate Responsibility: For Whom will Corporate Managers be Trustees?' in K J Hopt and G Teubner, *Corporate Governance and Directors Liabilities: Legal, Economic and Sociological Analyses of Corporate Social Responsibility* (De Gruyter, Berlin 1984) 3–54, 3

72 Ibid. at 44

institution for the unique benefit of its shareholders and workers but rather exists above all to fulfil a broader role in society'.[73]

The role of law in shaping the corporate enterprise is therefore significant and important and this is why Parkinson in 1993 surmised the overall question in relation to law as follows:

> Identifying appropriate modes of control over management demands we first decide what the objectives of the company should be. The questions of means and ends form the subject matter of other disciplines . . . They are also part of the subject-matter of law. Whether one emphasises the role of state or of contract in corporate existence, companies are creations of law, their objectives are defined by law and the law is a major source of the practical constraints on management behaviour.[74]

This is an opinion shared by Justice Douglas in his dissenting Supreme Court opinion, where he pointed out:

> The modern super-corporations . . . wields immense, virtually unchecked power, some say they are 'private governments', whose decisions affect the lives of us all. The philosophy of our times, I think requires that such enterprises be held to a higher standard than that of the 'morals of the market place' which exalts a single-minded myopic determination to maximise profits as the traditional be-all and end-all of corporate concern.[75]

The necessity for a more holistic approach towards CSR is strengthened by its linkage with globalisation. CSR as a concept spread to other countries alongside concerns over the spread of globalisation and the impact of large MNCs.[76]

73 G Teubner 'Corporate Fiduciary Duties and Their Beneficiaries: A Functional Approach to the Legal Institutionalisation of Corporate Responsibility' in K J Hopt and G Teubner (eds), *Corporate Governance and Directors Liabilities: Legal, Economic and Sociological Analyses of Corporate Social Responsibility* (De Gruyter, Berlin 1984) 149–177, 157

74 J E Parkinson, *Corporate Power and Responsibility: issues in the Theory of Company Law* (Clarendon Press, Oxford 1995) viii

75 *SEC v Medical Committee for Human Rights* (1972) 404 U.S. 403, 409–410

76 Dodd points out a comment by Dean Donham that '*the only way to defend capitalism is through leadership which accepts social responsibility*' (emphasis added). (Dodd n 9) 1155, Hopkins (n. 9) 2–3. Others argue that this has been an American concern since the late nineteenth century. See H Wells, 'The Cycles of Corporate Social Responsibility' (2002) *University of Kansas Law Review* 77–140, 77. See also J Llewellyn, 'Regulation: Government, Business and Self in the US' in S K May, G Cheney and J Roper, *The Debate over Corporate Social Responsibility* (Oxford University Press, New York 2007) 177–189. Blowfield and Murray point out that Adam Smith was concerned about the limited liability nature of the corporation and the potential for that nature to breed irresponsibility. M Blowfield and A Murray, *Corporate Responsibility: A Critical Introduction* (Oxford University Press, Oxford 2008) 41–50

An examination of recent CSR literature reveals a variety of issues covering different geographic regions including CSR in developing countries, CSR in various continents and CSR in several industry sectors.[77] Scherer and Palazzo point to the importance of large corporations in the global sphere, they state that:

> The world's biggest corporations have revenues that equal or exceed the gross domestic product of some developed states . . . (and this is further enhanced) by their mobility and capacity to shift resources to locations where they can be used more profitably and to choose among suppliers, applying a criteria of efficiency.[78]

This has re-ignited core questions about the role of these corporations but on a global scale translating questions raised in the 1930s with the multiplier effect.

Davis's landmark analysis in 1973 and Carroll's redefinition of CSR in 1979 stand out as central analytical points but the 1980s and 1990s resulted in an explosion of writing on alternatives and complementary themes such as corporate social performance, corporate social responsiveness, corporate citizenship, stakeholder theory and business ethics.[79] However Carroll observes that 'very few unique contributions to the concept of CSR occurred in the 1990s'.[80] It seems that at that time there was a micro-focus on highlighted aspects of CSR debates and the development of complementary themes.

By 2000 significant focus was being given to CSR research into the impact of globalisation and to complementary aspects such as corporate citizenship, corporate social performance, corporate accountability and business ethics. The normative debates also continued and several theories began to emerge. The overall picture emerges more clearly in the next section which examines the problems with definition, analysing the various theoretical bases and more specifically their link with the complementary themes.

77 An illustrative list includes: K Fukukawa and J Moon, 'A Japanese Model of Corporate Social Responsibility? A Study of Website Reporting' (2004)16 *Journal of Corporate Citizenship* 45–49; O DeSchutter, 'CSR European Style' (2008) 14(2) *European Law Journal* 203–236; C C Baughn, N L Bodie and J C McIntosh, 'Corporate Social and Environmental Responsibility in Asian and Other Geographical Regions' (2007) 14(4) *CSR and Environmental Management* 189–205; U E Ite, 'Multinational Corporation and CSR in Developing Countries: A Case Study of Nigeria' (2004) 1(1) *CSR and Environmental Management* 1–11; S Fritsch, 'The UN Global Compact and the Global Governance of CSR: Complex Multilateralism for a More Human Globalisation' (2008) 22(1) *Global Society* 1–28

78 A G Scherer and G Palazzo, 'Globalisation and Corporate Social Responsibility' in A Crane, A McWilliams, D Matten, J Moon and D Siegel (eds), *The Oxford Handbook of CSR* (Oxford University Press, New York 2008) 413–431, 418. See also A D Chandler and B Mazlish, *Leviathans: Multinational Corporations and the New Global History* (Cambridge University Press, Cambridge 2005)

79 These complementary themes will be analysed in the following section

80 A B Carroll, 'A History of Corporate Social Responsibility: Concepts and Practices' in A Crane, A McWilliams, D Matten, J Moon and D Siegel (eds), *The Oxford Handbook of CSR* (Oxford University Press, New York 2008) 19–46, 37

2.3 Multiple CSR theories and complementary themes

There is no unified theory of CSR, rather there are several theories reflecting the complex and dynamic CSR landscape. As a general guide, theories may be descriptive or normative. They can be descriptive in the sense that they describe what CSR practice is or could be for corporations or normative in the sense that they examine the rationale for corporations to adopt CSR. Normative theories therefore examine answers to questions about why corporations should pursue CSR thereby signifying what such corporations ought or ought not to be doing.

Melé points out that 'a good normative theory needs a good philosophical foundation which has to include a correct view of human nature, business and society and the relationship between business and society'.[81] The lack of a normative grounding for CSR is key to the inability to set clear and define agendas for achievement in the CSR field. Campbell points out that this lack of grounding of CSR 'threatens the credibility of CSR programmes and impedes the articulation and implementation of CSR policies within business, government and civil society'.[82]

The landscape of various theories and alternate themes makes it very difficult to identify the core issues within CSR. This is why the aim of this chapter is to address CSR as an essentially contested concept, in order to identify a common core from which contestation emerges. However this section will attempt to map out CSR theories and identify the role of complementary themes. The landscape of CSR theories is complex and tangled but certain authors have attempted to map out the theories involved. They include Windsor,[83] Klonoski,[84] Garriga and Melé[85] and, more recently, Melé.[86]

Windsor addressed three key approaches to CSR: ethical responsibility theory, economic responsibility theory and corporate citizenship. These approaches stem from ethical duties, economic responsibilities and political positions respectively. The ethical approach proposes the social advantage of morally sensitive business practices and policy using a range of moral frameworks. The economic approach argues that no costly responsibility action should be undertaken voluntarily.

81 D Melé, 'Corporate Social Responsibility Theories' in A Crane, A McWilliams, D Matten, J Moon and D Siegel (eds), *The Oxford Handbook of CSR* (Oxford University Press, New York 2008) 47–82, 76

82 T Campbell, 'The Normative Grounding of Corporate Social Responsibility: A Human Rights Approach' in D McBarnet, A Voiculescu and T Campbell (eds), *The New Corporate Accountability: Corporate Social Responsibility and the Law* (Cambridge University Press, Cambridge 2007) 529–564, 530

83 D Windsor, 'Corporate Social Responsibility: Three Key Approaches' (2006) 43(1) *Journal of Management Studies* 93–114

84 R J Klonoski, 'Foundational Considerations in the Corporate Social Responsibility Debate' (1991) 34(4) *Business Horizons* 9–18

85 Garriga and Melé, 'Corporate Social Responsibility Theories: Mapping the Territory' (2004) 53(1–2) *Journal of Business Ethics* 51–71

86 Melé (n. 81)

Windsor points out that this perspective also has a moral core based in utilitarianism as a variant of consequentialism with an outcomes orientation. Finally, Windsor sees the corporate citizenship approach as a political metaphor which falls between the earlier two approaches unsatisfactorily.

Klonoski, for his part, distinguished between 'fundamentalism' where the corporation dealt strictly with profit-making within the law, theories implying moral responsibility and theories that focused on the social dimension of the corporation.[87]

However, one of the most accepted classifications is that offered by Garriga and Melé in their essay on mapping out the territory of CSR theories. Other scholars point out that this attempt to map CSR theories is successful and presents a brilliant account of the foremost academic debate on CSR. [88]

Garriga and Melé identify four main types of CSR theories: instrumental theories advancing economic objectives through social activities; political theories advocating corporate power and its responsible use; integrative theories expressing the necessity for corporations to integrate social demands; ethical theories examining the morality and rightness of corporate social action. These theories will be examined briefly below but will also be studied in further detail later in the chapter as exemplifying multiple interpretations that have developed within CSR.

Instrumental theories are traditionally accepted theories on the role of the corporation as an instrument of wealth creation. This category covers theories which advocate maximisation of shareholder value. Friedman advocated that 'the only one responsibility of business towards society is the maximisation of profits to the shareholder within the legal framework and ethical custom of the country'[89] and in line with this modern theorists advocate an 'enlightened value maximisation'[90] accepting that certain social activities may contribute to the long-term shareholder value of the corporation. This group also includes theories that express corporate social activities in terms of gaining a competitive advantage either within a competitive context[91] or to generate new untapped markets such as in developing countries.[92] An example is the growth of telecommunications corporations in developing countries such as India and Nigeria.[93] It also covers

87 Klonoski (n. 84)

88 A Crane, D Matten and L J Spence, *Corporate Social Responsibility: Readings and Cases in a Global Context* (Routledge, Abingdon 2008) 58

89 M Friedman, 'The Social Responsibility of Business is to Increase Profits' *New York Times Magazine,* 13 September 1970, 32–33

90 M C Jensen, 'Value Maximisation, Stakeholder Theory and the Corporate Objective Function' (2002) 12(2) *Business Ethics Quarterly* 235–256

91 M E Porter and M R Kramer, 'The Competitive Advantage of Corporate Philanthropy' (2002) 80(12) *Harvard Business Review* 56–69

92 C K Prahalad and A Hammond, 'Serving the World's Poor Profitably' (2002) 80(9) *Harvard Business Review* 48–58

93 R Singh, 'Mobile Phones for Development and Profit' Overseas Development Institute Opinion April 2009 <http://www.odi.org.uk/resources/download/2846.pdf > accessed 18 March 2011

theories which place CSR as marketing and integral to building a reputation and a brand which adds to the bottom line of profit. This can be demonstrated by the adoption of fair-trade standards and then placing the logos on products. McWilliams and Siegel point out this link by stating that 'support for cause related marketing creates a reputation that a firm is reliable and honest [and] consumers typically assume that the products of a reliable and honest firm will be of a high quality'.[94] The focus is on CSR as an instrument of long-term wealth creation.

Political theories highlight the notion of corporate power and its relationship with responsibility within society. This category covers theories by Davis mentioned above,[95] such as the social power equation and the iron law of responsibility, which find fault with the classical economic theory of the notion of perfect competition by exposing the power roles of the corporate party and its ability to influence the market. However this category also covers newer perspectives such as corporate citizenship.

Corporate citizenship as a type of political theory is sometimes used synonymously with CSR and therefore has taken on various meanings. However at its root is the notion of the corporation as a citizen in society with rights and responsibilities.[96] Currently three views of corporate citizenship can be identified.[97] First a limited view which equates corporate citizenship with corporate philanthropy,[98] an equivalent view which equates corporate citizenship with CSR[99] and an extended conceptualisation which defines corporate citizenship as describing the role of the corporation in administering citizenship rights for individuals.[100] There has been severe criticism of the extended conceptualisation as 'an idea whose time has not yet come'[101] especially in the absence of credible accountability mechanisms for the increase of corporate power which this could entail.

Integrative theories examine how business integrates social demands into its business operations, this is embodied in the analysis by Preston and Post on public

94 A. McWilliams and D Siegel, 'Corporate Social Responsibility: A Theory of the Firm Perspective' (2001) 26(1) *Academy of Management Review* 117–127, 120

95 Davis 1973 (n. 34)

96 J Andriof and M McIntosh (eds), *Perspectives of Corporate Citizenship* (Greenleaf, Sheffield 2001)

97 D Matten and A.Crane, 'Corporate Citizenship: Towards an Extended Theoretical Conceptualisation' (2005) 30(1) *Academy of Management Review* 166–179

98 D J Wood and J M Lodgson, 'Business Citizenship: From Individuals to Organisations' (2002) 3 *Ethics and Entrepreneurship* 59–94 (The Ruffin Series of the Society for Business Ethics) 59–94; S A Waddock and S B Graves, 'The Corporations Social Performance-Financial Performance Link' (1997) 18(4) *Strategic Management Journal* 303–320 (a view of corporate citizenship as social investing)

99 A B Carroll, 'Four Faces of Corporate Citizenship' (1998) 100(1) *Business and Society* 1–7

100 Matten and Crane (n. 97); D Matten, A Crane and W Chapple, 'Behind the Mask: Revealing the True Face of Corporate Citizenship' (2003) 45(1–2) *Journal of Business Ethics* 109–120

101 J Van Oosterhout, 'Corporate Citizenship: An Idea Whose Time has not Yet Come' (2005) 30(4) *Academy of Management Review* 677–681

responsibility[102] as well as the more popular theories of corporate social performance and of stakeholder management. They include significant descriptive theories focused on the corporate response to CSR. Stakeholder management, publicised in the works of Freeman[103] and others,[104] advocates an approach where management takes into cognisance stakeholders or people who affect or are affected by corporate policies and practices.[105] This management theory is, however, underscored by an ethical theory that embraces a modified property rights position that requires the corporations to be run on behalf of stakeholders instead of its shareholders.

Corporate social performance involves an integrated theory that adopts the principles of CSR, processes of corporate social responsiveness and outcomes of corporate behaviour.[106] Integrative theories therefore represent a synthesis of other categories of theories to provide frameworks for gauging corporate response, analysis and developing corporate policy.

Finally, ethical theories focus on ethics and in this sense doing what is right for a good society. These ethical theories are often contested, hence they are susceptible to varied interpretation. These theories include stakeholder theory, universal rights based on human rights, sustainable development and the common good approach.[107] Stakeholder theory has used a number of ethical theories as the basis of the requirement of the corporation to take into consideration other persons that affect or may be affected by corporate actions.

They include normative moral theory based on Kantian theory,[108] Rawls theory of justice,[109] and other theories of property and distributive justice.[110] These varied theoretical stances are because of the necessity to justify the standpoint that the corporation can be run in the interests of stakeholders. This stakeholder perspective also requires a fundamental reform in the role of the corporation. For example,

102 L E Preston and J E Post, *Private Management and Public Policy: The Principle of Public Responsibility* (Prentice-Hall, Englewood Cliffs, NJ 1975)

103 R E Freeman, *Strategic Management: A Stakeholder Approach* (Pitman, Boston, MA 1984); R E Freeman and W M Evan, 'Corporate Governance: A Stakeholder Interpretation' (1990) 19(4) *Journal of Behavioural Economics* 337–359

104 S Ogden and R Watson, 'Corporate Performance and Stakeholder Management: Balancing Shareholder and Customer Interests in the UK Privatised Water Industry' (1999) 42(5) *Academy of Management Journal* 526–538; J Preston, L Post and S. Sachs, *Redefining the Corporation: Stakeholder Management and Organisational Wealth* (Stanford Business Books, Stanford, CT 2002)

105 Garriga and Melé (n. 85) 59

106 This notion was more recently popularised by D J Wood, 'Corporate Social Performance Revisited' (1991) 16(4) *Academy of Management Review* 691–718

107 See Garriga and Melé (n. 85) 60–61

108 W M Evan and R E Freeman, 'A Stakeholder Theory of the Modern Corporation: Kantian Capitalism' in T Beauchamp and N Bowie (eds), *Ethical Theory and Business* (Prentice-Hall, Englewood Cliffs, NJ 1988) 75–93

109 R A Phillips, 'Stakeholder Theory and a Principle of Fairness' (1997) 7(1) *Business Ethics Quarterly* 51–66

110 T Donaldson and L E Preston, 'The Stakeholder Theory of the Corporation: Concepts, Evidence and Implications' (1995) 20(1) *Academy of Management Review* 65–91

from a Kantian perspective, it requires the balancing of the property rights of the corporation as a legal person with Kant's principle for respect of a person.[111]

Garriga and Melé's attempt to map CSR theories is exemplary but it is immediately obvious that the boundaries are not clear-cut and there is a tendency for overlap within the theories and a mixed use of descriptive and normative approaches within the theories. In arriving at a workable definition of CSR, a pragmatic approach is advisable. Beesley and Evans point out that although CSR has suffered from a lack of definition as an issue and as a consequence discussion has been amorphous and ill-focused, it may still be an effective way of dealing with outstanding social problems, irrespective of whichever of the dominant ideologies is being asserted.[112] There is a significant overlap between the theories and the complementary themes and titles that have developed in association with CSR.

In his 2008 study[113] Melé further realigns his earlier model of theories with complementary themes or multiple interpretations of CSR that have developed. He analyses four contemporary mainstream theories: corporate social performance theory, shareholder value theory, stakeholder theory and corporate citizenship theory as exemplifying the integrative, instrumental, ethical and political theories respectively.

Therefore the next section follows this pattern when examining the theories further. This will mean that the complementary themes are examined in more detail as exemplifying the theories and multiple interpretations of CSR.[114]

The first three themes: corporate social performance, shareholder value theory and stakeholder theory draw from the dominant debates in management discourse representing justification and arguments for CSR from within. They represent integrative, instrumental and ethical theories respectively. The fourth theory, corporate citizenship begins to introduce language from political science but also represents attempts from practitioners to justify good behaviour in society. This is examined as an example of political theories.

111 In this regard, such a perspective applies Kant's practical imperative which requires that one 'act as to treat humanity, whether in thine own person or in that of any other, in every case as an end withal, never as a means only'and reinterprets this to mean that the business as a person should consider the interests of all affected stakeholders in any decision it takes. See I Kant, *Fundamental Principles of the Metaphysics of Morals*, reprinted in L Dennis (ed.), *Groundwork for the Metaphysisc of Morals – Immanuel Kant* (Broadview Press, Ontario 2005) 88. See also N E Bowie, 'A Kantian Approach to Business Ethics' in R E Frederick (ed.), *A Companion to Business Ethics* (Blackwell, Oxford 1999) 1–16, 10

112 M Beesley and T Evans, *CSR: A Reassessment* (Croom Helm, London 1978) 9–10

113 Melé (n. 81)

114 Amaeshi and Adi demonstrate that this is not an exhaustive list as they identify other multiple interpretations including business ethics and morality, corporate greening and green marketing, diversity management, sustainability and so on. However the categorisation covers the main themes in current CSR discourse. See K. Amaeshi and A B C Adi, 'Reconstructing CSR Construct in Utlish' (2007) 16(1) *Business Ethics: A European Review* 3–18

In addition a fifth complementary theme of corporate accountability is included. This sits outside the Garriga and Melé categorisation but it draws from normative legal debates on the role of the corporation and addresses those theories of CSR that have emanated from outside the management and social science fields. It dwells on the external aspects of CSR questioning how society holds corporations to account. Each of these complementary themes as multiple interpretations of CSR will be analysed in more detail in the following section.

2.3.1 Corporate social performance as integrative theory

The key proponents of the corporate social performance (CSP) theory include Carroll,[115] Wartick and Cochran,[116] Wood[117] and Swanson.[118] In 1991 Wood defined CSP as:

> the configuration in the business organisation of principles of social responsibility, processes of response to social requirements, and policies, programs and tangible results that reflect the company's relations with society.[119]

The emphasis is on the corporation or business organisation and its response to society, hence it is an integrative theory. The rationale is to demonstrate interrelationship among diverse topics and provide unifying themes.[120] Its history as a concept lies in the 1970s, with 'corporate responsiveness' and the writings of Ackerman[121] and Sethi.[122]

These writings were focused on corporation behaviour in response to changing societal demands. In 1975 Sethi proposed a model that included social obligations, societal responsibility and social responsiveness. Then in 1979 Carroll formally introduced the term 'corporate social performance' and suggested that corporate response or obligations to society must include the economic, legal,

115 Carroll 1979 (n. 35)

116 S L Wartick and P J Cochran, 'The Evolution of the Corporate Social Performance Model' (1985) 10(4) *Academy of Management Review* 758–769

117 D J Wood, 'Corporate Social Performance Re-visited' (1991) 16(4) *Academy of Management Review* 691–718

118 D L Swanson, 'Addressing a Theoretical Problem by Re-orienting the Corporate Social Performance Model' (1995) 20(1) *Academy of Management Review* 43–64; D L Swanson, 'Towards an Integrative Theory of Business and Society: A Research Strategy for Corporate Social Performance' (1999) 24(3) *Academy of Management Review* 596–621

119 Wood (n. 117)

120 T Jones, 'An Integrating Framework for Research in Business and Society: A Step Towards the Elusive Paradigm? (1983) 8(4) *Academy of Management Review* 559–564

121 R W Ackerman, 'How Companies Respond to Social Demands' (1973) 51(4) *Harvard University Review* 88–98

122 S P Sethi, 'Dimensions of Corporate Social Responsibility' (1975) 17(3) *California Management Review* 58–64

ethical and discretionary aspects.[123] Subsequently, in 1985, Wartick and Cochran addressed corporate response based on principles of social responsibility, the process of social responsiveness and the policy of issues management.[124]

Wood developed this model further and created a CSP model based on three aspects: principles of CSR expressed at institutional, organisational and individual levels as well as the processes of corporate social response and outcomes of corporate behaviour. In outlining this model, the principles of CSR include a drive for legitimacy at the institutional level,[125] 'public responsibility' at an organisational level, implying that business is responsible for outcomes related to its primary and secondary areas of involvement with society,[126] and managerial discretion at the individual level appealing to principles of moral action. The processes of corporate social responsiveness include environmental assessment, stakeholder management and issues management and the outcomes of corporate behaviour include social impacts, social programmes and social policies.

This theory provides an adequate strategy for business when faced with responding to societal pressures and demands for change, it also provides a structure for corporate response to society but it does not provide a rationale for CSR. It also acts like an integrated systemic response that business can produce in response to calls for CSR. When addressing responsibility, it addresses and draws from existing literature that merely identifies that corporations should be responsible. Nevertheless it focuses from a historical viewpoint on corporate response and involves arguments for CSR addressing its response from within the corporation.

2.3.2 Shareholder value theory as instrumental theory

Shareholder value theory (SVT) is a theory of CSR which is largely in line with the traditional view of the role of the corporation as maximising the profit of its shareholders.[127] It developed largely to realign responsibility with profit-making. The theory attempts to demonstrate that CSR is instrumental to shareholder value. Friedman encapsulated the original approach in his saying that 'the one and only responsibility of business towards society is the maximisation of profits to the shareholders within the legal framework and the ethical custom of the country'.[128] This therefore means that those who adhere to this view have to

123 This was developed in 1991 into the 'pyramid of CSR'. See A B Carroll, 'The Pyramid of Corporate Social Responsibility: Towards the Management of Organisational Stakeholders' (1991) (July/August) *Business Horizons* 39–48

124 Wartick and Cochran (n. 116)

125 This is focused on Davis 1973 (n. 34) – society grants legitimacy and power to business and in the long run misuse of such power may result in loss

126 This is based on the principle of 'public responsibility as advocated by Preston and Post (n. 102)

127 A contractual view of the corporation

128 Friedman (n. 89)

demonstrate that CSR could be profitable and was in the interest of business. They seek a justification that harmonises CSR with profit-making.[129]

This has led to the notion of 'enlightened self-interest', which gives rise to consequential giving and actions aligned to the long-run interests of the corporation.[130] It has also led to notions of 'strategic CSR', which refers to policies, programmes and processes which yield benefits to the firm, 'in particular by supporting core business activities and thus contributing to the firm's effectiveness in accomplishing its mission'.[131]

This is also the main source theory for notions of 'enlightened shareholder value', which Jensen describes as long-term value maximisation allowing trade-offs with stakeholders.[132]

In 2008 *The Economist* pointed out that:

> One way of looking at CSR is that it is part of what businesses need to do to keep up with (or, if possible, stay slightly ahead of) society's fast-changing expectations. It is an aspect of taking care of a company's reputation, managing its risks and gaining a competitive . . . So paying attention to CSR can amount to enlightened self-interest, something that over time will help to sustain profits for shareholders. The truly responsible business never loses sight of the commercial imperative.[133]

In spite of this, it is doubtful that all CSR practices can be profitable.[134] Vogel points out that an extensive body of academic research on the link between CSR and profitability is at best inconclusive.[135] The grounding for CSR must be beyond self-interest as the problems that CSR seeks to address are serious and do not rely on a narrow self-interested corporate philanthropy vision.

It is significant that in espousing what has eventually become strategic CSR Porter and Kramer refer to 'strategic corporate philanthropy' and point out that the 'acid test of good corporate philanthropy is whether the desired social change is so beneficial to the company that the organisation would pursue the change even

129 Encapsulated in notions of a business case for CSR or quotes like 'being good is good for business'

130 G D Keim, 'Corporate Social Responsibility: An Assessment of the Enlightened Self-interest Model' (1978) 3(1) *Academy of Management Review* 32–39

131 L Burke and J M Logsdon, 'How Corporate Social Responsibility Pays Off' (1996) 29(4) *Long Range Planning* 495–502, 496

132 M C Jensen, 'Value Maximisation, Stakeholder Theory and the Corporate Objective Function' (2001) 14(3) *Journal of Applied Corporate Finance* 8–21

133 *The Economist* 'Do It Right: Corporate Responsibility is a Matter of Enlightened Self-interest' 17 January 2008 < http://www.economist.com/node/10491124> accessed 19 March 2011

134 Vogel (n. 44)

135 D Vogel 'Is There a Market for Virtue? The Business Case for Corporate Social Responsibility' (2005) 47(4) *California Management Review* 19–45

if no one ever knew about it'.[136] It may be that the history of this theory, which lies in philanthropy, seeks to extend some of its justification to the much more foundational concept of CSR that has arisen from debates about the role of the corporation in society. Yet this theory draws from one of the central debates about the origin and role of the corporation. It relies heavily on a contractual view of the corporation and draws on the notion of property rights that stresses the shareholders as owners of the business and the managers as their employees.[137]

Therefore it inadvertently highlights that true fundamental change to grounding CSR must come from an examination of the role of the corporation in law. The heart of the matter revolves around the role of the corporation in society. One of the indications of this is that the notion of 'enlightened shareholder value' has been at the heart of the reform of the company's director's duties in the UK.[138] It links and contrasts with the next theory which seeks to demonstrate that there are other constituents within the corporation.[139]

2.3.3 Stakeholder theory as ethical theory

Stakeholder theory (ST) also analyses CSR from within the corporation and addresses how the corporation should be managed. However, in one sense, it is a counter-argument to the SVT because it seeks to demonstrate that in running the company management should 'balance the multiple claims of conflicting stakeholders'.[140] The stated objective of the stakeholder theory is to replace the duty to shareholders with a duty to 'stakeholders'.[141] The central concern is to address the question: 'for whose benefit and at whose expense should the firm be managed'?[142] The theory addresses two aspects, the descriptive aspect used to describe the interests that the manager should take into account in running the corporation and the normative aspects, which involve attempts to justify the adoption of these interests through various ethical theories adapted for business.

136 M Porter and M Kramer, 'The Competitive Advantage of Corporate Philanthropy' (2002) 80(12) *Harvard Business Review* 67

137 Melé (n. 81). See also P Ireland, 'Property and Contract in Contemporary Corporate Theory' (2003) 23 *Legal Studies* 453–493

138 See Ministerial Statements, DTI, June 2007 'Companies Act 2006, Duties of Company Directors' <http://www.bis.gov.uk/files/file40139.pdf> accessed 19 March 2011; A Keay, 'Enlightened Shareholder Value, the Reform of Director's Duties and the Corporate Objective' (2006) 3 *Lloyds Maritime and Commercial Law Quarterly* 335–361

139 This is demonstrated in the changes following the ESV principle that allowed for balancing of interests in s.172 of the Companies Act 2006. See L Cerioni, 'The Success of the Company in s.172(1) of the UK Companies Act 2006: Towards the Enlightened Directors' Primacy' (2008) 4(1) *Original Law Review* 1–31

140 R E Freeman, 'A Stakeholder Theory of the Modern Corporation' in T L Beauchamp and N E Bowie (eds), *Ethical Theory and Business* (5th ed., Prentice-Hall, Englewood Cliffs, NJ 1997) 66–76

141 Ibid.

142 Freeman 1997 (n. 140)

These theories have developed as a branch of business ethics promoting the ethical behaviour of business.

This concept was originally introduced by Freeman in 1984 as a strategic management principle on how the corporation should be managed.[143] Evans and Freeman in 1988 gave the following 'stakeholder management principles':

> The corporation ought to be managed for the benefit of its stakeholders: its customers, suppliers, owners, employees and local communities . . . Management bears a fiduciary relationship to stakeholders and to the corporation as an abstract entity. It must act in the interest of stakeholders as their agent, and it must act in the interest of the corporation to ensure the survival of the firm, safeguarding the long-term stakes of these groups.[144]

These principles were based on Kantian ethics and the respect for persons.[145] However, in trying to justify the stakeholder theory position others have based their arguments on several normative ethical positions: Donaldson and Dunfee's integrative social contracts[146] utilise notions of social contract as found in Locke and Rawls to derive hypothetical 'macro' contracts and extant 'micro' contracts for business, Argandona proposes an extension of the common good theory as a basis for the stakeholder theory,[147] Wicks and others extend feminist ethics and find a theoretical basis for stakeholder theory which is relational and caring[148] and Phillips extends principles of fairness to stakeholder theory.[149]

In failing to identify a strong ethical or normative basis, stakeholder theory does not provide a wholesome justification for its version of CSR but it does add to the debate on the role of the corporation in society. Yet Freeman endorses this plurality of theories as central to the stakeholder theory, citing that 'the stakeholder theory can be unpacked into a number of stakeholder theories, each of which has a "normative core" '.[150] The related nature of shareholder and stakeholders can be seen in Jensen's enlightened shareholder value theory which sought to distinguish itself from stakeholder theory and provided justification for considering other

143 R E Freeman, *Strategic Management: A Stakeholder Approach* (Pitman, Boston, MA 1984)

144 W M Evan and R E Freeman, 'A Stakeholder Theory of the Corporation' in T L Beauchamp and N E Bowie (eds), *Ethical Theory and Business* (Prentice-Hall, Englewood Cliffs, NJ 1988) 75–93

145 Ibid.

146 T Donaldson and T W Dunfee, *Ties that Bind: A Social Contracts Approach to Business Ethics* (Harvard Business School Press, Boston, MA 1999)

147 A Argandona, 'The Stakeholder Theory and the Common Good' (1998) 17(9–10) *Journal of Business Ethics* 1093–1102

148 Structuring value-creating activity along principles of caring and connection: A C Wicks, D R Gilbert and R E Freeman, 'A Feminist Re-interpretation of the Stakeholder Concept' (1994) 4(4) *Business Ethics Quarterly* 475–497

149 R A Phillips, 'Stakeholder Theory and a Principle of Fairness' (1997) 7(1) *Business Ethics Quarterly* 51–66

150 Freeman 1997 (n. 140)

interests in the form of trade-offs. Stakeholder theory has been crucial in highlighting that the stake and interest in corporations is not exclusive to shareholders. However, this is a theory emerging from within the corporation (management), justifying its actions or non-action as response or balancing.

In addition, the practical question of how these interests are to be balanced has also plagued practitioners. This has led to theories such as the team production theory, which suggest a reorientation of the corporation towards all stakeholders who contribute firm-specific resources towards corporate production.[151] Yet the search for a workable alternative model of managing the corporation's interests from within goes on because it is important that solutions are practical as well as theoretically sound. This is why stakeholder theory can be criticised as potentially self-serving. Sternberg proposes that 'a business that is accountable to all is actually accountable to none'.[152] This is suggested against the backdrop that the manager may attempt to justify self-serving behaviour by reference to considerations of one or more of the stakeholder groups.

Another limitation of this approach is that it focuses attention on a narrow aspect of the question, which is to determine which groups can be regarded as having a stake, but what is required is a functional basis of responsibility, as it is possible that the groups to whom responsibility is owed may vary from setting to setting.[153] CSR must also deal with the external question of its significant effect on society and responsibility for that effect. Therefore, to a large extent, the stakeholder theory still informs an internal management perspective.

2.3.4 Corporate citizenship as political theory

Corporate citizenship has at its root the notion of the corporation as a citizen in society with rights and responsibilities.[154] This is a term drawn from the political sciences. Presently three views of corporate citizenship can be identified:[155] First, a limited view which equates corporate citizenship with corporate philanthropy;[156] an equivalent view which equates corporate citizenship with CSR;[157] and an

151 M M Blair and L A Stout, 'A Team Production Theory of Corporate Law' (1999) 85(2) *Virginia Law Review* 247–328

152 E. Sternberg, *Just Business: Business Ethics in Action* (2nd ed., Oxford University Press, Oxford 2000) 51

153 Teubner (n. 73)

154 See J Andriof and M McIntosh (eds), *Perspectives of Corporate Citizenship* (Greenleaf, Sheffield 2001)

155 Matten and Crane (n. 97)

156 D J Wood and J M Lodgson, 'Business Citizenship: From Individuals to Organisations' (2002) 3 *Ethics and Entrepreneurship* 59–94 (The Ruffin Series of the Society for Business Ethics); S A Waddock and S B Graves,' The Corporations Social Performance-financial Performance Link' (1997) 18(4) *Strategic Management Journal* 303–320 (a view of corporate citizenship as social investing)

157 A B Carroll, 'Four Faces of Corporate Citizenship' (1998) 100(1) *Business and Society* 1–7

extended conceptualisation which defines corporate citizenship as describing the role of the corporation in administering citizenship rights for individuals.[158]

The term 'corporate citizenship' has developed from a practitioner perspective reflecting on the notion of participation in society and being a good corporate citizen. In 1951, whilst analysing management responsibility in a complex world Abrams pointed out that management as a 'good citizen'[159] who cannot function properly in an acrimonious and contentious atmosphere, has the positive duty to work for peaceful relations and understanding among men. He proposes management should balance the claims of various interested groups, similar to the basis of stakeholder theory.[160]

For some, corporate citizenship is seen as an extension to CSR that reflects how business should act towards stakeholders but there are severe limitations to this extension, as it is basically analysing and considering the same questions as CSR, question about the role of the corporation in society. The notion of a good citizen and a socially responsible corporation are not radically different.

Wood and Logsdon propose a view of business citizenship that is amenable to universal rights.[161] However, this does not advocate that the corporation is compelled by universal rights but that good behaviour via processes and practices that abide with these universal ethical standards is desirable. This results in:

> a set of policies and practices that allow a business organisation to abide by a limited number of universal ethical standards (called hyper norms), to respect local cultural variations that are consistent with hyper norms, to experiment with ways to reconciliate local practices with hyper norms when they are not consistent and to implement systematic learning processes for the benefit of the organisation, local stakeholders and the larger global community.[162]

This global business citizenship model outlines practical steps of corporate behaviour by appealing to respect the universal rights of citizens. The extended conceptualisation of corporate citizenship mentioned earlier even goes a step further in assigning a role for the corporation in administering citizen rights[163]

158 Matten and Crane (n. 97); Matten, Crane and Chapple (n. 100)

159 F W Abrams, 'Management's Responsibilities in a Complex World' (1951) 29(3) *Harvard Business Review* 29–34,30

160 Ibid.

161 D J Wood and J M Logsdon, 'Theorising Business Citizenship: From Individuals to Organizations' in J Androif and M McIntosh (eds), *Perspectives on Corporate Citizenship* (Greenleaf Publishing, Sheffield 2001) 83–103

162 J M Logsdon and D J Wood, 'Implementing Global Business Citizenship: Multi-level Motivations' in J Hooker (ed.), *International Corporate Responsibility: Exploring the Issues* (Carnegie Mellon University Press, Pittsburgh, PA 2005)

163 Matten and Crane (n. 97)

although this view is quite problematic in the absence of political electoral processes for corporations similar to those of governments.[164]

Windsor puts forward a severe criticism of corporate citizenship as an attempt to escape from the debate between the economic (SVT) and the ethical (ST) positions.[165] He points out that citizenship as a metaphor separates into two kinds: instrumental citizenship, which for him is economics in disguise, and idealised citizenship, which simply reflects ethics in disguise. Wood and Logsdon's view of corporate citizenship would be an idealised view of corporate citizenship, while the instrumental view is aligned with notions of obtaining a social licence to operate, which exploits an essentially economic position of strategic self-interest. Corporate citizenship represents an attempt to frame several aspects of the CSR debate from a political perspective and there is a lot of room for developing some of the ideas.

2.3.5 Corporate accountability

Corporate accountability is a complementary theme of CSR which realigns CSR with its history and drivers. It is sometimes identified as CSR and at others in opposition to CSR. The demand for corporations to become responsible has not only come from within the corporation. Corporate responses from within have been in reaction to other aspects of society pushing for change.[166] In a sense the corporate position of strict self-interest became untenable because there are many drivers of CSR practice.[167] They include civil society, communities, consumers, government and employees.[168]

One of the most important drivers is civil society and this can be defined as 'an area of association and action independent of the state and the market in which citizens can organise to pursue purposes that are important to them individually

164 J. (Hans) van Oosterhout, 'Corporate Citizenship: An Idea Whose Time has not Yet Come' (2005) 30(4) *Academy of Management Review* 677–684

165 D Windsor, 'Corporate Social Responsibility – Three Key Approaches' (2006) 43(1) *Journal of Management Studies* 93–114, 106

166 D L Owen, T A Swift, C Humphrey and M C Bowerman, 'The New Social Audits: Accountability, Managerial Capture or the Agenda of Social Champions' (2000) 9(1) *European Accounting Review* 81–98

167 Haigh and Jones identify six sets of influences: 'internal pressures on business managers, pressure from business competitors, investors and consumers and regulatory pressures coming from governments and non-governmental organisations'. M Haigh and M Jones, 'The Drivers of Corporate Social Responsibility: A Critical Review' (2006) 5(2) *The Business Review, Cambridge* 1–9

168 Department for International Development (DFID); DFID and Corporate Social Responsibility Issues Paper <http://www.dfid.gov.uk/pubs/files/corporate-social-resp.pdf> accessed 16 March 2011. These are all factors counter-influenced by globalisation to varying degrees

or collectively'.[169] Civil society, including non-government organisations and communities, highlighted the critical incidents that have occurred in several parts of the world recently and began to draw attention to the negative aspects of corporate power. These include: the Shell Brent Spar incident,[170] the Shell crisis in Nigeria,[171] the Bhopal chemical spill,[172] the Exxon Valdez oil spill,[173] the use of slave labour in Burma and the controversial working conditions in Asian factories,[174] the baby milk scandals,[175] the conflicts between indigenous peoples, mining communities and mining companies in South American countries, West Papua and other areas,[176] the pharmaceutical industry and the anti-retroviral drugs crisis[177] and the Enron collapse[178] among others.

169 L D Brown, S Khagram, M H Moore and P Frumkin, 'Globalisation, Non-governmental Organisations and Multi-sectoral Relations' in J S Nye and J D Donahue (eds), *Governance in a Globalizing World* (Brookings Institute, Washington, DC 2000) 271–286

170 Greenpeace controversially stopped the dumping of the Brent Spar (North Sea) oil storage facility in the ocean. See G Jordan, *Shell, Greenpeace and the Brent Spar* (Palgrave, Basingstoke 2001)

171 Shell's alleged complicity in the deaths of Ogoni human rights activists and other human rights violations. See D Wheeler, H Fabig and R Boele, 'Paradoxes and Dilemmas for Stakeholder Responsive Firms in the Extractive Sector: Lessons from the Case of Shell and the Ogoni' (2002) 39(3) *Journal of Business Ethics* 297–318; B. Manby, *Shell in Nigeria: Corporate Social Responsibility and the Ogoni Crisis,* Carnegie Council on Ethics and International Affairs Case 267 (Institute for the Study of Diplomacy, Georgetown University, Washington, DC 2000)

172 This was a chemical leak from a storage facility in Bhopal, India that resulted in the death of thousands of people. See R A G Monks and N Minow, *Corporate Governance* (3rd ed., Blackwell, Oxford 2004) 18–19

173 An oil tanker accident resulting in one of the largest oil spills ever. This occurred in a region of Alaska which is a habitat for many different species of sea creatures and fish. The livelihood of the local fishing population was also adversely affected. See M Baker, 'Companies in Crisis – What not to Do When It All Goes Wrong: Exxon Mobil and Exxon Valdez' <http://www.mallenbaker.net/csr/crisis03.html> accessed 10 April 2011

174 A Ramasastry, 'Corporate Complicity: From Nuremburg to Rangoon, an Examination of Forced Labour Cases and Their Impact on the Liability of MNC' (2002) 20 *Berkeley Journal of International Law* 91–137

175 Nestlé, the largest artificial baby milk producer, was implicated in allegations of scandalous marketing practices, especially in developing countries. The Business and Human Rights website details various baby food and baby milk controversies <http://www.business-humanrights.org/Categories/Sectors/Agriculturefoodbeveragetobaccofishing/Babyfoodbabymilk> accessed 10 April 2011

176 N Yakovleva, *CSR in the Mining Industries* (Ashgate, Aldershot 2005); T E Downing, J Moles, I McIntosh and C Garcia-Downing, *Indigenous Peoples and Mining Encounters: Strategies and Tactics* April 2002 Report No. 57 Mining, Minerals and Sustainable Development (MMSD), Institute for Environment and Development (IIED), World Business Council for Sustainable Development (WBCSD), 2002)

177 World Bank Development Report 2006 *Equity and Development* (IBRD/WB/Oxford University Press, Washington, DC 2005) 215

178 The sudden collapse of a large energy corporation, Enron, opened up questions on the ethical aspect of such corporations. Buhr and Grafstrom remark that 'the collapse of ENRON in the autumn of 2001 marked a watershed in the discussion of CSR'. H Buhr and

It gave rise to anti-globalisation feelings expressed vividly in the 1999 Seattle protests against the World Trade Organization and at large global or business meetings since then.[179] It is in this sense that scholars conclude that 'the emergence of organised civil society and of NGOs as an organisational manifestation of broader social movements has dramatically altered the global-political-economic landscape'.[180]

The large corporation is viewed as an archetype of globalisation and its actions symptomatic of its growing power and effect on society. Various aspects of civil society decidedly forced the issue of change onto the agenda and this occurred against a background of weak instruments and failed initiatives at the international level. NGOs have begun to target MNCs with increasing frequency and vigour in recent years.[181] They excelled in the use of media to disseminate information especially through the internet. This is demonstrated by the Greenpeace and Brent Spar campaign which galvanised media and consumer focus on Shell and prompted a change of tactics by the oil corporation.[182] These NGOs began to attack corporations directly because of the perception of an inability to govern multinational corporate conduct at an international level. At the international level states are deemed the only direct addresses of international law and attempts to directly regulate non-state actors such as MNCs have proved unsuccessful so far.[183]

The effectiveness of the NGO attack on transnational corporations was greatly assisted by the speedy and widely available communication networks that now exist under globalisation. An example is given below:

> a developing country protester with a digital video camera (perhaps provided by a developed country NGO) can film an indiscretion of oil company security forces and send the clip by e-mail instantly to influence media and developed country decision-makers). The internet essentially provides a big floodlight for NGOs to shine on the overseas operations of multinational corporations.[184]

M Grafstrom, 'The Making of Meaning in the Media, the Case of CSR in the FT' in F Den Hond, F G A De Bakker and P Neergaard, *Managing CSR in Action: Talking, Doing and Measuring* (Ashgate, Aldershot 2007) 15–32, 26

179 J Bendell, *Barricades and Boardrooms: A Contemporary History of the Corporate Accountability Movement* (Paper 13: United Nations Research Institute for Social Development, Geneva 2004)

180 H Teegen, J P Doh and S Vachani, 'The Importance of Non-governmental Organisations in Global Governance and Value Creation: An International Business Agenda' (2004) 35(6) *Journal of International Business* 463–483, 463

181 P Newell, 'Managing Multinationals: The Governance of Investment for the Environment' 13 *Journal of International Development* 907–919, 910

182 G. Jordan, *Shell, Greenpeace and Brent Spar* (Palgrave Macmillan, New York, 2001)

183 Examples include M Noortmann and C Ryngaert, *Non-state Actor Dynamics in International Law* (Ashgate, Aldershot 2010)

184 P Swanson, 'Corporate Social Responsibility and the Oil Sector' 11(1) *CEPMLP Journal* 1–4

Bendell points to a critical point in 2002 when a key divide in CSR discourse emerged between those who regarded corporate power as a problem and those who either accepted it or considered it as an opportunity, if used appropriately.[185] He referred to the first group as 'corporate accountability' and the second group as 'corporate responsibility'. This distinction is nevertheless an artificial one, as this may be said to represent varying levels of critique of corporate power and the corporation's role in society.[186] Corporate accountability focuses on the question of power and its accountability. The underlying justification is that for power to be legitimate, it must be subject to constraints. Stokes points out that:

> if private property (such as corporations claim to be) is to be legitimate within the framework of liberal society, it is also necessary to show that there are constraints which prevent it from becoming a source of power which threatens the liberty of the individual or rivals the power of the state.[187]

Therefore questions which come to the fore in corporate accountability are similar to those raised with governments in traditional questions of public accountability. That is, 'how to keep power under control, how to domesticate (tame) it, how to prevent its abuse, how to subject it to certain procedures and rules of conduct'.[188] Garvey and Newell extend this definition to corporate accountability pointing out the 'answerability aspects' and the 'enforceability' aspects.[189]

This area has also revitalised the interface between CSR and the law. It highlights law as an important aspect of the CSR toolkit[190] which can strengthen answerability or enforceability in varied frameworks. In her work Pillay identifies two strands of corporate accountability: 'post-voluntarist' strains and the 'challenge to the neo-liberal orthodoxy'.[191] Whereas the first strand deals with a hardening of voluntary CSR initiatives and the interplay between the voluntary and the legal, the second strand can be summed up in the question, 'Is CSR as it is currently being preached and practised by multinational corporations around the world actually a red

185 Bendell (n. 179) 18

186 M Kerr, R Janda and C Pitts, *Corporate Social Responsibility – A Legal Analysis* (LexisNexis, Ontario 2009)

187 M Stokes, 'Company Law and Legal Theory' in W. Twining (ed.), *Legal Theory and Common Law* (Blackwell, Oxford 1986) 155

188 A Schedler, *The Self-restraining State: Power and Accountability in New Democracies* (Lynne Rienner Publishers, Boulder, CO 1999) 13

189 N Garvey and P Newell, 'Corporate Accountability to the Poor? Assessing the Effectiveness of Community-based Strategies' UK Institute of Development Studies, Brighton, Working Paper 227, October 2004, 4

190 H Ward, 'Corporate Social Responsibility in Law and Policy' in N Boeger, R Murray and C Villiers, *Perspectives on Corporate Social Responsibility* (Edward Elgar, Cheltenham 2008) 8–38

191 R Pillay, *The Changing Nature of Corporate Social Responsibility: CSR and Development in Context – The Case of Mauritius* (Routledge, Abingdon 2015) 10–21

herring?', distracting attention from more fundamental reform of the capitalist model.[192]

In the second strand, some authors argue that corporate accountability within a neo-liberal structure is severely limited and vulnerable to corporate ideological capture.[193] This idea is also inherent in Pillay's characterisation of ameliorative CSR and transformative CSR, where ameliorative CSR emerges against a neo-liberal backdrop of markets, deregulation and shareholder primacy as paired respons-ibility to social obligations within the given framework, whereas a more radical transformative CSR would question the backdrop and push for 'public interest'.[194]

Corporate accountability is nevertheless an integral part of CSR. As Kerr and others[195] point out the relevant aspects of accountability are complementary to CSR. These include: giving justification or account of actions, receiving rewards or punishments for those actions and achieving results in line with stated business goals, legal requirements and social expectations.

2.4 Extending essentially contested concepts as an analytical tool to CSR

In view of the multiple interpretations and theories of CSR as well as the level of contestations, it is quite difficult to decipher a single definition of CSR. Nevertheless this section will apply Gallie's ECC theory as an analytical tool and examine CSR as an essentially contested concept. The aim is to propose a common core in the contest that unites themes of CSR. Therefore this section will explain the ECC theory and then apply it to CSR

2.4.1 Explaining essentially contested concepts

In 1956 Gallie proposed a '*single explanatory hypothesis calling for some fairly rigid schematization*' [196] which he had hoped would give us enlightenment of a much needed kind, with regard to concepts which perpetually engender disputes. Gallie pointed out that 'there are concepts which are essentially contested concepts, the proper use of which inevitably involves endless disputes about their proper uses on the part of their users'.[197]

192 J Bendell, *The Corporate Responsibility Movement* (Greenleaf Publishing, Sheffield, 2009) 216

193 A Grear and B H Weston, 'The Betrayal of Human Rights and the Urgency of Universal Corporate Accountability: Reflections on a Post-*Kiobel* Lawscape' (2015) 15(1) *Human Rights Law Review* 21–44

194 Pillay (n. 191) 10

195 Kerr *et al.* (n. 186) 25

196 W B Gallie 'Essentially Contested Concepts' (1958) 56 *Proceedings of the Aristotelian Society* 167–198, reprinted in M. Black (ed.), *The Importance of Language* (Prentice-Hall, Englewood Cliffs, NJ 1962) 121–146, 122 (emphasis added)

197 Ibid. at 123

In setting out his theory of ECC Gallie laid out the following seven important criteria:[198]

1. An ECC must be appraisive in the sense that it signifies or accredits some kind of valued achievement.
2. This achievement must be of an internally complex character; for all that its worth is attributed to it as a whole.
3. Any explanation of its worth must therefore include reference to the respective contributions of its various parts and features.
4. The accredited achievement must be of a kind that admits of considerable modification in the light of changing circumstances.
5. To use an essentially contested concept means to use it both aggressively and defensively.
6. The derivation of any such concept from an original exemplar whose authority is acknowledged by all the contestant users of the concept.
7. The probability or plausibility of the claim that the continuous competition between contestant users of the concept enables the original exemplar's achievement to be developed in optimum fashion.

Fortunately, in setting out these conditions Gallie also used examples to further our understanding of what he meant. For our purposes, one of the most appropriate is that of the political concept of democracy. For Gallie, democracy is appraisive or evaluative because a primary question in major policy decisions has come to be 'is it democratic?'[199] And the response signifies a valued achievement. This valued achievement is, however, dependent on other value judgements that may be made to assess if democracy is of good value.

In this vein Connolly points out that there is an inherent value judgement in assessing such concepts, therefore 'if we say a society is undemocratic or that a practice does not meet democratic standards . . . we are describing it from the vantage point of accepted standards of political participation, debate and accountability'.[200] For Connolly, therefore, the relationship between the criteria of a concept and its purpose is what makes notions such as democracy the subject of intense disputes. This may be the sense in which 'the evaluative nature' is the criterion and not the response as it may equally apply to concepts which may signify 'disapproved or denigrated phenomena'.[201] Therefore, for ECC the evaluative or appraisive nature is a multilayered one, first because we assess for valued achievement or disapproved phenomena and also because this assessment is based on inherent value judgements.

198 Ibid. at 125 and 136
199 Gallie (n. 196) 135
200 W E Connolly, *The Terms of Political Discourse* (3rd ed., Blackwell, Oxford 1993) 29
201 M Freeden, *Ideologies and Political Theory – A Conceptual Approach* (Oxford University Press, Oxford 1998) 56

For Gallie, the second and third conditions are linked, he points out that democracy is internally complex and therefore admits to a variety of descriptions in which its different aspects are graded in different orders of importance. In his example democracy could mean the power of the majority of citizens to choose or remove government, or equality of all citizens irrespective of race, sex, etc. to lead politically, or the continuous active participation of citizens in political life at all levels. In different political traditions, Western or otherwise, the aspects of democracy that are emphasised vary to a greater or lesser degree on the relevance to that tradition.[202] This nature of an ECC is occasionally referred to as 'diverse describability' because an ECC can be described in a variety of ways. It has also been highlighted that 'diverse describability' may involve an exclusive emphasis on one or more facets of the concept.[203]

The fourth criterion, which specifies the accredited achievement must be of a kind that admits of considerable modification in the light of changing circumstances, is usually suggested as rendering such a concept to be 'open in character'.[204] For Gallie, democratic targets will be raised or lowered as circumstances alter and democratic achievements will be judged in light of those changing circumstances.[205] This is another key factor which creates essential contestability; as such modification may create new facets previously unattributed to the original concept.

To satisfy the fifth requirement, democracy in his example can also be used aggressively and defensively hinging on its general use.[206] In this sense, it is used against other uses and recognised that it is to be maintained against other uses. Some analysts query this criterion pointing out that some proponents of an ECC use a concept in such a way as to differ from other usages;[207] however the aggressive and defensive use of concepts always exists within the contested uses of the ECC as a whole, although perhaps not within each individual work.

The sixth criterion is the most controversial as it points to an incontrovertible issue which is that there is the need for an 'exemplar', i.e. common basis. He elucidates on this point thus:

> This exemplar's way of playing must be recognised by all contesting teams . . . as the way the game is to be played, yet because of the internally complex and variously describable character of the exemplar's play, it is natural that different features in it should be weighted differently by different appraisers, and hence that our different teams should have come to hold different *conceptions* of how the game should be played.[208]

202 Gallie (n. 196) 135

203 D Collier, F D Hidalgo and A O Maciuceanu, 'Essentially Contested Concepts: Debates and Applications' (2006) 11(3) *Journal of Political Ideologies* 211–246, 217

204 Gallie (n. 196) 125

205 Ibid. at 136

206 Ibid.

207 Collier (n. 203)

208 Gallie (n. 196) 129

It is in light of this that other philosophers have chosen a concept/conceptions distinction,[209] correctly pointing out that there is a core notion and multiple interpretations.

It is in this sense of the 'exemplar' that Rawls in his book *A Theory of Justice* points to a distinction between a concept and its conceptions, when with regard to the concept and conceptions of justice he writes:

> those who hold different conceptions of justice can then still agree that institutions are just when no arbitrary distinctions are made between persons in the assigning of basic rights and duties and when the rules determine the proper balance between competing claims to the advantages of social life. Man can agree to this description of just institutions since the notion of an arbitrary distinction are left open for each to interpret according to the principles of justice that he accepts . . .[210]

In relation to our chosen example, democracy, Gallie points to an exemplar of 'a long tradition . . . of demands, aspirations, revolts and reforms of a common anti-inegalitarian character'.[211] For the final criterion, Gallie prescribes that continuous competition between contestant users enables the exemplar to develop in optimum fashion but he concedes that within democracy it may fan the flames of conflict.[212] He suggests some mitigation may be possible if the essentially contested nature of the concept is accepted. Still the additional point recognised at this juncture is that continuous competition can be beneficial or harmful to the development of an ECC.

Gallie's hypothesis has provoked a huge response[213] because a conflict resides within it that is replicated in many concepts of social sciences. The reality that even where we accept the essentially contested nature of a concept, there is a need to identify something in common if contestants are to claim that they partake in the same contest. As Gray points out:

> Unless divergent theories or world-views have something in common, their constituent concepts cannot be "contested" even though their proponents are in conflict. References to definitional "contests" have a point only if there is something which is not treated as "contestable".[214]

209 J Rawls, *A Theory of Justice* (Oxford University Press, Oxford 1971) 5–6; S Lukes, *Power: A Radical View* (Macmillan, London 1974)

210 Rawls ibid.

211 Gallie (n. 196) 136

212 Gallie (n. 196) 137

213 J Waldron, 'Is the Rule of Law an Essentially Contested Concept (in Florida)?' (2002) 21(2) *Law and Philosophy* 137–164, 149

214 J N Gray, 'On the Contestability of Social and Political Concepts' (1977) 5(3) *Political Theory* 331–348, 342

If from the following analysis CSR proves to be an ECC, this is also an inherent conflict which must be resolved.

2.4.2 CSR as essentially contested concept

To fit into Gallie's theory of ECC, CSR has to satisfy the seven conditions highlighted above. Gray points out more generally that 'essentially contested concepts occur characteristically in social contexts which are recognizably those of an ideological dispute'.[215] CSR is undoubtedly a social phenomenon which not only questions what sort of relationship business should have with society but if business should have any relationship with society and what form this relationship should take.

First, CSR can be perceived as appraisive or evaluative, in the sense that it is seen as accrediting a vital element to corporations. Therefore for CSR, similar to Gallie's example on democracy, the question has come to be 'is the corporation socially responsible?' And the response often signifies or accredits a kind of valued achievement. Social responsibility is seen as a valued achievement, valued by management, civil society and other stakeholders.

Websites of companies upload reports to affirm CSR activity and corporate reporting of CSR is now firmly established as desirable activity.[216] NGOs keep a firm watch on corporate behaviour to highlight irresponsibility. Connolly correctly points out that the value of the response will depend on the inherent value judgements to the questioner, in the same way that there are proponents for and against CSR in business, who still question whether CSR is a 'good' or a 'bad' thing although there is more consensus that CSR is desirable.

Next CSR can be shown to be internally complex as it admits 'a variety of descriptions in which its different aspects are graded in different orders of importance'.[217] The complexity of CSR reveals itself in the multiple interpretations and dimensions that have so far been analysed by several writers. Dimensions identified from CSR definitions include the economic, legal, ethical and discretionary dimensions or the human rights, environment and labour angles.[218] The emphasis placed on each of these dimensions depends on the motivation, interest or objective of the writer. The importance given to each of these different aspects has varied across different proponents.

Therefore a business definition of CSR will give credence to the economic interests and perhaps seek to prove that CSR is subsumed under a profit objective, an example is the Confederation of Business Industry (CBI) definition 'CSR requires companies to acknowledge that they are publicly accountable not only for

215 Ibid. at 333

216 J Allouche (ed.), *CSR: Concepts, Accountability and Reporting* (Palgrave Macmillan, London 2006)

217 Gallie (n. 196)

218 A. Dahlsrud, 'How CSR is Defined' (2008) 15 *CSR and Environmental Management* 1–13

financial performance, but also for their social and environmental record . . .';[219] whereas an NGO would seek to emphasise the legal and ethical angles. In his recent article Dahlsrud identifies the environmental, social, economic, stakeholder and voluntary dimensions from the frequency of words used in a Google search on the internet.[220]

Another indication of the internal complexity can be exemplified by attempts to map CSR scope, theories and approaches. This has been done in diverse ways. Lantos by distinguishing between ethical, altruistic and strategic CSR;[221] Garriga and Melé by identifying four groups of CSR approaches: instrumental, political, integrative and ethical.[222] For Garriga and Melé, instrumental theories perceive CSR as merely a means to an end of profit, while the political theories emphasise the social power of the corporation in relation to society and its responsibility. The integrative group consider that business ought to integrate social demands as it depends on society for continuity and growth, while ethical theories entrench their views in ethics pointing out that firms ought to accept social responsibility as an ethical obligation. For instance, ethical theories and approaches cover the use of sustainable development, human rights and the stakeholder theory. However, there are no clear-cut maps and overlaps occur in the use of theories and approaches.

Additionally there has been use of differing terminology to emphasise and attempt to distinguish certain aspects of CSR. One of the best examples is the attempt to apply the political concept of citizenship to CSR. Yet corporate citizenship is not defined very differently from CSR, 'good corporate citizenship . . . can be defined as understanding and managing a company's wider influences on society for the benefit of the company and society as a whole'.[223] A survey of competing terminology[224] reveals other terminology which include corporate sustainability,[225] corporate social performance[226] and corporate accountability[227] among others. These terms are often defined in similar terms and used interchangeably with CSR.

219 C A Hemingway, *An Exploratory Analysis of CSR: Definitions, Motives and Values* (2002) Research Memorandum 34, University of Hull Business School

220 Dahlsrud (n. 218)

221 G Lantos, 'The Boundaries of Strategic CSR' (2001)18(7) *Journal of Consumer Marketing* 595–630

222 Garriga and Melé (n. 85)

223 M McIntosh, R Thomas, D Leipziger and G Coleman, *Living Corporate Citizenship* (Financial Times/Prentice-Hall, London 2002); C. Marsden and J Andriof, 'Towards an Understanding of Corporate Citizenship and How to Influence It' (1998) 2(2) *Citizenship Studies* 329–352

224 Amaeshi and Adi (n. 114)

225 M Van Marrewijk, 'Concepts and Definitions of CSR and Corporate Sustainability: Between Agency and Communion' (2003) 44(2–3) *Journal of Business Ethics* 95–105

226 D J Wood, 'Corporate Social Performance Revisited' 16(4) *Academy of Management Review* 691–718

227 Bendell (n. 179)

Well-founded CSR debates refer to the different features ascribed to the term and these various features of CSR have changed over time. This diverse describability is the sense in which several CSR writers focus on specific features of CSR aligning it to their own situations and challenges. In the process, the content of CSR practice has varied over time to reflect the needs of the particular participants in the relationship. An example would be the inclusion of anti-corruption as the tenth principle in the UN Global Compact with the earlier nine principles drawn from human rights, labour standards and environmental principles.[228]

In addition the concept of CSR is used both aggressively and defensively. Perhaps a good illustration is the NGOs' campaign for MNCs to adopt CSR contrasted with the MNCs' defensive claims of CSR practice.[229]

The most significant criterion is whether discussions of CSR should claim authority from an original exemplar whose authority is acknowledged by all the contestant users of the concept. Perhaps the solution may be that while there can be varied conceptions; there is a core that links these debates. In Gallie's example of democracy he speaks of 'a long tradition of demands, aspirations, revolts and reforms of a common anti-inegalitarian character . . .'[230] and perhaps, in relation to CSR it would be the long tradition of societal demands for control of corporate power.

In a more generalised way, CSR is about the changing relationship and expectations of corporations and society, yet the debates are triggered by the increasing corporate power and the drive to make it legitimate in today's society. For example, in charting the modern era of CSR Carroll points out that 'Bowen's work in 1953 proceeded from the belief that the several hundred largest businesses were vital centres of power and decision-making and that the actions of these firms touched the lives of citizens at many points'.[231] This statement on power and its effect on the lives of citizens in society is even more applicable today. Donaldson points out that power is a morally neutral concept, capable of being used for good or evil.[232] It is that 'capability' and 'use' that is in contention.

Some of the resulting ideas include capability for good use such as questions about the corporate manager's role in society, the challenge of balancing

228 The UN Global Compact is an international CSR initiative aimed at creating voluntary global networks to enhance CSR practice. It draws on the Universal Declaration of Human Rights, the International Labour Organisation's Declaration on Fundamental Principles and Rights at Work, the Rio Declaration on Environment and Development and the UN Convention against Corruption. See D Leipziger, *The Corporate Responsibility Code Book* (2nd ed., Greenleaf, Sheffield 2010)

229 A Dahlsrud 'How CSR is Defined' (2008) 15 *CSR and Environmental Management* 1–13

230 Gallie (n. 196)

231 A B Caroll, 'CSR: Evolution of a Definitional Construct' (1999) 38(3) *Business and Society* 268–295, 269

232 T Donaldson, *The Ethics of International Business* (Oxford University Press, Oxford 1989) 32

competing claims to corporate resources and philanthropy[233] calls for social justice represented by appeals for a human face to global markets[234] and the role of business in sustainable development.[235] While also demanding responsibility for wrongful use of power such as in 'financial scandals, human rights violations, environmental side-effects, collaboration with repressive regimes . . .'[236] These issues demonstrate the increased impact of corporate power and society's need to constrain the ability to misuse such power. CSR also extends to channelling such power to constructive uses beneficial to society.

The final criterion is that the continuous competition between the contestant users of CSR sustains the development of CSR in optimum fashion. It could perhaps be argued that it is this contentious nature of CSR that has caused CSR to develop into a distinct field. However such a contentious nature can also be harmful. In his example of democracy Gallie questions whether contention within democracy is not rather more likely to fan the flames of conflict. He resolves this by proposing the possibility that an acceptance of the essentially contested nature of such a concept might affect such conflict. However, contention about its appropriate meaning has been detrimental to establishing and assessing the achievement of CSR. Van Marrewijk points out that the 'subsequent diversity and overlap in terminology, definitions and conceptual models hampers academic debate and on-going research'.[237] While Whitehouse comments that as a consequence 'the whirlwind of debate over the last 75 years has consumed substantial energy while ultimately going around in circles'.[238]

Perhaps the view of CSR as an ECC will serve a purpose if other participants in the contest will take more time to get a wholesome view of the various conceptions before adding theirs. However, hopefully the view taken in this book will help to derive an exemplar for CSR whilst leaving room for contextual interpretations of CSR.

2.5 Deriving a corporate social responsibility exemplar

This examination reveals that, at a general level, CSR's exemplar is the relationship between business and society. However, it is important to derive a more specific reference point. This can be done with the assistance of the criteria laid out in McMahon's models of the relationship between corporation and society, where

233 W Frederick, *Corporation be Good! The Story of CSR* (Dog Ear Publications Inc, Indianapolis, IN 2006)

234 McIntosh *et al.* (n. 223)

235 J. G. Frynas, 'The False Developmental Promise of CSR: Evidence of Multinational Oil Companies'(2005) 81(3) *International Affairs* 581–598

236 G Palazzo and A G Scherer, 'Corporate Legitimacy as Deliberation: A Communicative Framework' (2006) 66 *Journal of Business Ethics* 71–88

237 Van Marrewijk (n. 225)

238 L Whitehouse, 'CSR as Regulation: The Argument from Democracy' in J O'Brien (ed.), *Governing the Corporation* (Wiley, London 2005) 141–162

he identifies two types of ways or models of looking at all such relationships.[239] These two ways can be conceived of as the power models and the rights models.[240] The power models stress the significance of power and power relations in relationships between corporations and society while the rights models draw from a contractual theme in society.

This distinction coincides with the approaches to questions about the nature of the corporation as a legal person. In essence, the question of persons as individual beings with priority given to contract and property rights or persons as social beings with priority given to democracy, fairness and trust. This is perhaps why rights approaches are firmly rooted in contractual origins whereas the power models draw on notions of fairness and democracy.

The rights approaches are usually based on an interpretation of contract theories. They are of four types as identified by McMahon:

Explicit contract: This involves rights arising from explicit contracts between firms and the local community or group. This clearly identifies rights and obligations in a written or oral form. McMahon gives the example of planned cities in Reston, Virginia and Columbia, Maryland in the United States, where there is an accord between claimants including business firms like General Electric Corp. over rights and obligations.[241] Within CSR these explicit contracts could be said to give rise to consequential rights in the case of framework agreements where signatories accept that there are mutual commitments and obligations relevant to both parties. An example would be the agreement between the Norwegian Oil and Petrochemical Workers Union and the International Federation of Chemical, Energy, Mine and General Workers Union and Statoil.[242] Or a better example might be the 'good neighbour agreements', described as compacts, drawn up by major companies in co-operation with local residents.[243] These have been promoted by community activists in the United States as a means of achieving environmental justice.[244] The explicit contract is not very common; it is used in a few specific circumstances. When these contracts are spelt out, they form obligations only as between the parties involved to the extent of the terms specified within the contract. This is static and limited. It is therefore a very limited basis on which to place the justification for CSR, it is rather more closely associated to obligations arising from pure contracts.

239 T F McMahon, 'Models of the Relationship of the Firm to Society' (1986) 5 *Journal of Business Ethics* 181–191. McMahon refers to corporations as firms

240 Ibid.

241 McMahon (n. 239)

242 D Leipziger· *The Corporate Responsibility Code Book* (Greenleaf Publishing, Sheffield 2003) 351

243 B M Illsley, 'Good Neighbour Agreements: The First Step to Environmental Justice' (2002) 7(1) *Local Environment* 69–79

244 Ibid.

Implied contract: Within this approach, proponents describe the idea that continued association between the firm and society could give rise to legitimate expectations of mutual rights and obligation. Garrett, an advocate of this perspective, identifies three potential areas for the use of implied contracts. They could arise between firm and employee, between employer and employee and between firm and local community where such mutual rights and obligation arise out of continuing relationships.[245] In many respects this is similar to the CSR notion of the MNC needing a 'licence to operate' from communities.

In the same vein Gamble and Kelly indicate that 'in many national jurisdictions the granting of a "licence to operate" to companies inevitably raises questions as to what they should give in return'.[246] However similar problems arise chiefly from using a contractual basis. Namely, in contracts expectations do not usually give rise to rights and obligations, they are more akin to aspirations. McMahon points out that expectation may only give rise to rights in cases where there is a pre-established criterion, but CSR relations between corporation and communities are often novel, pre-established standards do not exist. Even where these exist in other operational areas of the company, it will be arguable whether or not it can be extended to new areas as of right.[247] Interestingly, in his article on corporate governance, Williamson points out that the community occupies a unique position; needing specially crafted[248] protection but falling short of direct representation on boards. The protection, in his view, must be adequate to address externalities and the hazards of appropriation.[249] This in itself raises power issues, as the communities may not be able to achieve this protection without adequate authority.

Market contract: This refers to the simple buyer-seller contract within a free competitive environment. This is the traditional economic position towards corporate social relations where the local community is in the same position as any other citizen who may choose to buy the company's products. This is

245 'Business normally expects that the local community will maintain a reasonable and orderly tax policy and encourage good labor relations. The community on its side assumes the business will strive to maintain stable employment patterns as well as pay its taxes and protect community resources . . .' See T M Garrett, *Business Ethics* (Prentice-Hall, Englewood Cliffs, NJ 1966) 185

246 A Gamble and G Kelly, 'The Politics of the Company' in J Parkinson, A Gamble and G Kelly (eds), *The Political Economy of the Company* (Hart Publishing, Oxford 2000) 21–49

247 This has implications for the double standards debate regarding standards in developing and developed countries

248 This refers to his statistical representation of the relationship between corporation and other actors. See O Williamson, 'Corporate Governance' (1984) 93(7) *Yale Law Journal* 1197–1229, 1215

249 Ibid.

the rights analogy used by classical economists like Milton Friedman,[250] who simply argue that the community has no special privileges, except that it has a buyer-seller contract; the local community is no more than the operating environment. McMahon is at odds with this view as he points out that the economic, social and political power which firm and local communities possess come into play in this relationship.[251] Markets are not power neutral and therefore may not result in adequate limitations on corporations in the interests of buyers, and this may be especially the case in community interests. As Coleman points out, 'in the control of a large corporate body, however, a perfect market for such exchange does not exist . . .'[252]

Social contract: This theory seeks to extend jurisprudential social contract theories into the relationship between corporations and society.[253] Donaldson, a major proponent of this approach, argues that the point of applying social contract theory to business is to clarify the moral foundations of productive organisations.[254] He therefore views the social contract in this light:

> As we look at the moral foundations of business, we are to presume that rational individuals living in a state of 'nature' in which everyone produces without benefit of direct cooperative efforts of others – attempt to sketch the terms of the agreement between themselves and the productive organisations upon which they are considering bestowing status as legal, fictional persons and to which they are considering allowing access both to natural resources and the existing employment pool.[255]

The social contract is more apt for the political context than the social context. It is challenged on the grounds of not having identifiable real community or corporation representation. However, the social contract theory is also seen as a basis for applying human rights to corporate social contexts. The argument being that the United Nations Declaration of Human Rights is a new social contract which shares responsibilities in the post-world war era.[256] While this

250 For his position, see M. Friedman, *Capitalism and Freedom* (University of Chicago Press, Chicago 1962) 12–16

251 McMahon (n. 239)

252 See J S Coleman, 'Reply to Hayduk' (1976) 41(6) *American Sociological Review* 1081

253 Traditional exponents of the social contract theory include Hobbes, Locke, Rousseau and Rawls. See D Boucher and P Kelly, *The Social Contract from Hobbes to Rawls* (Routledge, Abingdon1994); T Hobbes, *Leviathan* (new ed., Longman, Harlow 2008); J. Rousseau, *The Social Contract* (Wordsworth, Ware, Hertfordshire 1998); J. Locke, *The Second Treatise of Government* (Hackett Publishing, Indianapolis, IN 1980)

254 T. Donaldson, *The Ethics of International Business* (Oxford University Press, Oxford, 1989) 47

255 Ibid.

256 W Cragg, 'Human Rights and Business Ethics: Fashioning a New Social Contract' (2000) 27 *Journal of Business Ethics* 205–214; O. Amao, 'CSR, Social Contract, Corporate Personhood and HR Law – Understanding the Emerging Responsibilities of Modern Corporations' (2008) 33 *Australian Journal of Legal Philosophy* 100–133

is an appealing emotive view, there are limitations in making this the central basis for CSR. First CSR affects more than human rights issues. Furthermore human rights themselves are contentious as it is not yet settled that there is a universal basis of application or a universal social contract. This theory may justify a demand for rational and acceptable behaviour for business but it cannot set a compelling agenda for CSR; rather it appeals to what corporations ought to do.

The alternative to the above approaches is the power approaches or models. These models identify power as the crucial element in the relationship between corporations and society. The following analysis identifies four models. McMahon identifies three but the fourth model can be derived from more recent literature on this issue.

Power-responsibility model: This was first propounded by Davis.[257] He felt that the firm or corporation had social relationships reflective of its social power.[258] He developed two principles: first, the social power equation, which indicated that the greater the power of the firm, the greater the firm's social responsibility. Second, the iron law of responsibility predicting that whoever does not use his social power responsibly will lose it. The highly persuasive element to this model is the notion that power incurs responsibility. This is the reason why this model has proved popular and is perhaps the reasoning behind titles such as 'Big Business, Big Responsibilities'[259] and corresponding assertions that unless business takes proactive a CSR step then the pressure to legislate CSR elements will grow.[260] This model has also proved attractive to businesses, who entertain a certain benevolence in acts of CSR to offset opinions of reproach at huge profit margins and the matching economic power.

This model is exemplified by a statement by the Swedish insurance corporation Skandia. The corporation points out that 'since the world's economic development resources are in the hands of the companies, they are recognizing that they must take greater responsibility for global and local development matters'.[261] This also implies that as long as corporations use their power responsibly, then possession of such significant power is justified for large corporations. As further power models reveal, while this is a sincere and convincing model it is not entirely adequate. It still fails to provide a compelling agenda for CSR. It explains what the possessor of power should do but not

257 Davis 1980 (n. 34)

258 Not his economic or political power, although I would argue that economic and political power allow for attainment of social power

259 See L Gardiner, C Rubbens and E Bonfiglioli, 'Big Business and Big Responsibilities' (2003) 3(3) *Corporate Governance* 67–77

260 Ibid. at 74

261 J Tullberg, 'Illusions of Corporate Power: Revisiting the Relative Power of Corporations and Governments' (2004) 52 *Journal of Business Ethics* 325–333, 325

why it should be done. In a sense it fails to complete the picture and answer the questions of justification for such possession of power in the societal framework. For instance, what happens when some corporations are irresponsible and yet very powerful?

Techno-structure model: This term can be credited to Galbraith, who in his work, *The New Industrial State*[262] identified techno-structure as the bureaucratic apparatus of the firm. This corporate part of the economy exercises influence and control over the larger economic, political and social context. In surveying the extent and purpose of this control he refers to 'the planning system', which going beyond prices includes the ensuring and controlling of sources of supply, the associated cost management, the shaping of consumer response and obtaining the relevant government action and support.[263] This view is somewhat exaggerated but differs only in degree from Monks and Minnow's statement that corporations are such a pervasive element in everyday life that it is difficult to step back far enough to see them clearly.[264] It is also similar to the premise in Bakan's bestselling book, *The Corporation*, where he describes the corporation as a pathological institution. In his view it is 'a dangerous possessor of great power it wields over people and society'.[265]

There are quite cogent reasons for this view of the corporation, however, for our purposes, they are rather limited. The focus is on answering the questions what has the corporation become ands how has the corporation got to this point without providing an authoritative account of why this is the case. The focus sought for the 'exemplar' should be on the purpose of CSR. There is also a slight amplification element which lies in the assumption that the use of power is always planned. The use of power is not always a result of *intentional* action; it is more accurately described by Lukes as 'a capacity',[266] the capacity to produce significant effects.

Interpenetrating model: Preston and Post first proposed this model to examine what the relationship is between the corporation and society.[267] They stress the need for a long-term central core of relationships inherent to the corporate structure: a system of inter-penetration with society affecting business, as business affects society, a kind of symbiotic relationship. They had

262 J K Galbraith, *The New Industrial State* (3rd ed., Houghton Mifflin Company, Boston, MA 1978) 74–87

263 J K Galbraith, 'The New Industrial State after 20 Yrs Time' (1988) 78(2) *American Economic Review* 373–376, 375

264 See R A G Monks and N Minow, *Corporate Governance* (3rd ed., Blackwell Publishing, Oxford 2004) 14

265 J. Bakan, *The Corporation:The Pathological Pursuit of Profit and Power* (Constable, London 2004) 2

266 S. Lukes, *Power: A Radical View* (2nd ed., Palgrave Macmillan, Basingstoke 2005)

267 L E Preston and J E Post, *Private Management and Public Policy* (Prentice Hall, Englewood Cliffs, NJ 1975)

examined previous models and faced a dilemma of how to interpret the relationship in a way which gives credence to both the individualistic nature of the corporation and the pluralist nature of society.[268] Preston and Post point out that:

> the extreme separation of the managerial unity from the 'rest of society', whether for purposes of pure exchange or unfettered exploitation required in these models contrasts too sharply with common experience reflecting cohesiveness and a broad commonality of interests – and hence bases for cooperation rather than conflict along social entities. On the other hand, the full-blown technostructure model appears to overstate both the integration and the rationality of social relationships and to under-estimate the importance of pluralism, adaptability, initiative, and innovation.[269]

Their proposed solution was a focus on the 'public policy' concept which will involve a gradual change in corporate structure as a form of public responsibility and social responsiveness. The focus once again is on a realistic approach that envisages what could happen in the business and society relationship. It is not centred on why that relationship has emerged or is necessary.

Power legitimacy model: This is a more recent model which does not feature in McMahon's original essay. However, it is derived from my analysis and some recent literature, which stresses the re-emergence of questions of legitimacy of the power of the corporations within society.[270] The model questions the legitimacy of corporate power, stressing that the legitimate exercise of power within liberal society means that such power should be subject to effective constraints and control. Stanfield and Carroll point out that 'power is exercised legitimately when it is deployed within the bounds of dominant rules and norms, that is, when it is transparently deployed such that the information is available to those who must hold its use accountable'.[271] Possession of such strategic power can be found in large MNCs and blurs the distinction between private property and public entity. This is akin to

268 L E Preston, 'Corporation and Society: The Search for a Paradigm' (1975) 3 *Journal of Economic Literature* 434–453; R A Buchholz, 'Private Management and Public Policy – Another Look at the Interpenetrating Systems Theory' (1996) 35(4) *Business and Society* 444–453; T M Jones, 'An Integrating Framework for Research in Business and Society: A Step towards the Elusive Paradigm?' (1983) 8(4) *Academy of Management Review* 559–564

269 Preston and Post (n. 269) 25

270 Mary Stokes, 'Company Law and Legal Theory' in W Twining (ed.), *Legal Theory and Common Law* (Blackwell, Oxford 1986) 155.

271 J R Stanfield and M C Carroll, 'Governance and the Legitimacy of Corporate Power: A Path for Convergence of Heterodox Economics?' (2004) 38(2) *Journal of Economic Issues* 363

the assertion that 'the attack on the public/private distinction was the result of widespread perception that the so-called private institutions were acquiring coercive power that had been formerly reserved to governments'.[272]

The crucial assertion is that, where the legitimacy of government power is ensured through accountability processes to the electorate, sufficient accountability must be devised for such corporate power. Alternatively exercise of such power must be constrained and brought under the ambit of adequate democratic or representative control.

Stokes proposes that:

> if private property is to be legitimate within the framework of liberal society, it is also necessary to show that there are constraints which prevent it from becoming a source of power which threatens the liberty of the individuals or rivals the power of the state'[273]

This model provides justification for the argument that corporate power must have corresponding social responsibility. It stands out as an adequate response to questions about why CSR has become necessary. CSR is the result of societal concerns about the corporation, which are centred on the theme of corporate power and its significant effect on society. For increased legitimacy, such power needs to show that it is accountable and therefore subject to certain constraints for continued legitimacy.

This relationship has many variables and tends to change over time. On the one hand, there is the nature of this corporation, questions of its ownership, structure and role and, on the other, there is its impact on society. However, initially the triggers for CSR were all questions predicated on notions of corporate power and with time they have spread to concerns of the social impact of such use or misuse of power.

Kercher in his work on CSR draws a contextual historical timeline from the 1930s to the present day, emphasising that traditionally CSR debates have been focused on power but that this has evolved over time to cover the social impacts of such corporate power.[274] This links in with the growing concern with social, labour, human rights, environmental degradation, community rights and corruption issues as the social impacts of the corporate misuse of power as well as questions of how

272 Alex Mills, 'The Private History of International Law' (2006) 55 *International and Comparative Law Quarterly* 1

273 Mary Stokes, 'Company Law and Legal theory' in W Twining (ed.), Legal Theory and Common Law (Blackwell, Oxford 1986) 155

274 K Kercher, 'Corporate Social Responsibility: Impact of Globalisation and International Business' (2007) *Corporate Governance e-journal* (Bond University) <http://epublications.bond.edu.au/cgej/4> accessed 10 December 2011

corporations can rightly use their power to contribute to global development. These concerns and issues are symptomatic of the social impact of corporate power and capacity.

Therefore the crucial questions within CSR are those of corporate power: its use by management, responsibility for its use, accountability for its use or non-use and the capabilities which such powers provide. This is why CSR has become more important as perceptions of increasing corporate power have developed. The exemplar or central theme of CSR has become the drive for legitimacy of corporate power.

The drive for such legitimacy has come from several perspectives. The traditional instrumental perspective sees corporate power within the law and posits that it should have an economic area of competence which is profit and thereby contribute to society through payment of taxes and relevant levies. The ethical perspective highlights that corporate power implies responsibility to society but fails to fully demonstrate a universal basis of responsibility because there may be no such universal basis. At best what must be found is a functional basis that takes context into account, identifying above all the objectives which such responsibility seeks to achieve at that point in time.

There is also the political citizenship perspective, which focuses on rights and obligations that flow from existence in a societal context and therefore views corporate power in the context of citizenship rights and responsibilities. Or the corporate accountability perspective, which demands a more explicit focus on accountability for such power.

Applying Gallie's ECC analysis, it becomes evident that the core or central theme of these CSR debates is based on questions of corporate power in the business and society relationship. It reveal conceptions based on varying aspects of corporate power and its impact on society prompting questions and re-evaluation of its proper role in today's society. The core can then be outlined as the legitimacy of corporate power.

2.6 Conclusion

This chapter established that CSR can be seen as an essentially contested concept. So the level of contention and variety within CSR begins to make sense as one understands that the possibility of a uniform interpretation of such a concept is a difficult one. ECCs are concepts open to continuous contestations but Gallie provides a framework that allows for an exemplar or a central idea. This means that contestation can be fashioned in a constructive direction.

It has also been pointed out that the level of reflection that contestation provokes is deepened when participants understand the implications of essential contested-ness.[275] This is because it allows parties to develop a sense of lack of

275 Waldron (n. 213)

exclusivity of definition or issues and to garner an understanding of other aspects of such contestations surrounding the central idea of the concept.

CSR embodies issues regarding the relationship of the corporate form to society. These are issues which provoke extensive debate as a result of the theoretical viewpoints of the parties in this debate. There are theories relating to corporation which privilege contract over community and vice versa. There are also theories about the role of corporations within society and these theories are constantly being reviewed in the light of changing circumstances. An illustration would be the impact of multinational oil corporations on areas of human rights, the environment, labour and anti-corruption which has shifted CSR in those practical directions.

However, the anchor for those issues has been the changing perception and questions about corporate power in the corporate-society relationship. The perception of power and its perceived impact in the hands of these corporations has also meant that there has been a corresponding increase in the responsibility demanded of these corporations. This chapter reveals that a core or central theme of CSR is focused on the legitimacy of corporate power. CSR is about debates on issues arising from the relationship between corporation and society which are centred on the impact of corporate power. This important reference point is further explored in the following chapters.

3 Legitimacy of power as core to CSR

> The issue of power is central for the normative discussion about CSR.[1]

> The existence of power wielded by corporations means that the question of legitimacy can be applied to the private sector.[2]

3.1 Introduction

Where the core question is 'Why CSR?', the answer would indicate that demands for CSR have been primarily driven by perceptions of power in the hands of large corporations and the need to justify such power. The analysis within this chapter therefore examines what 'power' means both as a theoretical concept and within a given context. It then contextualises the analysis by examining the power of MNCs.

While there is some agreement as to the centrality of power[3] there are two further issues which arise: first the notion of some distinction between power and perceptions of power and second the division between those who regard power as an issue or problem and others who regard power as an opportunity.[4] Thus it is essential to explore what is meant by power and in doing so address three sub-questions: first, 'Why define power?', second, 'What does power mean?' and, third, 'Are there different modes of power?'

The existence of power can only be established when some understanding of the concept is acquired. This is because it is a complex and dynamic concept which

1 J Tullberg, 'Illusions of Corporate Power: Revisiting the Relative Power of Corporations and Governments' (2004) 52 *Journal of Business Ethics* 325–333, 325

2 C Coglianese,'Legitimacy and Corpoorate Governance' (2007) 32(1) *Delaware Journal of Corporate Law* 159–167, 161

3 Tullberg (n. 1)

4 J Bendell, *Barricades and Boardrooms: A Contemporary History of the Corporate Accountability Movement* (Paper 13, UNRISD, Geneva 2004) 18

does not lend itself to exact scientific and verifiable measurement.[5] This exploration of power will also clarify its centrality to CSR. This chapter will also set in place the context for examining the corresponding requirement that such power should be subject to limitations that render corporations accountable. The need to justify or legitimise the exercise or possession of power is a task that corporations face and CSR has developed as a result of this need.[6] The role of law in legitimacy will be the subject of the next chapter.

3.2 Why define power?

Power is an extremely common word yet its meaning as a concept is highly contested. Nevertheless it is irreplaceable as a notion which assists with the assigning of authority or responsibility in social relations. The importance of defining power is primarily to be able to identify this concept in given situations. Therefore, if the notion of power is central to CSR, defining power helps the identification of this concept as a trigger for CSR demands. However, such identification is not be made for its own sake. There are a number of reasons why it is necessary to identify power. It may have an allocation role, in the sense of allocating responsibility for action but it is also essential for identifying persons of authority. The reasons for identifying power must be seen in context.

In his important work on power Moriss identifies three contexts within which we talk of power. They are the practical, moral and evaluative contexts.[7] The practical context involves knowing 'the power of others'. That is, identifying and knowing those who can get things done. They are the ones with the 'capacity to affect outcomes'. The second context is the moral context and this involves allocating responsibility. And the third context is the evaluative context, in the sense of evaluating social systems to locate power distribution.[8]

These contexts can be identified in everyday life. For instance, the practical context is used when governments are said to be in power, having control over certain aspects of public life. However, it is also used to call upon the power of

5 R A Dahl, 'Power as the Control of Behaviour' in S Lukes (ed.), *Power: Readings in Social and Political Theory* (Basil Blackwell, Oxford 1986) 37–58, indicates the problems that exist with any attempt to empirically measure power. However, this is relevant when examining political systems as he notes that 'attempts to arrive at a better understanding of the more concrete phenomena of political life and institutions often sacrifice a good deal in the rigor of logic and verification in order to provide more useful and reliable guides to the real world'." He also further notes that 'at a very general level, attempts to analyze power share with many – perhaps most – other inquiries in the social sciences the familiar dilemma of rigor versus relevance'

6 N Mitchell, 'Corporate Power, Legitimacy and Social Policy' (1986) 39(2) *The Western Political Quarterly* 197–212, 199–200

7 P Moriss, *Power: A Philosophical Analysis* (2nd ed., Manchester University Press, Manchester 2002) 37–42

8 Ibid.

the MNC to get things done. Donaldson speaks of great power enhancing the possibility of effecting great good. He points out that 'attributing power to multinational corporations is not the same as attributing morality. Power is seen as morally neutral. Great power enhances the possibility of effecting great evil but similarly the possibility of effecting great good.'[9]

In the moral context, power and responsibility have a reciprocal relationship. Within his power responsibility model Davis points out that the greater the power of the firm, the greater the firm's social responsibility and concludes whoever does not use his social power responsibly will lose it.[10] This context is very important to the focus of this book, however it is modified by the view that such power and responsibility is not only important for social status but also for accountability and legitimacy in society. This is also linked with the evaluative context which assesses power within social systems because it is through such evaluation that reform of laws and administrative responsibility occurs. This is similar to the assertion that power must be legitimately accountable within liberal society. Power within social systems can be analysed with the aim of assessing the legitimacy of such power.[11]

The moral and evaluative contexts are crucial to our analysis. This is because although distinct they are related. It is possible to find that those who have acquired power in society are not fully accepting of consequential responsibility, this could prompt a re-evaluation of the social system where the use of power within that society is judged as falling short of the required legitimate standards. This can lead to a push for changes in social systems.

The relationship between power and responsibility is a complex one. The initial presumption is, as Moriss points out, that 'you are not usually considered responsible for something if you did not do it'.[12] However, he concedes that you can fail to do something for two reasons, 'disinclination' or 'inability', and that the first is more blameworthy. In this regard responsibility can be for action or omission, especially where omission is as a result of 'disinclination' within a sphere where there lies the ability. For our purposes it is important to identify MNCs as one of the powerful global actors and then assign responsibility for action which falls squarely within the sphere of such power and influence. This will include responsibility for their direct acts but also responsibility for the failure to act in certain circumstances. This is the key issue of CSR. For as Ball states:

> When we say that someone has power or is powerful we are . . . assigning responsibility to a human agent or agency for bringing (or failing to bring)

9 T Donaldson, *The Ethics of International Business* (Oxford University Press, Oxford 1989) 32

10 K Davis, 'The Case For and Against the Assumption of Social Responsibilities' (1973)16(2) *Academy of Management Journal* 312–322

11 M Stokes, 'Company Law and Legal Theory' in W Twining (ed.), *Legal Theory and Common Law* (Basil Blackwell, Oxford 1986) 155–183

12 Moriss (n. 6) 38

> about certain outcomes that impinge upon the interests of other human beings.[13]

In his seminal work on power Lukes agrees that the second context is not only moral but political as well. He notes that 'the powerful are those whom we judge or can hold to be responsible for significant outcomes'.[14] In other words, 'the point of locating power is to fix responsibility for consequences held to flow from the action, inaction of certain specifiable agents'.[15] This is the difference that strengthens a power legitimacy relationship: the fact that it is not only important that power be responsible but also that power can be *held* responsible. As a result it is essential that 'power must be defined prior to locating responsibility for its exercise'.[16] Thus, in this examination of CSR, the initial task is to lay a foundation for defining the power of the corporation in relation to society. This is to further justify the position that power is central to the discussion of CSR.

It is also important at this point to note that the general notion of responsibility is a variable concept. There are different levels of responsibility, one can be fully responsible or partially responsible,[17] Responsibility as a concept can be classified into different types. Whitehouse[18] identifies three categories. They are personal, obligatory and causal responsibility. Personal responsibility refers to a qualitative judgement that an individual or person is responsible; obligatory responsibility invokes a sense of compulsion; while causal responsibility denotes responsibility for a certain situation arising. However, these categories are not rigid.

In applying responsibility to individuals it becomes important to apply moral or legal rules. Moral rules have a significant link with causal responsibility to the extent that moral responsibility has been described as:

> responsibility for a given harm or defect if the person's conduct played a significant causal role in that harm or defect, the person's conduct was blameworthy or it was morally faulty in some other way and the aspect of the act that was faulty was also one of the aspects in virtue of which it was a cause of the harm.[19]

13 T Ball, 'Review of S. Lukes, *Power* and J. Nagel, *The Descriptive Analysis of Power*' (1976) 4 *Political Theory* 246–249, 249

14 S Lukes, *Power: A Radical View* (2nd ed., Palgrave Macmillan, Basingstoke 2005) 66

15 S Lukes, *Power: A Radical View* (1st ed., Macmillan, London 1974) 56

16 A Kernohan, 'Social Power and Human Agency' (1989) 86(12) *Journal of Philosophy* 712–726, 722

17 Kernohan, ibid. 'Responsibility Comes in Degrees Ranging from Full through Partial to None and This is Relevant to Identifying Power' 723

18 L A Whitehouse, 'The Company: Property, Power and Responsibility' in A Hudson (ed.), *New Perspectives on Property Law, Obligations and Restitutions*' (Cavendish, London 2004) 331–344

19 G F Mellema, *Collective Responsibility* (Rodopi, Atlanta, GA 1997) 7

Legal responsibility is based on legal rules which may not always be based on causal responsibility in the direct sense but does infer compulsion and obligation. Whitehouse puts it this way:

> Although both legal and moral responsibilities are [usually] only attributed to those who are causally responsible for the outcome in question either by act or omission, it is possible to impose responsibility on an individual when they are not directly responsible for the harm.[20]

Within CSR responsibility hinges on both moral and legal rules. Even where one is interested in legal responsibility, it is important to also establish moral responsibility as it is a good starting point.[21] Power has a role in finding out who is morally or causally responsible by act or omission. Power's role in this detection may sometimes be theoretical because a corporation's responsibility for its actions stems from the power that imbues to the corporation as a whole giving it capacity to achieve great good or evil. Nevertheless, in practical terms, this can also be given effect by the actions or inactions of its employees.

Yet studies of power become practical when it is linked with the law's prospective regulatory role of assigning responsibility, that is, duties and liabilities. The law may look to the power of an entity and then prescribe duties and responsibilities. In light of this, the political theorist Connolly correctly points out that:

> To acknowledge power over others is to implicate oneself in responsibility for certain events and to put oneself in a position where justification for the limits placed on others is expected. To attribute power to another, then is not simply to describe his role in some perfectly neutral sense but is more like accusing him of something, which is then denied or justified.[22]

This assertion is strengthened by the lengths to which corporate groups went in the past to deny possession of power.[23] However, power in itself is just a dispositional concept indicating ability or capacity.[24] The possession of power therefore points to possession of capacity. Power is linked to the responsible and legitimate use of such capacity.

Where significant power over others is established, it implies responsibility for the exercise of such power. This is inclusive of both moral responsibility, in the

20 Whitehouse (n. 18) 338

21 J Feinberg, 'Problematic Responsibility in Law and Morals' (1962) 71(3) *Philosophical Review* 340–351, 344

22 W Connolly, *The Terms of Political Discourse* (Heath, Boston, MA 1974) 97; also Kernohan (n. 16)

23 It obviously matters that they have such power. 'There must be some misuse of power when those who obviously possess it are so at pains to deny having it.' J K Galbraith, *The Anatomy of Power* (Houghton Mifflin, Boston, MA 1983) 142

24 Lukes 2005 (n. 14) 63

sense of taking care, and also responsibility that can be held to account within legitimate frameworks. This is why it is necessary to define power and apply it to our context as this will determine the importance of the drive for accountable and legitimate frameworks for such power.

3.3 Meaning of power

The task then is to define what power means.[25] This is not an uncomplicated task but it is important to outline what it means within the context of this book. In the literature there is a distinction between 'power to' and 'power over'. Where the former refers to ability as evidenced by Hobbes' definition involving the power of man (to take it universally) in his present means to obtain some future end.[26] While, in the latter sense, 'power over' turns our attention to those on the giving and receiving end of the relationship.[27] Yet they are closely related as Lukes views power over 'protestas' as a sub-concept of power to 'potentia'.[28]

The meaning of power as a concept is not settled and there are different views of power resulting from disparate foci on certain aspects of power.[29] However, one of the most comprehensive and persuasive definitions of power is that given by Lukes. In his assessment of the concept of power, he considers three views of power. He accepts that the views of power considered can be seen as alternative interpretations and applications of one and the same underlying concept of power, according to which '*A exercises power over B when A affects B contrary to B's interests*' (emphasis added).[30] He later amended this definition in 2005 to reflect power as capacity, not just exercise.[31] Beyond this he identifies three views

25 'Few words are used so frequently with so little seeming need to reflect on their meaning as power.' J K Galbraith, 'Power and Organization' in S Lukes (ed.), *Power: Readings in Social and Political Theory* (Basil Blackwell, Oxford 1986) 211–228, 211

26 T Hobbes, *Leviathan* (Oxford University Press, Oxford 2008) Chapter X

27 Connolly (n. 22) 87. Lukes 2005 (n. 14) 69 proposes 'that there is, indeed, a single generic concept of power common to all cases and that, in application to human agents [individual and collective] it exhibits two distinct variants (which we can provisionally, but misleadingly label as concepts of "power to" and "power over") where the latter is a sub species of the former and that alternative ways of conceiving a version of the latter exhibit what has been called "essential contestedness" with significant consequences for our understanding of social life'

28 Power over reflects for him the ability to have another or others in your power, by constraining their choices, thereby securing compliance

29 Connolly (n 22) 86–88

30 Lukes 1974 (n 15) 27

31 This is his opinion 30 years later in the second edition of his book, see Lukes 2005(n. 14) at 109. Still standing by his work on power, he finds the definition unsatisfactory for the following reasons. 'Firstly it focuses on the exercise of power committing the exercise fallacy; power is a dispositional concept, identifying an ability or capacity, which may or may not be exercised. Secondly it focuses entirely on the exercise of "power over" . . . thirdly it equates over with domination . . . thereby neglecting the manifold ways in which power can be productive, transformative, authoritative and comparable with dignity, fourthly, assuming that

or conceptions of power in the one-dimensional, two-dimensional and three-dimensional modes.

In the one-dimensional category, Lukes points to Dahl, who describes his intuitive idea of power as '*A has power over B to the extent that he can get B to do something that B would not otherwise do*' (emphasis added)[32] and in addition his intuitive view of power relations also involves a successful attempt by *A* to get *B* to do something he would not otherwise do. Polsby, another proponent of this view, points out that 'one can conceive of power . . . as the capacity of one actor to do something affecting another actor, which changes the probable pattern of specified future events . . .'[33] This view focuses on behaviour in making decisions over key or important issues as involved in actual observable conflict.

In the second category, the two-dimensional view accepts this first view but only as one part of power, it raises a second role observing that '*to the extent that a person or a group – consciously or unconsciously – creates or reinforces barriers to the public airing of policy conflicts, that person or group has power*' (emphasis added).[34] Therefore power may involve initiating, deciding and vetoing but it could also be exercised by confining or limiting the scope of decision-making to relatively 'safe' issues.

Finally Lukes himself proposes a three-dimensional view, which is rather a critique of the behavioural focus of the first two views.

He writes that:

> the first two views . . . allow for consideration of the many ways in which potential issues are kept out of politics whether through the operation of social forces and institutional practices or through individual decisions. This can moreover occur in the absence of actual observable conflict, which may be successfully averted – though there remains here an implicit reference to potential conflict. The potential may never be actualised. What one may have here is a latent conflict between the interest of those exercising the power and the real interests of those they exclude. The latter may not express or even be conscious of their interests . . .[35]

power thus defined . . . offers no more than a perfunctory and questionable account of what those interests are and finally it operates with a reductive and simplistic picture of binary power relations'

32 R A Dahl, 'The Concept of Power' (1957) 2 *Behavioural Science* 201–210; Lukes 1974 (n. 15) 11

33 N W Polsby, *Community Power and Political Theory* (Yale University Press, New Haven, CT and London 1963) 3–4; see also Lukes 1974 (n. 391) 12

34 This view is expounded by Bachrach and Baratz . See P Bacharach and M S Baratz, *Power and Poverty. Theory and Practice* (Oxford University Press, New York 1970) 8. They importantly bring the idea of 'mobilisation of bias' into the discussion of power. This is 'a set of predominant values, beliefs, rituals and institutional procedures that operate systematically and consistently to benefit certain persons and groups at the expense of others'. See pp. 43–44; see also Lukes 1974 (n. 15) 16–17

35 Lukes 1974 (n. 15) 24

The third radical view, despite its difficulties in application, allows the language of power to be applied to certain relevant situations where power is more pervasive and less easily identifiable. Broadly speaking he points out that:

> A may exercise power over B by getting him to do what he does not want to do, but he also exercises power over him by influencing, shaping or determining his very wants. Indeed is it not the supreme exercise of power to get another or other to have the desires you want them to have – that is to secure compliance by controlling their thoughts and desires.[36]

Thus both Lukes' actions and inactions show power. He highlights certain examples such as where the consequence of inaction may lead to a further non-event of a political issue. He cites the case of Crenson's analysis of US Steel.

In his case study Crenson concluded that US Steel, which had built Gary and was responsible for its prosperity, had for a long time effectively prevented the issue of pollution from even being raised through its power reputation operating on anticipated reactions and then, for a number of years, thwarted attempts to raise the issue and, finally, decisively influenced the content of the anti-pollution ordinance enacted. Crenson pointed out that 'US Steel exercised influence from outside the range of observable political . . . behaviour though the corporation seldom directly intervened directly in the deliberations of the town's air pollution policymakers, it was nevertheless able to affect their scope and direction'.[37]

This analysis also answered questions for him about why many cities and towns in the United States delayed or failed to make a pollution issue of their air pollution problems. This third view also affirms that 'unconsciousness', disinclination or omission can be another variant of inaction.[38]

In this category, a relevant example is that of a drug company which markets a dangerous drug. Lukes points out that the allegation that power is being exercised cannot be refuted by merely showing that 'the company's scientists and managers did not know the drug's effects were dangerous where they could have taken steps to find out'.[39] Power, therefore, can manifest in many forms. While it is not always important that the powerful actor intends the consequences of his action, he needs to be aware of his power.

This may seem a far-fetched notion of power but it is decidedly relevant to the relationship between society and large corporations, as it is undeniable that these corporations have become essential to our everyday life and thinking.

36 Lukes 1974 (n. 15) 23

37 Lukes 1974 (n 15) 42 and 51

38 He deals with a three-way split [a] one may be unaware of what is held to be the 'real' motive or meaning of one's action or [b] one may be unaware of the consequences of one's action or [c] one may be unaware of how others interpret one's action. The example highlighted deals with scenarios from the third group.

39 Lukes 1974 (n 15) 52

As Monks and Minnow highlight, corporations are such a pervasive element in everyday life that it is difficult to step back far enough to see them clearly.[40] It is perhaps best described by Hertz in her use of the apt title *The Silent Takeover*, when analysing the new global relations involving MNCs.[41] Cotoi puts forward a Foucauldian perspective where the current system, termed 'neo-liberalism', 'governs by giving the impression it is not governing'.[42] Cotoi stresses that this is done by 'creating and consuming a regime of "freedoms"'.[43] This ideological power of the regime of 'freedoms' empowers certain interests which include multinational corporate interests. Harvey points out that ;the freedom it embodies reflects the interests of private property owners, businesses, multinational corporations and financial capital'.[44] The everyday language of choice, preferences and competition engenders societal thinking that empowers corporate interests.

This also ties in with Galbraith's classification of power into three types: condign, compensatory and conditioned power.[45] The first two types, condign power and compensatory power are visible and objective. Condign power involves the use of physical force and sanction while compensatory power involves the use of inducement and incentive. He describes the third type, conditioned power, as follows:

> Conditioned power, in contrast, is exercised by changing belief. Persuasion, education, or the social commitment to what seems natural, proper or right causes the individual to submit to the will of another or of others. The submission reflects the preferred course; the fact of submission is not recognised.[46]

This implies that this type of power can be applied in a very subtle way to manipulate and create preferences. Again these preferences are not necessarily wrong or evil but the capacity to influence is in itself power. This is similar to the sense in which the media is sometimes referred to as powerful in as much as it can influence public opinion, but this is even more subtle. Perhaps this view of power becomes less radical in light of the examples that follow, on modes of power. Nonetheless it can be deduced that power is a capacity which may be

40 R A G Monks and N Minow, *Corporate Governance* (3rd ed., Blackwell, Oxford 2004) 14

41 N Hertz, *The Silent Takeover: Global Capitalism and the Death of Democracy* (Heinemann, London 2001)

42 C Cotoi, 'Neo-liberalism: A Foucauldian Perspective' (2011) 1(2) *International Review of Social Research* 109–124, 114

43 Ibid.

44 D Harvey, *A Brief History of Neo-liberalism* (Oxford University Press, Oxford 2005) 7 – these are features of the neo-liberal state now embraced in various forms globally

45 J K Galbraith, 'Power and Organisation' in S. Lukes (ed.), *Power – Readings in Political Philosophy* (Basil Blackwell, Oxford 1986) 211–228. See also J K Galbraith, *The Anatomy of Power* (Houghton Mifflin, Boston, MA 1983) 24

46 Ibid. 214

overt or covert, exercised or unexercised, evidenced by action or omission. This capacity to affect others includes influence as well as compulsion.

3.4 Modes of power

Power is often classified in different modes or types. The most important classification of modes of power when dealing with MNCs can be found in the works from the international political economy (IPE) field. Strange, one of the foremost writers on this issue in this field, refers to the two modes of power as: *relational or agency power* and *structural power*. According to Strange:

> The concept of relational power is clear and consists in the ability of A to get B by coercion or persuasion to do what B would not otherwise do. The concept of structural power is less clear and requires some definition. It consists in the ability of A to determine the way in which certain basic social needs are provided.[47]

She cites four basic societal needs, that is, security, knowledge, production and credit, with production as the fundamental essential.[48] Production has a vital role for credit, knowledge and even security. Beyond provision of basic societal needs structural power reveals an indirect and subtle way of influencing the structural system of society. Strange points out the link between the dominant position of the United States in world affairs and the desire of MNCs to invest and trade in the US economy.[49] Indeed, the most interesting analogy she makes is about the use of knowledge as structural power. In her opinion:

> the acceptance by intellectuals in the ex-socialist countries of central Europe, for instance, of the idea that the less the state intervenes in the market economy the better, that protection of local firms is always against national interest, and that keeping inflation to a minimum is always the first priority of the central bank, is all a classic instance of power exercised through the knowledge structure.[50]

These examples of knowledge power are replicated in several countries through the new and dominant ideology within foreign investment, which is promoted

47 S Strange, 'Towards a Theory of a Transnational Empire' (1989) in R Tooze and C May (eds), *Authority and Markets: Susan Strange's Writings on International Political Economy* (Palgrave Macmillan, Basingstoke 2002) 141–156

48 There is considerable agreement on this; although it has its roots as a Marxist concept

49 Strange (n. 47) 147

50 S Strange, 'Who Governs? Networks of Power in World Society' (1994) in R Tooze and C May (eds), *Authority and Markets: Susan Strange's Writings on International Political Economy* (Palgrave Macmillan, Basingstoke 2002) 171–184, 176

by world financial institutions and large corporations and, as a result, has opened access and afforded protection to huge markets globally.[51] This not simply a question about value judgements on whether this wholesale export of an ideology has been a good choice, rather it is an acceptance of the fact that it undoubtedly affords these corporations and institutions power.

Farnsworth pinpoints another method of addressing the agency-structural power classification.[52] He points out that agency power has been employed at an international level to guard against the adoption or implementing of international policies contrary to business interests and conversely this has helped protect structural power which allows corporations to play states off against each other. In addition, agency power is played out through lobbying, institutional participation, sponsorship and funding of political parties as well as direct corporate social provision. Structural power, on the other hand, is used to control investment, labour and state revenue dependency.

While his focus was on the British welfare economy, it holds out some vital points which apply equally to our analysis of MNCs in the international sphere. These views also highlight the interdependency of power and structures.[53] Power takes place within structural limits which expand and contract over time. While those structures determine who exercises power and how power can be exercised, the powerful can reshape those structures through action and influence.[54] Indeed, power relations are fluid in nature and may vary over time but within the context of globalisation, and the resulting global market economy, business interests are set to remain powerful for quite some time.

To speak of multinational corporate power is not to assume that all these corporations think and act in the same way but rather that there is oneness of purpose which is easier to identify at an international level. The landscape of large MNCs is changing with the increasing impact of large corporations originating from developing country home states and of the state-owned MNCs.[55]

51 This echoes the modified replication of ideas that are attributable to Gramsci's theory of securing consent for hegemony. See Antonio Gramsci, *Selections from the Prison Notebooks* (International Publishers, New York 1971). In one interpretation, Gramsci's view was that in the West it was ideology that constituted the mode of class rule secured by consent by means of bourgeoisie's monopoly over ideological apparatuses. See Lukes 2005 (n. 14) 7–9. For analysis of Gramsci's works in relation to the International Political Economy, see R W Cox, 'Gramsci, Hegemony and International Relations: An Essay in Method' (1991) 12(2) *Millennium: Journal of International Studies* 162–175; J Femia, 'Gramsci, Machiavelli and International Relations' (July 2005) 76(3) *Political Quarterly* 341–349

52 K Farnsworth, *Corporate Power and Social Policy – British Welfare Under the Influence* (Policy Press, Bristol 2004)

53 Lukes states in his analysis of power and structure in *Essays in Social Theory* (Macmillan, London 1977) 29 that 'Social life can only be properly understood as a dialectic of power and structure, a web of possibilities for agents, whose nature is both active and structured, to make choices and pursue strategy within given limits that expand and contract over time'

54 Farnsworth (n. 52) 22

55 UNCTAD World Investment Report 2015, *Reforming International Investment Governance* 4–5. See also A Cuervo-Cazurra, A Inkpen, A Musacchio and K Ramaswamy 'Government

However they are affected by the globalisation process and the emphasis on capital. Bremner points to this broader picture which is 'one of economies embracing capitalism and the state loosening its grip on economic activity'.[56]

The question has been whether these newer entrants have a markedly difference policy and the answer appears to be that they simply reflect different varieties of capitalism including state capitalism.[57] The pursuit of capital provides a cohesion around business principles which afford MNCs a certain unity of purpose. Farnsworth finds that 'in some ways, cooperation between various business groups at an international level has facilitated a greater degree of cohesion than that which often emerges at the level of the nation state'.[58] With this background on power and its manifestations, the next section will specifically address the modes of power of large MNCs as an exemplar for CSR.

Perceptions of power and the evidence of its significant effects on society has been the main trigger for calls for CSR. The aim within this section is to attempt to demonstrate this power. Coleman suggests that 'one may measure the power either by measuring the investments which show the power thus collected or by measuring the outcomes of transactions which show power in use'.[59] This use of multinational corporate power in practical terms can be divided into agency and structural power. Agency power involves the exercise of direct power and influence over the policy process; structural power is more pervasive, as it involves 'power to influence without taking direct action'.[60]

The analysis will show the use of structural power, to control foreign direct investment, trade and its influence in dealings with the state, on the one hand, and the use of agency power for participation, lobbying and funding, on the other hand. Farnsworth points out that business does not always *desire* to influence all forms of policy-making and that where and how such corporations act depends on policy areas and the prevailing political context,[61] but the crucial issue for MNCs is that they demonstrate a *capacity* to exercise significant power. In several

as Owners: State-owned Multinational Companies' (2014) 45(8) *Journal of International Business Studies* 919–942

56 I Bremner, 'The End of Free-market: Who Wins the War Between States and Corporations?' (2010) 9(2) *European View* 249–252, 252

57 At this juncture, some note must be taken of new varieties of state capitalism described thus: influence of government ' either owning majority or minority equity positions in the companies (direct) or by providing subsidized credit and/or other privileges to private companies (indirect)' see A Musacchio and S G Lazzarini, *Reinventing State Capitalism* (Harvard University Press, Cambridge, MA 2014) 2. Free-market capitalism is often compared to state capitalism, see Bremner, ibid. Further work on the varieties of capitalism include P A Hall and D Soskice, *Varieties of Capitalism* (Oxford University Press, Oxford 2001)

58 Farnsworth (n. 52) 81

59 J S Coleman, 'Reply to Hayduk' (1976) 41(6) *American Sociological Review* 1080–1082, 1081

60 Farnsworth (n. 52) 1–8, 6

61 Farnsworth (n. 52)

instances this capacity is reflected in actual exercise of power, which can be detrimental or beneficial.

Indeed the evidence suggests MNCs have a significant capacity to make decisions in private with substantial public effects.[62] This may be one reason for the substantial catalogue of abuses of power by MNCs, especially in the oil and natural resources industry, from the involvement of International Telephone and Telegraph (ITT) in US plans to overthrow the government of Salvador, Allende in Chile to the Bhopal tragedy, the antics of Shell in Nigeria and the Enron crisis, extending to the use of slave labour in Burma, repression of opposition groups in Nigeria and Colombia, dangerous working conditions in the toy factories of Asia, intimidation of trade unionists on banana plantations in Costa Rica, the rights of indigenous communities threatened by a mining company in West Papua, to consumer's rights abuses by manufacturers of baby milk and cigarettes.[63]

Possession of such strategic power can be found in large MNCs and blurs the distinction between private property and public entity. This is analogous to the assertion that 'the attack on the public/private distinction was the result of a widespread perception that the so-called private institutions were acquiring coercive power that had been formerly reserved to governments'.[64] In this sense power acquisition, its exercise and the control of its exercise in the relationship between corporation and society at different levels becomes the key issue for CSR.

The following sections will take an in-depth look at factual evidence of 'power-in-use' by the large MNCs. This examination will be classed under structural power and agency power. However, as we have seen, these modes of power are intertwined. The singular most important factor attributable to these corporations is that they make decisions that can significantly affect not only related parties like investors and employees but society and, in this case, global trends. Therefore as Parkinson states: 'the scope of significant choice open to [an actor]. . . his power over others is the power scope of his choices which affect them significantly'.[65] He notes that the two key elements are discretion and significant effects. Therefore these 'companies are able to make choices which have important social consequences: they make private decisions with public results'.[66]

The World Bank Institute (WBI) demonstrates this capacity in a significant way, when it posits that:

62 J E Parkinson, *Corporate Power and Responsibility* (Clarendon Press, Oxford, 1993) 10

63 See J Woodroffe, 'Regulating Multinational Corporations in a World of Nation States' in M K Addo (ed.), *Human Rights Standards and the Responsibility of Transnationals* (Kluwer International, The Hague 1999) 131–140, 131

64 A Mills, 'The Private History of International Law' (2006) 55 *International and Comparative Law Quarterly* 1–50

65 Parkinson (n. 62) quoting C Kaysen, 'The Corporation: How Much Power? What Scope?' in E S Mason (ed.), *The Corporation In Modern Society* (Harvard University Press, Cambridge, MA 1959) at 85

66 Parkinson (n. 62) 10

> in the era of economic globalisation, political transition and technological transformation, rapid changes are taking place which are bringing more than three billion people into economies operating on market principles. The private sector is the main engine of growth and development something which has raised a number of new and fundamental questions about the role of the private sector in sustainable development, in particular for multinational companies . . .[67]

Indeed the bottom line in global affairs is that large MNCs possess significant power.

3.5 Multinational companies and structural power

It is in the context of globalisation that the large MNCs have become structurally powerful. Globalisation is the process of opening up states and national markets to create more global interaction and interdependency. This process began with the gradual global adoption of the market economy as the successful economic model and then the subsequent global integration as a consequence of a major ideological shift among states towards capitalism.[68] This ideological shift is sometimes captured in the term 'neo-liberalism'. It is a brand of capitalism that advocates 'liberalisation, privatisation and stabilisation'.[69] Its focus is on 'the glorification of individual choice, markets and private property'[70] and thus it places state control in opposition to individual autonomy and markets. The ideology empowers vehicles of free enterprise.

'National and international economic policies shifted sharply in the 1970s and 1980s towards more reliance on the market—diminishing the role of the state.'[71] This was further facilitated by the end of the Cold War between 1989–1991 with the fall of the Berlin Wall and the collapse of the Soviet Republic. Since this time, huge merit has been placed on the opening up of national markets of goods and

67 See document: 'CSR: Main Concepts' World Bank Institute Section on CSR <http://www.worldbank.org/wbi/corpgov/csr/pdf/csr_mainconcepts.pdf> accessed 10 December 2008

68 The ideological perspective of states before 1991 could easily be categorised into Eastern bloc with its socialist ideas and the Western bloc with capitalist ideas

69 D M Kotz and T McDonough, 'Global Neoliberalism and the Contemporary Social Structure of Accumulation' in T McDonough, M Reich and D M Kotz (eds), *Contemporary Capitalism and Its Crises* (Oxford University Press, Oxford 2010) 93–120

70 Ibid. 94

71 This was 'driven by technocrats [and] the changes were strongly supported by the International Monetary Fund [IMF] and World Bank financing as part of comprehensive economic reform and liberalisation packages. Conditions of membership in the WTO and the Organisation for Economic Cooperation and Development [OECD] were important incentives'. See the UNDP Human Development Report (HDR) 1999 *Globalisation with a Human Face* (Oxford University Press, New York 1999) 29

services to foreign investment by MNCs through liberalisation and privatisation.[72] Dunning points out that:

> the current round of globalisation[,] . . . can be traced back to the fall of the Berlin Wall in 1989; to the renaissance of market economies, spearheaded by Margaret Thatcher in the United Kingdom and Ronald Reagan in the United States. Also to the emergence of new wave technological advances that culminated in the global embrace of e-commerce in the late 1990's; inter-alia it has been fashioned by a widening and deepening of all forms of international business activity, especially of foreign direct investment (FDI) [*by multinational corporations*].[73]

MNCs have benefited immensely from this process of globalisation. They have continued to grow even bigger as a result of the increase in foreign direct investment and global interconnectivity to become substantial and very powerful global actors.[74] The UNDP Human Development Report 1999 suggests that this trend of global integration and opening up of markets has been of immense benefit to MNCs giving them more economic power than some states.[75] The MNC has thus acquired the capacity to influence society through its actions in ways which affect how society provides its basic needs.

The emergence of a strong global economy was heralded as the cure to most of the ills in society so emphasis was placed on states rolling back on the creation of a welfare state to embrace liberalisation of markets, privatisation of economic activity and even public services. However, the success of globalisation has been limited in dealing with society and its problems. The effect of globalisation has left unevenness in its success, there are core areas of human rights, labour standards and environmental practices that are unsatisfactory, furthermore there is some

72 'Growing cross-border interconnectivity of economic activity'. J H Dunning, 'More and Yet More – on Globalisation' (2005) 14(2) *Transnational Corporations* 159–168. He relevantly comments that 'As a result, for good (or bad), what, 60 years ago, were a collection of economically protected states are now, for the most part, better regarded as inter-related parts of a global village' 160

73 Ibid. (words in italics are mine)

74 In January 2006, for example, Exxon Mobil and Shell announced record profits of £18 and £12.9 billion respectively. In spite of this, the state is still the only primary subject of international law although it is acknowledged that ultimately international rules affect the behaviour of human beings and may impose direct obligations such as in compliance with the international humanitarian law rules applicable in international armed conflict or may grant direct rights such as access to international adjudicatory organs without support from any home state. The situation for multinational enterprises under international law is unclear and therefore in need of review, they are aptly referred to as 'controversial candidatures'. See I Brownlie, *Principles of International Law* (6th ed.) (Oxford University Press, Oxford 2003) 65

75 See UNDP HDR 1999 (n. 71) 1

evidence that public services are failing and do not work for the world's poor.[76] This has created the necessity to hold all global actors accountable, that is, to set limits and define responsibilities for all actors through legitimate frameworks. To outline the structural power of large MNCs, the following issues will be examined in the following sections: control of foreign direct investment; control of trade; influence over the state; ideological control.[77]

3.5.1 Foreign direct investment[78]

MNCs finance foreign direct investment through equity capital, intra-company loans and reinvested earnings.[79] MNCs are sometimes defined in terms of foreign direct investment; a multinational or transnational enterprise can be defined as an 'enterprise that engages in foreign direct investment and owns and controls value-adding activities in more than one country'.[80] Although this may not be a wholly satisfactory definition, it highlights one of the most important activities of MNCs.[81]

76 The World Bank (WB) in its World Development Report (WDR) 2004 admits that 'the private sector if left to its devices will not achieve the level of health and education the society desires'. See World Bank WDR 2004 *Making Services Work for Poor People* (Oxford University Press/WB, New York 2004) 3 (Box 2-services – a public responsibility)

77 Farnsworth concludes that the structural power of capital rests on its control over investment, the dependency of the state on economic success for its revenue, the asymmetrical power over labour and its hegemonic power. Farnsworth (n. 52)

78 In spite of the inability to conclude a multilateral agreement on investment, the United Nations Conference on Trade and Development [UNCTAD] World Investment Report 2000 estimates that the number of Bilateral Investment Treaties had risen to 1,856 at the end of 1999 and these all contain varied levels of investor protection (now estimated by UNCTAD as over 2,000 by 2005; see N Gal-Or 'NAFTA Chapter Eleven and the Implications for the FTAA: The Institutionalisation of the Investor Status in Public International Law' (2005) 14(2) *Transnational Corporations* 129–158.

Newfound rights have been accorded to investors under the North American Free Trade Agreement Chapter 11 and the Energy Charter Treaty (both multilateral investment treaties), which permit investors to sue the state for violations of the treaty standards of investor protection. Liberalisation of foreign direct investment policy is also often conditionality in the IMF and World Bank adjustment programmes for developing countries, further guaranteeing open doors for MNC investment. See also H Ward, 'Corporate Citizenship: International Perspectives on the Emerging Agenda' Conference Report Royal Institute of International Affairs Energy and Environment Programme June 2000

79 See UNCTAD World Investment Report (WIR) 2005 *Transnational Corporations and Internalization of R&D* (UN, New York and Geneva 2005) 10

80 J H Dunning, *Multinational Enterprises and the Global Economy* (Addison-Wesley Publishing Ltd, Wokingham 1993) 3. He also notes two distinctive features of the multinational enterprise: first, it organises and coordinates multiple value-adding activities across national boundaries and, second, it internalises the cross-border market for the intermediate products arsing from these activities, see p. 4

81 The relationship between MNCs and foreign direct investment is important but not synonymous. Mira Wilkins puts it best, when she states that '*multinational enterprises make*

Foreign direct investment can be defined as:

> an investment involving a long-term relationship and reflecting a lasting interest and control by a resident entity in one economy (foreign direct investor or parent enterprise) in an enterprise resident in an economy other than that of the foreign direct investor (FDI enterprise or affiliate enterprise or foreign affiliate). FDI has three components: Equity capital is the foreign direct investor's purchase of shares of an enterprise in a country other than its own; Reinvested earnings comprise the direct investor's share (in proportion to direct equity participation) of earnings not distributed as dividends by affiliates or earnings not remitted to the direct investor. Such retained profits are re-invested; Intra-company loans or intra company debt refer to short or long term borrowing and lending of funds between direct investors (parent enterprises) and affiliate enterprises.[82]

Foreign direct investment seen in global terms has made huge leaps, outpacing world output as the stock of outward foreign direct investment grew from US$1.7 trillion in 1990 to US$6.6 trillion in 2001.[83] The UNCTAD World Investment Report 2005 considers that "the universe of transnational corporations is large, diverse and expanding . . . (and) the role of transnational corporations in the world economy has thus continued to grow as reflected in the expansion of FDI stock and in the operations of affiliates'.[84]

In 2011, the World Investment Report pointed out that these 'transnational corporations worldwide in their operations both home and abroad, generated value-added of about $16 trillion in 2010 – about a quarter of total world GDP'.[85]

foreign direct investment and carry on other tasks as well. The investment of capital flows are only part of the activities of a multinational enterprise. These companies must have a business association with foreign operations' (emphasis added). This is because there are different kinds of MNCs but in spite of the differences there is congruence in the behaviour of multinationals from different countries. See M Wilkins, 'European and North American Multinationals 1870–1914: Comparisons and Contrasts' in M Casson, *Multinational Corporations* (Edward Elgar, Cheltenham 1990) 541

82 See UNCTAD WIR 2005 (n. 79) 297. Dunning perceives foreign direct investment as '(1) The investment is made outside the home country of the investing company, but inside the investing company. Control over the use of resources transferred remain with the investor; (2) It consists of a package of assets and intermediate products such as capital, technology, management skills, access to markets and entrepreneurship.' This is contrasted with portfolio or contractual transfer of resources as (1) Specific assets and intermediate products (e.g. capital, debt or equity, technology) are separately transferred between two independent economic agents through the modality of the market. Control over resources is relinquished by the seller to the buyer; (2) Only these resources are transferred. See J H Dunning (n. 80) 5

83 UNCTAD WIR 2002, *TNC and Export Competitiveness* (UNCTAD, Geneva 2002) 1

84 UNCTAD WIR 2005 (n. 79) 13

85 UNCTAD WIR (2011) *Non-Equity Modes of International Production and Development* (UNCTAD, Geneva 2002) 4

This major growth in the significance of foreign direct investment can be mainly attributed to globalisation. The decision to invest is a private decision but with very important consequences.

Przeworski and Wallerstein confirm that 'investment decisions have public and long-lasting consequences, they determine the future possibilities of production, employment and consumption for all, yet they are private decisions'.[86] Several states in today's global economy are without strong domestic investment as important markets have been opened up to foreign direct investment, thus lending power to the investors. A case in point is the developing countries that borrowed from the IMF in the 1980s and bought into the whole package of structural adjustment programme (SAP) policies which include privatisation, removal of restrictions on foreign investment and trade barriers.[87] This conditionality for loans regime has helped spread the dominant neo-liberalist economic framework with its insistence on economic reform towards state fiscal and monetary austerity, trade liberalisation, investment deregulation and privatisation.[88] Although there is now a more conciliatory conditionality lending regime, Tan concludes that 'this new configuration has not extinguished the policies of structural adjustment nor altered the dynamics of power or conditions of resource dependency inherent in the use of conditionality as a regulatory instrument'[89] of the new configuration enabled foreign investment to reach new markets in developing countries.

The sectors of the economy now open to business stretch from traditional industries such as manufacturing, financial services, commodities to former public services such as telecommunications, water provision, energy, hospital services and so on. The old narrow confine of responsibility to shareholders does not begin to comprehend the sphere of influence currently bestowed on business and MNC in particular by society. There are also implications for developed countries. For example, the 2016 UK steel industry crisis and the negotiations between the UK government and Tata indicate how private investment decisions affect whole communities.[90] Investment decisions, which often focus on pure capital principles of maximisation of profits, also have the power to significantly affect the lives of employees and communities. This indicates the level of power that foreign direct investment affords.[91]

86 A Przeworski andM Wallerstein, 'Structural Dependence of the State on Capital' (1988) 82(1) *American Political Science Review* 11–29, 12

87 J Stigilitz, *Globalisation and Its Discontents* (Allen Lane, London 2002) on the impact of the World Bank and IMF on globalisation

88 C Tan, 'The New Disciplinary Framework: Conditionality, New Aid Architecture and Global Economic Governance' in J Faundez and C Tan, *International Economic Law, Globalization and Developing Countries* (Edward Elgar, Cheltenham 2010) 121

89 Ibid. 124

90 'No Thank you' *The Economist* 2 April 2016 <http://www.economist.com/news/britain/21695872-why-it-would-be-wrong-government-bail-out-britains-steel-industry-no-thank-you> accessed 2 April 2016

91 This is similar to the effect of Pfizer's decision to pull out of Sandwich, Kent in 2011. R Cooper, 'Pfizer's Kent Site Closure Sets Tone for Drug Exodus' *Daily Telegraph* 6 February

3.5.2 Trade

Another issue that demonstrates the significance of corporate power is trade. MNCs account for an important and growing proportion of world trade. For instance, Dunning and Sauvant suggested that:

> The production of the affiliates [of transnational corporations (TNC)] exceeds world exports; For most of the past three decades, FDI flows have been increasing at a higher rate than both the world's gross national product and world's exports; TNC account for between 25% to 30% of the world's gross national product, about three-fifths of non-agricultural trade and about three-quarters of the world's stock of privately generated innovatory capacity; TNC employ directly some 73 million people or 10% of employment in non-agricultural activities world-wide.[92]

They conclude that as wealth-producing institutions MNCs have played a critical role in shaping the international allocation of economic activity, the pace and structure of development, the ownership of resource production capabilities and the distribution of income between countries.[93]

Cowling and Tomlinson point to evidence of a greater concentration of commodities in the international market citing that a significant proportion of commodity market trade of special significance to domestic countries rests with a few large MNCs.[94] They confirm that between three to six of the largest MNCs have the following proportions of commodity trade: 85–90 per cent for coffee; 85–90 per cent for jute, 75–80 per cent for tin.[95] Interestingly they point out that the:

> Dominant position of a few transnationals is rarely pointed out in the debates that revolve around access to markets in the developed world by the developing world. It is the governments who are generally seen as the villain of the piece, when it is likely that the power of corporate giants in commodity markets is likely to be of similar significance in determining export earnings, and thus development strategies, in the developing world.[96]

2011 <http://www.telegraph.co.uk/finance/newsbysector/pharmaceuticalsandchemicals/8305427/Pfizers-Kent-site-closure-sets-tone-for-drug-exodus.html> last accessed 2 April 2016

92 J H Dunning and K P Sauvant, 'Transnational Corporations in the World Economy' in *Transnational Corporations and World Development* (ITBP/UNCTAD publications, London 1996) p. xi

93 See ibid.

94 K. Cowling and P R Tomlinson, 'Globalisation and Corporate Power' (2005) 24(1) *Contributions to Political Economy* 33–51, 35

95 Ibid.

96 Cowling and Tomlinson (n 94)

If a comprehensive look is taken at the position of MNCs in the trade market, it reveals a very potent and dominant force, where generally these corporations account for two-thirds of world exports and approximately one-third of world exports intra-firm, notwithstanding sub-contracted relationships.[97] This can be seen as cornering the market. It is ironic that, in this aspect, the law regards the market as competitive as long as each single unit of the corporation is separately incorporated or registered as a different legal person. This problematic governance issue is even starker when it comes to tax debates because MNCs have cross-border corporate structures which seek tax minimisation and profit maximisation.[98]

The 2011 World Investment Report also points out a middle ground and growing area of influence in the area of international production, which is neither foreign direct investment nor trade. This area is referred to as 'non-equity modes' of production and includes newer forms of contractual relationships which MNCs now enter to influence production. This covers contract manufacturing, services outsourcing, contract farming, franchising, licensing, management contracts and so on. The report points out that through these relationships, MNCs coordinate activity in their global value chains and influence the management of host country firms without owning an equity stake in it.[99] It is estimated that these kinds of activities generated US$2 trillion in sales in 2010.[100] UNCTAD confirms this expanding international production by pointing out that in 2014 it 'generated value-added of approximately $7.9 trillion and the sales and assets of MNE's [multinational enterprises's] foreign affiliates grew faster than their domestic counterparts'.[101]

3.5.3 State dependence

The influence of corporations over the state in the light of globalisation is proportionate to their status as a significant economic power.[102] This is important because states remain the only fully-fledged recognised actor in international law. Traditionally the state depends on taxation for revenue. Taxation of business is supposed to be a major income earner. There is disputed evidence to show lower taxation as a result of globalisation and the competition to create adequate and attractive investment climates.[103]

97 Ibid.

98 See some debates UNCTAD WIR 2015 *Reforming International Investment Governance* (UNCTAD, Geneva 2015) xiii

99 UNCTAD WIR 2011 (n. 85) 16

100 UNCTAD WIR 2011 (n. 85) 15

101 UNCTAD WIR 2015 (n. 98) ix

102 'The growing influence of corporate power over the state should be seen in the context of globalisation and as going hand-in-hand with the emergence of the transnational corporation as the dominant business entity.' See Cowling and Tomlinson (n. 94) 44

103 Farnsworth (n. 52) 44. See also P Genschel, 'Globalisation, Tax Competition and the State' (2002) 30(2) *Politics and Society* 245–275; M P Deveraux, R Griffith and A Klemm,

Problems also arise when the bargaining power of these corporations is enhanced by the competition between states for foreign investment.[104] These corporations have an integrated structure of business activities which reaches beyond state borders but in spite of the strong activity of MNCs on the international plane, they are regarded as entirely private bodies subject to the jurisdiction of the states in which they are located. What this does, in effect, is to give these corporations the protections of a private person and the powers of a significant public international actor. As Muchlinski puts it, there is a mismatch between, on the one hand, the integrated character of business activities with its managerial and operational reach and the jurisdictional reach of the state that seeks to regulate the MNE, resulting in situations where such regulation may be ineffective.[105]

Often states will not pursue policies contrary to business interests. This in itself may imply coercive power when it affects policies which may be in the wider public interest. This may be perceived as regulatory capture,[106] but it is best described as a form of conditioned power where business would like to see society make its decisions within a business friendly framework. Reagan puts forward the argument that in essence:

> corporations are not only much concerned to protect their own immediate legislative interests but are reaching out in an attempt to create a business-orientated political and social framework within which all public decision-making would be constrained. Instead of the society channelling business decisions within the bounds of public interest, the corporation[s] seek to channel public-interest decisions within business-interest bounds.[107]

In the same vein, Cowling and Tomlinson conclude from their research that the transnational base of the corporation provides it with significant leverage in bargaining situations.[108] Such leverage can be applied against nation states since it is often the case that these corporations bargain with governments over measures that enable them to increase profits. Such measures may include the introduction and maintenance of favourable investment subsidies, infrastructural support, employment legislation and tax regimes. Since there are political rewards in attracting and retaining such investment, governments are often compelled to accommodate such measures.[109] This has a spiral effect as such corporations

'Corporate Income Tax Reforms and International Tax Competition' (2002) 17(35) *Economic Policy* 449–495

104 P J Buckley and M Casson, *The Future of the Multinational Enterprise* (Palgrave Macmillan, New York 2002)

105 P T Muchlinski, *Multinational Enterprises and the Law* (Blackwell, Oxford 1999) 108

106 Cowling and Tomlinson (n 94)

107 M D Reagan, *The Managed Economy* (Oxford University Press, New York 1963) 129–130 cited in Parkinson (n. 62) 21

108 Cowling and Tomlinson (n. 94) 44

109 Ibid.

will use this influence to deter policies that are detrimental to their interests. Furthermore, when taking decisions on the conduct of their business in some very dependent countries these corporations can influence decisions on employment, revenue and production, this in turn instantly affects the social life of the country.

Leonard finds that, by virtue of their normal conduct of business, MNCs in developing countries can help shape the broader social forces that influence how a government relates to its constituents, social forces that influence how a government relates to its constituents, the relationship between the elite groups, the relationships between the urban and rural sectors and the ability of a developing country to pursue autonomous development strategies.[110] He accepts that one need not take a cynical view of corporate intentions or fall back on past legacies of sinister corporate conduct to conclude that multinationals have power, rather he points out that:

> by affecting a society's capacity to control the rate, direction and beneficiaries of change – [MNCs] are a significant force in a country's political development and that whether intentionally or not, the multinational corporation is a distinct political actor in the domestic politics of any state within which it operates.[111]

The MNC as a significant force may be more observable in developing countries but it is not restricted to them. An example of this is the decision to outsource jobs from communities in the United States to India which has had a huge impact on the social lives of such communities both in the United States and in India.[112] The decision to close or sell steel plants in the UK has a huge impact on communities in the UK.[113] The issue is often that the influence or impact, though easily felt, is very difficult to describe in tangible terms. In addition, the problem with the use of such power over the state lies not only in its effect but in the lack of such power being called to account.

3.5.4 Ideological influence

A fourth aspect of the evidence of structural power can be found in the subtle use of ideological influence. This is sometimes referred to as 'hegemonial power' and can be traced to the writings of Marxists and Lindblom. An Italian Marxist,

110 H J Leonard, 'Multinational Corporations and Politics in Developing Countries' (1980) 32(3) *World Politics* 454–483, 457

111 Ibid.

112 To read an emotional account of the situation in West Virginia, read the Shell-economist prize-winning essay by Claudia O'Keefe, 'The Travelling Bra Salesman's Lesson' <www.shelleconomistprize.com> (*The Economist* 17 November 2004)

113 See *The Economist* (n. 90)

Gramsci, brought this aspect of power to the fore in his writings.[114] In one preferred interpretation of his work, he sees culture and ideology as means of class rule secured by consent. The issues he points out at that time are particularly relevant today.

Our society reinforces our view of business with pro-business ideology and this strengthens the power of business. Then business through advertising and marketing can shape consumer preferences. In the context of globalisation, business has been nominated as the vehicle of choice for greater prosperity. Conventional wisdom in society teaches that business is the best way. This in turn makes us turn to business for advice and solution.

Lindblom sees it this way; 'businessmen achieve indoctrination of citizens so that citizens serve not their own interests but the interests of businessmen. Citizens become allies of businessmen'.[115] However, this is not a brain-washing process, individuals give tacit consent because there is no viable alternative. Indeed, to become independent of the influence of MNCs in daily life is very difficult in most countries of the world. They have a stake in your energy supply, food, household goods and so on. Galbraith puts forward a probable picture of a corporate system that is able to create demand for particular goods and also shape prevailing social values.[116]

Strange also points out that production is the basic and fundamental essential requirement of society because she makes the point that 'who or what provides for these needs in society enjoys structural power through the capacity to determine the terms on which those needs are satisfied and to whom they are made available'.[117] Through foreign direct investment, trade and even new non-equity modes of international production MNCs have a substantial say in determining the production needs of society. The section above on trade demonstrated that these corporations directly control a huge proportion of production. Production, with its link to finance, has become a driving force in most economies in the world. Finance determines the sort of knowledge the population can acquire through advertising and marketing but especially through funding the research and development of newer technologies or sciences such as in pharmaceutical drugs. It also has strong links with credit.

114 A Gramsci, *Selections from the Prison Notebooks* (International Publishers, New York 1971). In one interpretation, Gramsci's view was that in the West it was ideology that constituted the mode of class rule secured by consent by means of bourgeoisie's monopoly over ideological apparatuses. See Lukes 2005 (n. 14) 7–9. For an analysis of Gramsci's works in relation to the International Political Economy see R W Cox, 'Gramsci, Hegemony and International Relations: An Essay in Method' (1991) 12(2) *Millennium: Journal of International Studies* 162–175; J Femia, 'Gramsci, Machiavelli and International Relations' (July 2005) 76(3) *Political Quarterly* 341–349. There are many interpretations of Gramsci's work

115 C E Lindblom, *Politics and Markets* (Basic Books, New York 1977) 202

116 J K Galbraith, *The New Industrial State* (2nd ed., Penguin, Harmondsworth, 1972) 217 cited in Parkinson (n. 62) 15

117 Strange (n. 47) 145

Interestingly, in 2006 the IMF World Economic Outlook[118] pointed out that the corporate sector of the G-7 countries had moved from being a net borrower to a substantial net saver and that this, coupled with the earlier move by emerging market countries to a net saver status following the financial crisis of the late 1990s, had substantially altered the financial landscape of the global economy. It concluded that 'these changes in behaviour are one factor behind the relatively low level of global long-term interest rates at present'.[119] This statement substantiates the view that the behaviour of these corporations affects global saving significantly which in turn affects society, in this case with relatively low level interest rates. There is also a link between finance and security. Funding and capital generation is often necessary for security.[120] The UNCTAD Report 2015 points out that 'looking at a far larger sample of 5000 MNEs, the cash reserve picture is consistent. At the end of 2014, these MNEs had an estimated $4.4 trillion cash holdings nearly double the level before the global financial crisis.'[121]

The 2008 financial crisis and the drive for restored capital generation only further the ideological stronghold of big business as questions raised by the crisis have not forced a rethink on the role of global business; rather it appears to have reinforced the idea that business and capital generation are key to development and success.[122] Crouch refers to this as the strange non-death of neo-liberalism and he points to 'the way in which far from casting doubt on the role of giant corporations especially financial ones, in contemporary society, the financial crisis of 2008–9 has only served to reinforce power'.[123] There is a perception that the lack of ideological options and therefore convergence around the dominant neo-liberal ideological position enhances the corporate power of MNCs.

3.6 Multinational corporations and agency power

Another mode of power is agency power. This refers to more direct forms of power that will also fall within the two earlier views of power in Lukes' model. In this section, ways in which MNCs directly participate in the affairs of the state will be examined. Agency power is less overt in view of the evident structural power in the corporation's favour but it can be demonstrated at the international or transnational level.[124] The ability of an MNC to influence is strong enough to significantly affect the society or state within which it is located by virtue of

118 IMF, World Economic and Financial Surveys, *World Economic Outlook, 2006, Globalisation & Inflation* (IMF, Washington, DC 2006) 153

119 Ibid.

120 However, there is a converse side to this as insecurity breeds unproductiveness, which cripples economies and breeds yet more instability

121 UNCTAD WIR 2015 (n. 98) 19

122 J Reed, 'Corporate Governance: Lessons from the Financial Crisis' *OECD Observer* No. 273 June 2009

123 C Crouch, *The Strange Non-death of Neo-liberalism* (Polity Press, Cambridge 2011) viii-ix

124 Farnsworth (n. 52) 59

its unique multinational position and economic strength, therefore it should be regarded as also having agency power.[125]

This includes direct participation in international affairs, lobbying and sponsorship/funding.

3.6.1 Direct participation and action in international affairs

International law has little or no recognition of non-state actors, especially as MNCs do not have a single international legal personality. nevertheless MNCs are active at the international level.[126] International investment treaties confer significant benefit on MNCs [127] and they have been the focus of international law–making, albeit soft law.[128] The debate over whether MNCs are 'subjects' of international law, that is whether they are 'capable of possessing international rights and duties' masks the considerable activity of MNCs at the international level.[129]

Some of the key organisations who represent strategic business interests at the international level, such as the International Chamber of Commerce (ICC), the World Economic Forum (WEF) and the World Business Council for Sustainable Development (WBCSD) have consultative status with the UN Economic and Social Council (ECOSOC.[130] In the case of the ICC, this status was gained in 1946.[131] The notion of the consultative status has its foundation in Article 71of Chapter X of the UN charter, which permits engagement of the ECOSOC) with NGOs.[132] This involvement is not contentious as the ECOSOC engagement with NGOs is wide-ranging.

125 Parkinson (n. 62) defines agency power as the ability to influence governmental policy and law-making, see p. 19

126 The focus is on states but the Reparations for Injury Suffered in the service of the United Nations Advisory Opinion (1949) *ICJ Rep 174* (Reparations case) showed UN as an international organisation with limited recognition, the international criminal courts do deal with individuals and there is a recognition of the rights of peoples to self-determination

127 P Muchlinski, 'Corporations and the Uses of Law: International Investment Arbitration as a "Multilateral Legal Order"' (2007) 1(4) *Onati Socio-Legal Series* 1–28

128 J Wouters and A Chane, 'Multinational Corporations in International Law' *Leuven Centre for Global Governance Studies Working Paper No.129* December 2013

129 Ibid. See also P Muchlinski, 'Corporations in International Law' in Rüdiger Wolfrum (ed.), *Max Planck Encyclopedia of Public International Law* (Oxford University Press, Oxford 2010)

130 List of NGOs with consultative status with the Economic and Social Council as of 18 September 2008 E/2008/INF/5 < http://www.un.org/esa/coordination/ngo/pdf/INF_List.pdf> accessed 10 March 2011

131 Ibid.

132 'The Economic and Social Council may make suitable arrangements for consultation with non-governmental organizations which are concerned with matters within its competence. Such arrangements may be made with international organizations and, where appropriate, with national organizations after consultation with the Member of the United Nations concerned'

The specific impact of corporate power at the international level has prompted the drive to assign formal responsibilities to MNCs, a drive which the corporations have so far successfully opposed. This is reflected in the failure of the draft UN Code of Conduct for Transnational Corporations, which had been drafted by the then UN Commission on Transnational Corporations in 1982,[133] and the vehement opposition to the Draft Norms on the Responsibilities of Transnational Corporations and Other Business Enterprises with Regard to Human Rights as this was intended to be a set of binding principles drafted in 2004 by the sub-commission of the then UN Commission on Human Rights.[134] The MNCs were directly involved through the ICC in opposing the norms and its binding nature at the international level.[135] This failure resulted in the UN Secretary-General's appointment of a Special Representative of the Secretary General on Human Rights and Transnational Corporations and Other Business Enterprises to make recommendations of a non-binding nature.[136]

The evidence of the impact and power of MNCs can also be demonstrated in the key areas of global governance of trade and investment. The impact is visible in the privileging of private interests on a global level on in these key areas. This can be seen in the use of WTO law by the United States and the EU through s. 301 of the Trade Act under the trade barrier regulation to permit some private entities to invoke WTO law at the national level.[137] Shaffer speaks of the blurring of public and private interests on this issue, pointing out that 'private firms collate with governmental authorities in the US and the EU to challenge foreign trade barriers before the WTO legal system and within its shadow'.[138]

In the area of specific investment, the investment agreements give MNCs in their role as investors' access to arbitration for the defence of their protected rights of non-discrimination or other relevant aspects of the treaty, thereby enabling

133 Muchlinski (n 105)

134 T Sorrell, 'UN Norms' in J Dine and A Fagan, *Human Rights and Capitalism: A Multidisciplinary Perspective on Globalisation* (Edward Elgar, Cheltenham 2006) 284–299

135 Ibid.

136 UN, The UN 'Protect, Remedy and Respect Framework for Business and Human Rights-Background' September 2010 <http://198.170.85.29/Ruggie-protect-respect-remedy-framework.pdf> accessed 10 March 2011. The Human Rights Council endorsed the guiding principles on business and human rights – Resolution 17/4 16 June 2011. There has been another attempt to draft an international binding agreement – HRC resolution 26/9 (adopted 26 June 2014) but this lacks the support of the Unites States and Western countries – N R Tuttle 'Human Rights Council Resolutions 26/9 & 26/22 Towards Corporate Accountability?' 19(20) *American Society of International Law Insights* 3 September 2015. This idea seems doomed to failure as it does not fit in with the dominant ideological powers

137 G C Shaffer, *Defending Interests: Public-private Partnerships in WTO Litigation* (Brookings Institution, Washington, DC 2003) 3

138 Ibid. 5. He also notes that 'the reaction of private parties throughout the world in opposition to or support of the WTO system and its stream of legal complaints and verdicts is just one indication of WTO law's relevance to the states and its constituents' 4

them to use the procedure of arbitration to override state law.[139] This is driven by a dominant philosophy which sees the corporate instrument as overwhelmingly useful. Hurst points out that 'we treated the corporate instrument as so useful for desired economic growth as to warrant using law to make it available on terms responsive to the businessman's needs and wishes'.[140]

These trilateral and bilateral investment agreements are signed by states to attract foreign investment and there has been a huge surge in the numbers signed. In their study of investment treaties Newcombe and Paradell give the following estimation:

> By the end of 2006, this network comprised of some 2573 [bilateral investment treaties[and 241 bilateral and trilateral free trade and investment agreements. The network also includes a number of regional and sectoral agreements that include investment protection provision notably NAFTA, The ECT and *Framework Agreement on the ASEAN Investment area.* In addition there is a network of 2,651 double taxation treaties.[141]

The driving force behind this is corporate power, both from an ideological standpoint and from the capability perspective. It ties in with the global trend where governments are committed to ideals of liberalisation and enhancing international flows of goods, services and investment, making foreign investment a key resource for state funds.[142]

A further indication of corporate power and its influence is the existence of tax havens which create a bargaining environment for MNCs. These tax havens can be viewed as jurisdictions which minimise taxes and reduce or eliminate other restrictions on business operations.[143] The desire to offer privileges and to make the jurisdiction attractive to foreign investment can lead to commercialisation of sovereignty.[144] Palan points out that corporations were given the opportunity to spread themselves to different localities and they went shopping for the jurisdictions

139 G Van Harten, *Investment Treaty Obligations and Public Law* (Oxford University Press, Oxford 2007)

140 J W Hurst, *The Legitimacy of Business in the Law of the United States 1780–1970* (University of Virginia Press, Charlottesville, VA 1970) 62

141 A Newcombe and L Paradell, *Law and Practice of Investment Treaties* (Kluwer Law International, Netherlands 2009) 57–58. In 2011 the UNCTAD WIR 2011 (n. 85) 100 pointed out that this regime of International Investment Agreements was close to 6,100 treaties with many ongoing negotiations and multiple dispute-settlement mechanisms. A significant number of these treaties provide for investor-state arbitration and UNCTAD WIR 2015 (n. 98) estimates 'the total number of known treaty-based claims' from investor-state dispute settlement to be 608

142 Ibid. 48

143 R Palan, 'Tax Havens and the Commercialisation of State Sovereignty' (2002) 51(1) *International Organisations* 151–176, 154

144 Ibid.

that offered the best arrangement and consequently commercial sovereignty has spread.[145]

This highlights the strength and bargaining position of corporations in global affairs.

It has also resulted in a different drive to engage with the corporations on their own voluntary terms. A good example of this is the UN Global Compact (UNGC) which was suggested at the World Economic Forum, Davos in 1999.[146] The UNGC is a drive for these corporations to join UN agencies, labour and civil society in the promotion of ten core principles of human rights, labour, the environment and anti-corruption. It demonstrates the current indispensability of MNCs for the success of any global agenda.

The former Secretary-General of the UN, Kofi Annan, pointed out that:

> we have to choose between a global market driven only by calculations of short-term profit and one which has a human face; between a world which condemns a quarter of the human race to starvation and squalor and one which offers everyone at least a chance of prosperity, in a healthy environment; between a selfish free-for-all in which we ignore the fate of the losers and a future in which the strong and successful accept their responsibilities showing global vision and leadership[147]

thereby making it clear that in this huge global developmental challenge, MNCs must lend their power to the endeavour.

The question remains whether for such fundamental issues should international society continue to cajole corporations or devise productive frameworks and systems to legitimate such power through CSR goals. In its 2011 report UNCTAD helpfully suggests that governments can maximise the development benefits deriving from CSR standards through appropriate policies that harmonise corporate reporting regulations, provide for capacity-building programmes and integrate CSR standards into investment regimes.[148] This suggestion can also be acted upon by other actors in society by constructively fashioning their engagement with MNCs within the CSR agenda towards legitimate objectives.[149]

145 Palan (n. 143) 172

146 It appears to be an acknowledgement of business power; accepting that corporations cannot be compelled to observe the fundamental rules of society and thus pleading with them at their own forum to reconsider. See the website: <www.unglobalcompact.org>

147 Kofi Annan's World Economic Forum, Davos Speech UN Press Release SG/SM/6881 1 February 1999

148 UNCTAD WIR 2011 (n. 85) 14–15

149 It has been pointed out that the actualities have changed and the law is changing. See E Duruigbo, 'Corporate Accountability and Liability for International Human Rights Abuses: Recent Changes and Recurring Challenges'(2008) 6(2) *North-western Journal of International Human Rights* 223–261

3.6.2 Lobbying and funding

Research suggests that large corporations often have access to political platforms at national and international level to significantly influence policy.[150] Sklair points out that 'corporations work quite deliberately and often rather covertly as political actors and often have access to those at the highest levels of formal political and administrative power with considerable success'.[151] Farnsworth indicates that large corporations and organisations play a major role as lobbyists and participants in the IMF, World Bank and WTO.[152] This is also supported by the research by Braithwaite and Drahos showing evidence of lobbying for favourable rules on the international scene.[153]

This could be due in part to informal links within both the commercial, financial interests and international organisations as Stigilitz draws attention to the fact that the governing committee of these institutions tend to be finance ministers and central bankers with former links with the business community.[154] The business organisations are increasingly vocal on their policy preferences on certain issues: for example, the Business Industry Advice Council (BIAC) insists that the OECD guidelines for multinational enterprises must remain voluntary.[155]

While it is undeniable that business has a right to be heard, the underlying issue is that it is a powerful bloc which participates on its own terms and dictates the agenda. Korten points out that 'the corporate interest rather than the human interest defines the policy agendas of states and international bodies'.[156] Large businesses can ultimately lobby governments to influence policy. Schepers therefore suggests that:

> fundamental questions remain about the objectives and methods of business-government relations or lobbying, not least about the lack of coherence between CSR and lobbying, about compromise building between private and public interests or about innovative, responsible value based business-government cooperation, beyond the present lobbying.[157]

150 Crouch (n. 123)
151 L Sklair, ' Transnational Corporations as Political Actors' (1998) 3(2) *New Political Economy* 284–287, 286
152 Farnsworth (n. 52) 65
153 J Braithwaite and P.Drahos, *Global Business Regulation* (Cambridge University Press, Cambridge 2000)
154 Stigilitz (n. 87) 18–20
155 D Lewis and S MacLeod, 'Transnational Corporations – Power, Responsibility and Influence' (2004) 4(1) *Global Social Policy* 77–98, 81
156 D Korten, *When Corporations Rule the World* (Kumarian, London 1995) 54
157 S Schepers, 'Business-government Relations: Beyond Lobbying' (2008) 10(4) *Corporate Governance* 475–483, 478

Lobbying seems stronger when teamed up with funding, for example Cowling and Tomlinson point to the reversal of US policy to ratify the international Kyoto Protocol agreement after the election of the Bush Administration, as a fact which may be attributable to the fact that the Bush campaign was largely funded by the oil industry.[158] Funding is given to think-tanks and research institutes to influence their way of thinking and foist that onto the political arena.

The work of the Institute of Economic Affairs and the Centre for Policy Studies is given as an example of developing and fostering neo-liberal ideas in the 1980s.[159] Shamir also points to the establishment of corporate-sponsored and corporate-oriented NGOs as a form of hegemony (corporate power) in the CSR field.[160]

It is evident that in carrying out action at the international level, the large MNCs use a variety of tactics which add to our perception of their agency power. Sands confirms this position when he points out that:

> Deregulating international flows, promoting private investment overseas and increasing global trade have greatly extended the international role of private and corporate sectors. Not surprisingly, these players are not content with a backseat role in the making and applying of International law. They want to influence the content of the rules and contribute to its enforcement. They do so by pressuring governments and increasingly participating directly in International treaty negotiations.[161]

There is significant evidence to indicate that the power and impact of MNCs is significant, with the effect felt at national and international levels.

3.7 Power and legitimacy

Establishing power brings up the question of legitimacy. This is simply to ask: 'Do large corporations have power and if so, is it legitimately exercised?'[162] Legitimacy can be measured against three kinds of standards: legal, sociological and moral.[163] Legal legitimacy focuses on the legality of action. Such legality is adjudged both from a procedural sense and a substantive sense. Its focus is

158 Cowling and Tomlinson (n. 94)

159 R Desai, 'Second-hand Dealers in Ideas: Think-tanks and Thatcherite Hegemony' (Jan/Feb 1994) 203 *New Left Review* 27–64, cited in Farnsworth (n. 52) 12

160 R Shamir, 'Corporate Social Responsibility: A Case of Hegemony and Counter-hegemony' in B De Sousa Santos and C A Rodriguez-Garavito (eds), *Law and Globalisation from Below – Towards a Cosmopolitan Legality* (Cambridge University Press, Cambridge 2005) 92–117, 95

161 P Sands, *Lawless World* (Penguin, London 2006) 19

162 J R Stanfield and M C Carroll, 'Governance and the Legitimacy of Corporate Power: A Path for Convergence of Heterodox Economics?' (2004) 38(2) *Journal of Economic Issues* 363–370, 363

163 R Fallon, 'Legitimacy and the Constitution' (2005) 118 *Harvard Law Review* 1787–1835. He analyses debates about the legitimacy of the constitution

on conformity to a law that has been properly made. For example, government actions can be viewed as legally legitimate when they conform to a constitution properly made.[164] Sociological legitimacy focuses on popular consent.[165] Weber, as its foremost proponent, focused on the active belief of citizens. He stated that 'every system of authority, attempts to establish or to cultivate the belief in its legitimacy'.[166] And moral legitimacy addresses legitimacy through moral justification; justification based on norms or accepted external social standards such as human rights, democratic principles and so on.[167] While these three are regarded as different concepts of legitimacy they are interconnected.[168]

The interconnected nature of these aspects of legitimacy can be seen in the work of Beetham. He points out that 'a given power relationship is not legitimate because people believe in its legitimacy, but because it can be justified in terms of their beliefs'[169] and these beliefs are often based on normative standards. In his view legitimacy will depend on conformity with the rule of law, the justification of those rules by reference to congruent beliefs of the state and its citizenry and the evidence of consent by citizenry. Within this context Beetham demonstrates the necessity for legitimacy to include justification and accountability. In line with this interconnectedness, Jones defines legitimacy as referring to 'a system of widely accepted rules and standards governing the way in which power is achieved and exercised',[170] Mitchell asserts that legitimacy refers to 'the belief among groups within the affected population, workers, consumers and managers themselves that the exercise of power is justified',[171] and Suchman defines legitimacy as 'a generalised perception or assumption that actions of an entity are desirable, proper or appropriate within some socially constructed system of norms, values, beliefs and definitions'.[172] The various authors outline belief and justification but also belief based on justification.

In this CSR context, legitimacy not only refers to the cultivation of belief that corporate power and its uses are legitimate (that is, through the use of public relation, marketing and the use of corporate policies on social responsibility) but also, more fundamentally, it refers to rules, standards and processes that govern the exercise of corporate power in a way that affects society. This perspective

164 Ibid. 1806
165 Fallon (n. 163)
166 M Weber, *Economy and Society* (Vol. 2, first published 1968, University of California Press, Berkeley, CA 1978) 213
167 Fallon (n. 163)
168 Ibid.
169 D Beetham, *The Legitimation of Power'* (Palgrave, Hampshire, 1991) 11 For critique of his position see R H T O'Kane, 'Against Legitimacy' (1993) 41 *Political Studies* 471–487
170 R H Jones, 'The Legitimacy of the Business Corporation' 1977 20(4) *Business Horizons* 5–9, 6. Jones was the Chairman and Chief Executive of the General Electric Company
171 N Mitchell, 'Corporate Power, Legitimacy and Social Policy' (1986) 39(2) *Western Political Quarterly* 197–212, 202
172 M C Suchman, 'Managing Legitimacy: Strategic and Institutional Approaches' (1995) 20(3) *Academy of Management Review* 571–610, 574

asserts that legitimate power is limited power and the limitations may be largely conventional or legally defined.[173]

3.8 Conclusion

In general demands for CSR arise from questions regarding the relationship between corporations and society. These questions are based on the impact of significant corporate power on society. Power is a capacity, therefore it includes action (exercise) and inaction (omissions) in the relevant circumstances. In the case of MNCs power is the capacity to significantly affect the interests of others. Power itself is a morally neutral concept, it can be used for right or wrong purposes.

This chapter examined the existence of corporate power and its centrality to CSR demands. It revealed that MNCs have significant power and capacity to affect and influence society. This power can be utilised in structural or agency modes. The specific examination of the oil industry shows how incidents and inadequate corporate responses have changed perceptions of corporate responsibility and caused awareness of the impact of corporate action. This has driven society through its various actors to begin to demand legitimacy and accountability from corporations because corporations wield power that affects and impacts significantly on society's interests.

These demands and responses are encapsulated within CSR. Yet the corporations' response has been to attempt to set the agenda. CSR is driven by demands in the communitarian spirit, demands adjusted to the present liberal society which requires that power held within such society must be legitimate, and yet it is also driven by the corporate response from a basis of self-interest.

The challenge is that corporate power demands legitimacy because of the significant impact which it has on society. Dahl proposes that 'every large corporation should be thought of as a social enterprise, that is, an entity whose existence and decisions can be justified only in so far as they serve public or social purposes'.[174] This also ties in with Dodd's assertion in the classical CSR debate with Berle that business is permitted and encouraged by law because it is of service to the community rather than because it is a source of profit to its owners.[175]

173 Beetham (n. 169), 35. This is succinctly stated in the following quote: 'Who selected these men, if not to rule over us, at least to exercise vast authority and to whom are they responsible? The answer to the first question is quite clearly: they selected themselves. The answer to the second is at best nebulous. This in a nutshell constitutes the problem of legitimacy.' L Rayman-Bacchus, 'Reflecting on Corporate Legitimacy' (2006) 17 *Critical Perspectives on Accounting* 323–335, 324 citing E S Mason, *The Corporation in Modern Society* (Harvard University Press, Cambridge, MA 1959); B Sutton (ed.), *The Legitimate Corporation* (Basil Blackwell, Bodmin 1993)

174 R A Dahl, 'A Prelude to Corporate Reform' (1972) *Business and Society Review* 17–23

175 E M Dodd, 'For Whom are Corporate Managers Trustees?' (1932) 45 *Harvard Law Review* 1145–1163

The purpose of CSR, therefore, is to present a platform for debates about legitimising corporate power. These legitimacy debates have already taken various forms and perspectives in view of various demands and responses. Yet the overwhelming focus of CSR has been on corporate responses and voluntary undertakings.[176]

Law has so far played a limited role focusing only on the traditional perspectives and highlighted in mainly reactionary circumstances, i.e. contravention of laws (if any) and litigation after the alleged wrongdoing or wrongful use of power. However this book would like to focus on the potential contribution that newer perspectives of law could bring to the legitimacy debate. Law does not claim to be the only aspect of legitimacy but it is a vital yet neglected aspect. The next three chapters will form the second part of the work focusing on legitimacy and law's role therein. The next chapter begins this second part of the examination with a general overview of the role of law and regulation within legitimacy.

176 Vogel (n 182); S B Banerjee, *Corporate Social Responsibility: The Good, the Bad and the Ugly* (Edward Elgar, Cheltenham, 2007) 16–18; A Crane, D Matten L J Spence(eds), *CSR Readings and Cases in a Global Context* (Routledge-Cavendish, Abingdon 2008) 6–9 identifies six core characteristics of current CSR practice as voluntary, internalizing and managing externalities, multiple stakeholder orientation, alignment of social and economic responsibilities, practices and values beyond philanthropy

4 Law, structure and legitimacy

> That legitimacy means responsibility – that an institution with power must be accountable to some judgement other than that of the power holders – expresses the prime emphasis this culture puts on the individual as the ultimate measure of institutions.[1]

4.1 Introduction

This chapter begins the second aspect of our analysis which addresses what potential law and a law-jobs approach may hold for the legitimacy of corporate power. To do this the chapter addresses the concept of legitimacy and its link with law, the meaning of law in this context, the relationship between law and regulation and finally law's current manifestations within CSR. This chapter does this in order to point out approaches of law which this work analyses in detail for relevance to CSR's exemplar.

There are many classifications of law but in general, law can be perceived from a traditional state-centred perspective or from a non-traditional decentred pluralist perspective. Law can also be classed as hard law and soft law and this does not imply that state law is always hard law or vice versa. This analysis of these perspectives is important because it demonstrates the argument that how law is conceived will affect its relationship with contemporary concepts such as CSR. At the outset it is important to identify that legitimacy is used in the sense which implies accountability.

Within CSR it has been established that the existence of corporate power that significantly affects societal interests raises the issue of legitimacy for the possession and exercise of such power. Berle points out that '*Whenever there is a question of power, there is a question of legitimacy and this means that the power holder must find some claim of legitimacy which also means finding a field of responsibility and*

1 J W Hurst, *The Legitimacy of Business in the Law of the United States 1780–1970* (University of Virginia Press, Charlottesville 1970) 58

a field of accountability'.[2] Consequently, in view of the societal interest driving for corporate legitimacy, 'compliance with whatever "social responsibility" demands is seen as a prerequisite, a defining condition for the possession of power'.[3] It has been demonstrated that corporations exert significant power and influence over people's lives.[4] This concern with power perceived and expressed in varied ways is the core issue in the debates within CSR. It can be seen as the power-legitimacy exemplar within CSR.[5]

CSR discourse has arisen as a result of the crucial necessity to justify and constrain the possession and exercise of such corporate power. When this issue of justification or constraints within legitimacy is raised the role of law in facilitating this accountability should be explored. However, in CSR discourse the role of law is largely contested.[6] The stumbling block has been that CSR is often portrayed as intrinsically voluntary while law is perceived as mandatory rules.[7] Though it is important to stress that such simple categorisation is problematic at various levels, the way law is defined will influence the depth and intensity of relationship between the two concepts. Kerr and colleagues point out that 'at first glance the concept of CSR does not appear to fit comfortably within a traditional legal setting'.[8] This is because CSR is in a constant state of evolution as the 'notion of what is socially responsible is situated by contemporary needs and concerns and thus cannot be pinned down in precise and unchanging terms'.[9]

2 A A Berle, 'Economic Power and the Free Society' in A Hacker (ed.), *The Corporation Takeover* (Anchor Double Day, New York 1965) 86, 98–99 (emphasis added), also cited in R Chen and J .Hanson, 'The Illusion of Law: The Legitimating Schemas of Modern Policy and Corporate Law' (2004) 103(1) *Michigan Law Review* 1–149; 148–149

3 J E Parkinson, *Corporate Power and Responsibility: Issues in the Theory of Company Law* (Clarendon Press, Oxford 1995) 25

4 This is illustrated in Chapter 3 through some of the critical incidents in the oil industry. See also L Rayman-Bacchus, 'Reflecting on Corporate Legitimacy' (2006) 17 *Critical Perspectives on Accounting* 323–335

5 M Stokes, 'Company Law and Legal Theory' in W Twining (ed.), *Legal Theory and Common Law* (Blackwell, Oxford 1986) 155–183; T F McMahon, 'Models of the Relationship of the Firm to Society' (1986) 5 *Journal of Business Ethics* 181–191, details an overall analysis of the various models of relating corporations (firms) to society contrasting the rights approaches to the power models

6 D McBarnet, 'Corporate Social Responsibility beyond Law, through Law, for Law: The New Corporate Accountability' in D McBarnet, A Voiculescu and T Campbell (eds), *The New Corporate Accountability: Corporate Social Responsibility and the Law* (Cambridge University Press, Cambridge, 2007) 45–56

7 This is entrenched in the positivist view of law especially with regard to narrowing law to state law or regarding state law as central and core. See D Galligan, *Law in Modern Society* (Clarendon Press, Oxford 2006) 177–178

8 M Kerr, R Janda and C Pitts, *Corporate Social Responsibility – A Legal Analysis* (LexisNexis, Ontario, 2009) 5

9 Ibid.

Yet it is accepted that there are other contemporary legal notions which embody this flexible nature.[10] The law is an integral aspect of the drive for legitimacy and can fulfil the role of accountability. It frames legal action and can provide tools which enhance the corporate-society relationship. The challenge is to reveal the potential that law may hold for contemporary concepts such as CSR. In demonstrating such potential, theoretical conceptions of law allow us to indicate the potential of meeting contemporary challenges of legitimising concepts without inhibiting their natural growth and flexibility.

To discover what potential chosen legal approaches can contribute to this fundamental aspect within CSR requires an analysis of law itself and how law may choose to engage with CSR in traditional and non-traditional ways.

This chapter examines law and regulation as a key component of legitimacy in order to derive two chosen approaches which will be examined in the following chapters. Chapter 5 will then analyse traditional corporate law to indicate the limitations which traditional conceptions of law such as corporate law now face in achieving this legitimising role. This is what drives the suggestion of a non-traditional law-jobs approach which holds the potential to view law within CSR through a new lens.

4.2 Legitimacy and law

The assertion that law can contribute to the legitimacy of corporate power requires that the linkage between law and legitimacy is established. Legitimacy as a concept embraces three interrelated conceptions: legal, sociological and moral.[11] Legitimacy embodies the notion of justification and accountability from these different conceptions. The legal conception of legitimacy is concerned with justification by reference to governing legal norms.[12] In line with this, Jones defines legitimacy as referring to 'a system of widely accepted rules and standards governing the way in which power is achieved and exercised'.[13]

The sociological conception of legitimacy premises people's obedience or respect. It adopts the Weberian view of legitimacy as deriving from people's belief

10 Kerr, Janda and Pitts (n. 8) give examples such as corporate governance, best interests of a child, but other examples would include precautionary principle and sustainable development. See T O'Riordan and J Cameron, *Interpreting the Precautionary Principle* (EarthScan, London 1994); J Cameron and J Abouchar, 'The Precautionary Principle: A Fundamental Principle of Law and Policy for the Protection of the Environment' (1991) 14(1) *Boston College International and Comparative Law Review* (Article 2) 1–27; M Decleris, 'The Law of Sustainable Development' (a report produced for the EC, 2000); A Ross, *Sustainable Development Law in the UK: From Rhetoric to Reality?* (Routledge, Abingdon 2011)

11 R Fallon, 'Legitimacy and the Constitution' (2005) 118 *Harvard Law Review* 1787–1801

12 Ibid.

13 R H Jones, 'The Legitimacy of the Business Corporation' 1977 20(4) *Business Horizons* 5–9, 6. Jones was the Chairman and Chief Executive of the General Electric Company

in its legitimacy.[14] In this sense the justificatory source is people's beliefs. It is in line with this that Mitchell asserts that legitimacy refers to 'the belief among groups within the affected population, workers, consumers and managers themselves that the exercise of power is justified'[15] and Suchman defines legitimacy as 'a generalised perception or assumption that actions of an entity are desirable, proper or appropriate within some socially constructed system of norms, values, beliefs and definitions'.[16]

Lastly, the moral conception of legitimacy refers to ethics and therefore seeks a moral or ethical justification for the exercise of such power. It is this sense that it is asserted that use of force should be morally legitimate. This conception of legitimacy derives from an ethical justificatory core. This can be exemplified by focusing on ethical standards such as human rights and rights of participation.[17] When speaking of moral legitimacy Buchanan argues that 'an entity that exercises political power is morally justified in doing so only if it meets a minimum standard of justice, understood as the protection of basic human rights'.[18] This categorisation assists in the use of standards in analysis and in the clarity of the conception that one adopts but these conceptions are also interrelated.[19]

Beetham crucially points out that 'a given power relationship is not legitimate because people believe in its legitimacy but because it can be justified in terms of their beliefs' and these beliefs are often based on normative standards.[20] These normative standards are frequently embodied in laws in that given context. Often such normative standards must have a moral or ethical content, if they are to appeal to people's obedience or beliefs. This can be appreciated in the light of long-standing debates within law on the role of morality or, more recently, the integral nature of fundamental human rights to law.[21] This is why Doak and O'Mahony point out that legitimacy that rests purely on the legal nature of a particular action can provide a veneer of technical legality to practices that might be otherwise regarded as illegitimate, especially where it does not depend on any external moral or normative values.[22]

14 M Weber, *Economy and Society* (University of California Press, Berkeley, CA 1968)

15 N Mitchell, 'Corporate Power, Legitimacy and Social Policy' (1986) 39(2) *Western Political Quarterly* 197–212, 202

16 M C Suchman, 'Managing Legitimacy: Strategic and Institutional Approaches' (1995) 20(3) *Academy of Management Review* 571–610, 574

17 J J Kirkpatrick, *Legitimacy and Force: Political and Moral Dimensions* (Transaction Inc, New Brunswick, NJ 1988) 10–11

18 A Buchanan, *Justice, Legitimacy and Self-determination: Moral Foundations for International Law* (Oxford University Press, New York 2004) 234; A Buchanan, 'Political Legitimacy and Democracy' (2002) 112(4) *Ethics* 689–719

19 A Simmons, *Justification and Legitimacy* (Cambridge University Press, Cambridge 2001)

20 D Beetham, *The Legitimation of Power* (Palgrave, Basingstoke 1991) 11

21 T Bingham, *Rule of Law* (Allen Lane, London 2010)

22 J Doak and D O'Mahony, 'In Search of Legitimacy: Restorative Youth Conferencing in Northern Ireland' (2011) 31(2) *Legal Studies* 305–325, 307

When this interconnectedness of legitimacy perspectives is applied to CSR it is easy to see why there is an interplay of marketing, public relations, reporting (all playing to people's beliefs) and normative quasi-legal standards (codes and regulations) often derived from ethical standards and basis (such as human rights) driving towards creating legitimacy for corporate power. The problem, however, is that the sociological perspectives focusing on people's beliefs have been dominant, and to a large extent captured, by the powerful corporations who seek to centre CSR on the notion of changing perceptions through appeals to normative ethical standards.[23] Yet the veracity of legitimacy also lies primarily in legality, the ability to have a legal framework that encourages or induces corporate responsibility. Hurst points out that 'what the law permits, what it enforces or compels, should be socially useful and socially responsible'.[24]

Whilst legality is not the self-sufficient criterion of legitimacy, it is a primary criterion. It is a focal area of interest for legal scholars who seek to ensure that 'power is legitimate, where its acquisition and exercise conform to established law'.[25] They also seek to examine the definition and interpretation of legal rules and examine how these can be initiated, revised and enforced.[26] Nevertheless such scholars are not only preoccupied with conformity to the 'rule of law', there is also a significant amount of legal literature which questions the legitimacy of law itself in particular contexts and accepts that procedures for forming the law, the ethical content of the law and the subjection of laws to accountability are an integral part of legitimacy.[27]

This may be why Hart acknowledged that the legal order provided for law as a union of primary and secondary rules; with the secondary rules concerned with how the primary rules may be 'conclusively ascertained, introduced, eliminated, varied and the fact of their violation conclusively determined'.[28] Society through law should provide for processes of reform of the law to a greater or lesser extent.

The content of law is often complex: on the one hand, law can be used as an instrument for the powerful[29] that frames and enables power and organisations such as corporations, but, on the other hand, it is also capable of providing limitations and giving valid expression to opponents of such power, providing room for contest and for change.[30]

23 B O'Dwyer, 'Conceptions of CSR: The Nature of Managerial Capture' (2003) 16(4) *Accounting, Auditing and Accountability Journal* 523–557; R Shamir, 'The De-radicalization of CSR' (2004) 30(3) *Critical Sociology* 669–689
24 Parkinson (n. 3) 25, Hurst (n. 1) 58
25 Beetham (n. 20) 4
26 Beetham (n. 20) 4
27 Fallon (n. 11)
28 H L A Hart, *The Concept of Law* (Clarendon Press, Oxford 1994) 94
29 Beetham (n. 20) 67. This is also a Marxist perspective of law
30 B De Sousa Santos (ed.), *Law and Globalisation From Below: Towards a Cosmopolitan Legality* (Cambridge University Press, Cambridge 2005)

As a result of this juxtaposition legal scholars' centre on the analysis of the moral and sociological conceptions intertwined with law. One recurrent theme is often whether the duty to obey the law requires a moral reason and whether legitimacy of law is drawn from this moral core.[31] The focus could also be on procedures that allow for the consent, participation and acquiescence of the people or on the fundamental nature of human rights to rules that make for such integral moral legitimacy.[32] The aim of such introspection is to avoid a situation where law is used exclusively as an instrument of power rather than also being a limitation to power.

Here the focus is primarily on the legal aspect of this interconnected conception of the legitimacy of corporate power but it will also become apparent that law of the type suggested must also acknowledge the sociological and ethical perspective. The aim is to suggest that law will need to develop flexibility to frame normative aspects of CSR and to fully perform the legitimating function. The assertion is not that only law can help CSR achieve its legitimising function but that it is a fundamental aspect of such a legitimating agenda. Law has to appear in its fully dynamic guise to embrace and assist the complexity that is CSR.

Within CSR the question of corporate legitimacy has often been put in the following way:

> Who selected these men, if not to rule over us, at least to exercise vast authority and to whom are they responsible? The answer to the first question is quite clearly: they selected themselves. The answer to the second is at best nebulous. This in a nutshell constitutes the problem of legitimacy.[33]

When the question of the legitimacy of corporations is analysed from a legal perspective, two aspects become visible: the internal aspects of how the corporation is run and the external aspect of the responsibility for such running. Stanfield and Carroll outline what this may mean by stressing that 'power is exercised legitimately when it is deployed within the bounds of dominant rules and norms, that is, when it is transparently deployed such that the information is available to those who must hold its use accountable'.[34]

31 J Raz, *The Authority of the Law: Essays on Law and Morality* (Oxford University Press, Oxford, 1979, 2002). Raz defined power over others as authority over them, see p. 19. Cotterrell points out that 'law controls and expresses power at the same time, as two sides of the same process. And since . . . the nature and distribution of power is complex, legal doctrine and the workings of the legal institutions necessarily show complex and often contradictory patterns.' See R Cotterrell, *The Sociology of Law* (2nd ed., Butterworths, London 1992) 113

32 A E Buchanan, *Human Rights Legitimacy and the Use of Force* (Oxford University Press, Oxford 2010)

33 L Rayman-Bacchus, 'Reflecting on Corporate Legitimacy' (2006) 17 *Critical Perspectives on Accounting* 323–335, 324, citing E S Mason, *The Corporation in Modern Society* (Harvard University Press, Cambridge, MA 1959); B. Sutton (ed.), *The Legitimate Corporation* (Basil Blackwell, Bodmin, 1993)

34 J R Stanfield and M C Carroll, 'Governance and the Legitimacy of Corporate Power: A Path for Convergence of Heterodox Economics?' (2004) 38(2) *Journal of Economic Issues* 363–370

Thus the question could be that where the legitimacy of government power is ensured through accountability processes to the electorate, sufficient accountability must be devised for such corporate power. Or, in the alternative exercise of such power must be constrained and brought under the ambit of adequate democratic or representative control, the over-riding issue is that of transparent constraints. This book focuses on the link between the accountability aspects of legitimacy and law's ability to foster accountability. The nature of the corporation differs from that of the government, so their accountability processes will not mirror each other, but this does not negate the need for visible constraints.

Stokes vein stresses that:

> If private property is to be legitimate within the framework of liberal society, it is also necessary to show that there are constraints which prevent it from becoming a source of power which threatens the liberty of the individuals or rivals the power of the state.[35]

Law's ability to frame or facilitate accountability frameworks is therefore the core issue, however, in the globalised society, law itself has not remained unaffected. The following section will define perspectives of law in this context to capture a significant picture of law's potential role and outline the emergence of traditional and non-traditional approaches in this context.

4.3 Perspectives of law

The concept of law is not easily defined but it is necessary to outline conceptions of law because the way law is defined spells out the role for law within contemporary debates. In other words the legal theoretical conception of law will dictate to a large extent the role of law in the task of legitimising corporate power. Hart reminds us that 'few questions concerning human society have been asked with such persistence and answered by serious thinkers in so many diverse, strange and paradoxical ways as the question "what is law?" '[36] So this section aims to address what is meant by law within this book to provide a framework for the legal approaches that will be analysed.

Whilst CSR is a global phenomenon, the notions of law often do not travel well.[37] International law which has a fair claim to universality remains the primary preserve of state actors[38] so the challenge becomes the ability to frame a conception

35 M Stokes, 'Company Law and Legal Theory' in W Twining (ed.), *Legal Theory and Common Law* (Basil Blackwell, Oxford 1986) 155–183

36 Hart (n. 28) 1

37 For example, R Dworkin, *Law's Empire* (Hart Publishing, Oxford 1998) 102 points out that 'Interpretative theories are by their nature addressed to a particular legal culture, generally the culture to which the authors belong'

38 The International Court of Justice points out that it is the fundamental principle of state sovereignty on which the whole of international law rests – *Case concerning military and*

of law that can be viewed from a global perspective. This challenge is identified by Twining as suggesting a way of constructing one or more general conceptions of law that may be useful when looking at legal phenomena from a global perspective.[39]

The need for a broad conception of law that is useful for examining legal phenomena from a global perspective is predicated on the novel nature of actors and actions within CSR. This attempt to define our chosen conceptions of law will only form a brief analysis of the much wider discourse about law's nature. This wider discourse, often termed 'jurisprudence', covers several theoretical questions 'about the nature of laws and legal systems, about the relationship of law to justice and morality and about the social nature of law'.[40] The seminal debates on the relationship between natural law school and legal positivism between Hart[41] and Fuller[42] as well as the fundamental addition of Dworkin[43] on rules and principles will not be covered in great detail. The interesting debates about the relationship of law to justice covered extensively by Nozick[44] and Rawls[45] as well as the issue of rights as expounded by Hohfeld[46] and Kant[47] are of little relevance to this work.

This analysis will dwell on the nature of law in the much narrower sphere of 'law and society' and the attempt to derive a conception of law applicable to global concepts such as CSR. It will seek to draw out views on legal centralism and legal pluralism as well as debates on hard law and soft law. In other words, it raises the question 'Is law limited in form to state made law conditional on certain key features or is law multifarious and of different kinds on different levels tied together by the role it performs?' The aim is to discover the conceptions of law that bear the most relevance to globalisation and our analysis of legitimacy of corporate power within CSR.

para-military activities in and against Nicaragua (Nicaragua v US) Merits (1986) ICJ Reps 14, para. 263

39 W Twining, *General Jurisprudence: Understanding Law from a Global Perspective* (Cambridge University Press, Cambridge 2009) 103

40 M D A Freeman, *Lloyds Introduction to Jurisprudence* (Sweet & Maxwell, London 2008) 3

41 H L A Hart, 'Positivism and the Separation of Law and Morals' (1958) 71(4) *Harvard Law Review* 593–629

42 L L Fuller, 'Positivism and Fidelity to Law' – A Reply to Professor Hart' (1958) 71(4) *Harvard Law Review* 630–672

43 R Dworkin, *Law's Empire* (Hart Publishing, Oxford 1998)

44 R Nozick, *Anarchy State and Utopia* (Wiley-Blackwell, Oxford 2001)

45 J Rawls, *A Theory of Justice* (Oxford University Press, Oxford 1971) 5–6; S Lukes, *Power: A Radical View* (Macmillan, London 1974)

46 W N Hohfeld, *Fundamental Legal Conceptions as Applied in Judicial Reasoning* (Yale University Press, New Haven, CT 1964)

47 I Kant, *Fundamental Principles of the Metaphysics of Morals,* reprinted in L Dennis (ed.), *Groundwork for the Metaphysics of Morals – Immanuel Kant* (Broadview Press, Ontario 2005)

4.3.1 Traditional legal perspectives (legal centralism)

One of the most influential definitions of law is given by H L A Hart in his book *The Concept of Law*.[48] Hart sees law as a system of rules, with the union of primary and secondary rules at the core of a legal system. This modifies the earlier theories of law which placed law in the realm of orders given by a sovereign and backed by threats.[49] For Hart these rules derived their validity from the rule of recognition which itself is a social fact accepted by officials of the legal system.[50] This definition has remained definitive in explaining legal systems and in explaining social structures of laws in many developed countries,[51] but this definition is mainly concerned with municipal law in the modern state.[52]

Galligan outlines features of Hart's definition of law that narrows it to the 'modern legal order' and a view which is centred on the state. The features are as follows[53]: primarily enacted law made by legislative bodies in their exercise of will, specialised organisations and institutions of officials with authority to make, apply and enforce that law, coercion as a central aspect, state law as final authority over other systems of rule within jurisdiction, the regulatory aspect of law as facilitating and protecting social relations of citizens, officials with extensive power constrained by sets of standards and this results in a distinctive normative structure based on the idea of rule of law. Griffiths calls this legal centralism and defines this as the view that 'law is and should be law of the state uniform for all persons, exclusive of all other laws and administered by a single set of state institutions'.[54]

48 Tamanaha points out that John Austin and H L A Hartare, respectively, the most influential early and current theorists of legal positivism. B Z Tamanaha, *A General Jurisprudence of Law and Society* (Oxford University Press, Oxford 2001) 22. Tamanaha points out the problem of the definition of law and suggests that 'until this problem is resolved, however, the concept of legal pluralism will not have a sound foundation'. B Tamanaha 'A Non-essentialist Version of Legal Pluralism' (2000) 27(2) *Journal of Law and Society* 296–321, 297. It is doubtful whether the question of the definition of law can ever be settled for it is an essentially contested concept but I do accept that each debate must be founded on an identified definition of law. In other words you must define 'law' in a given context

49 J Austin, *The Province of Jurisprudence Determined,* ed. H L A Hart (Weidenfeld & Nicolson London, 1954)

50 Hart (n. 28) 79

51 Tamanaha 2001 (n. 48) 133 notes that Hart's core analysis has survived relatively unscathed following 40 years of critique. See also D Galligan, *Law in Modern Society* (Clarendon Press, Oxford 2006) 7

52 Twining notes that 'with the exception of public international law as it was conceived in 1960, this model is confined to state or municipal law'. Twining (n. 39) 89. However Hart acknowledges the existence of other 'pre-legal' norms

53 Galligan (n. 51) 21–22

54 J Griffiths 'What is Legal Pluralism?' (1986) 24 *Journal of Legal Pluralism* 1–56, 3

This traditional definition is often the most recognisable form of law and ties in with the institutional nature of law identified by Raz as a component for the test for law's existence and identity.[55] Raz points out that:

> It is widely agreed . . . that a system of norms is not a legal system unless it sets up adjudicative institutions charged with regulating disputes arising out of the applications of norms of the system. It is also generally agreed that such a normative system is a legal system only if it claims to be authoritative and to occupy a position of supremacy within society that is: it claims the right to legitimise or outlaw all other social institutions.[56]

He therefore identifies the legal system as 'a system of guidance and adjudication claiming supreme authority within a certain society and therefore where efficacious also enjoying effective authority'.[57] The consequence of such analysis has been to link law with state institutions such as courts. Kelsen also identifies law as norms addressed to court,[58] Hart points to laws as standards courts are bound to apply and use in adjudication.[59] The advantage of this way of identifying law is that it becomes fairly distinctive from other forms of social rules and its enforceability is linked to the state institution. Corporate laws can be derived from the body of rules enjoying the effective legal authority of the state and regulating the formation and running of corporations. While this approach is desirable for its simplicity, it is difficult to apply such traditional law to CSR as it is a concept that demonstrates some of the more significant effects of globalisation on law. It does not currently utilise forms of rules clearly linked to the traditional perspectives of state law and it is influenced by a variety of actors. Furthermore there are limitations within corporate law itself that will be demonstrated in the next chapter that require that law within CSR should be a broader concept than the traditional view permits.

Examining the role of traditional state law in CSR Barnet points out three general limitations. These are the effect of business lobbying, the lack of regulatory enforcement and creative compliance.[60] The influence of business on the substance of law at national and international level is evident. This is done through lobbying and negotiation which is an aspect of agency power and may result in backtracking on an agenda.[61] State regulation has a cost attached and resources are limited,

55 Raz points out that the test for the identity of a legal system involves three elements: efficacy, institutional character and sources. J Raz, *The Authority of Law: Essays on Law and Morality* (Oxford University Press, Oxford 2009) 42

56 Ibid. 43

57 Raz (n. 55) 43

58 H Kelsen, *The General Theory of Law and State* (New York, 1945) 29

59 Hart (n. 28) 89

60 D McBarnet (n.6)

61 Ibid. The climb-down on initiatives such as the binding UK Operating and Financial Review (OFR) reporting requirement for companies is indicative of the pressure on governments to favour business interests in decision-making

penalties may be weak and enforcement may not be effective.[62] Finally, compliance can be 'creative'. Barnett speaks of complying with the letter of the law, not the spirit of the law. She gives examples of tax avoidance and creative accounting.[63]

Although these limitations are not exclusive to traditional law,[64] the key issue is that new ways of thinking are relevant within CSR and this includes new ways of thinking about law. The effect of globalisation on law has resulted in the search for a definition of law that is more reflective of global concepts. Although it is important that law retains its distinctive nature, it also needs to retain relevance. This search for relevance is made more urgent by the inherent limitations of traditional state law in the context of global concepts like CSR.[65] Nelson helpfully points out that 'the core issue is about changing attitudes, values and approach. It is about thinking and acting in non-traditional ways. It is about a new way of governance – at both societal and corporate level.'[66] It is for this reason that broader pluralist perspectives analysed in the next section which includes perspectives that are more inclusive of rules emerging from various actors and could be harnessed towards the goal of legitimacy of corporate power.

4.3.2 Non-traditional legal perspectives (legal pluralism)

Long before notions of 'globalisation', legal scholars had an interest in law as a social phenomenon and this school was termed 'sociological jurisprudence'. The influential thinkers in this group were scholars such as Durkheim, who distinguished between formal laws and informal laws,[67] and Ehrlich, who distinguished between the 'living law' and state law administered by courts.[68] Ehrlich is most relevant for this analysis because he points to the reality of a 'living law' that underlies the formal rules of the legal system and suggests that the task of the judge or jurist is to integrate the two types of law.[69] Ehrlich gives the example of commercial law which tries to keep up with commercial usage as an example that the 'centre of gravity of legal development therefore from time immemorial has not lain in the activity of the state but in society itself'.[70]

This analysis is subsequently highlighted in the work of Teubner who analyses the *lex mercantoria* – the transnational law of economic transactions – as one of

62 Ibid.
63 Ibid.
64 As questions of enforcement and compliance plague other non-formal ways of regulation as well as other informal laws and regulations
65 Kerr (n. 8)
66 Jane Nelson, cited in J Elkington, 'The Triple Bottom Line for Twenty-first Century Business' in J V Mitchell, *Companies in a World of Conflict* (Royal Institute of International Affairs/Earthscan, London 1998) 32–61, 63
67 E Durkheim, *Division of Labour in Society* (Macmillan, New York 1933)
68 E Ehrlich, *Fundamental Principles of the Sociology of Law* (Russell & Russell, New York 1936)
69 Ibid.
70 Ehrlich (n. 68) 390

the most successful examples of global law without the state. He points out, with regard to business, that 'technical standardisation and professional self-regulation have tended towards world-wide co-ordination with minimal intervention of official international politics'.[71] Globalisation and its resulting complexities of relationships have reignited and posed additional questions about the nature of law within global concepts such as CSR.

Writers point out transnational law that is emerging under the processes of globalisation of the second half of the twentieth century.[72] In the case of MNCs this is partially the result of inapplicability of international law to MNCs as identified subjects and the resulting exploitation of 'a vacuum between ineffective national laws' as a result of the preservation of the corporate legal personality concept.[73] This has been referred to as the invisibility of MNCs under international law but this has not prevented rule-making and normative activity globally because of the reality of MNC actions and their impact on a global scale.[74] It has led to the emergence of an enormous amount of non-state law and rules guiding the conduct of various actors at various levels of global society.

These non-state law and rules emanate from various bodies including trade associations, international institutions, corporations themselves and NGOs. Jenkins identifies five types of codes of conduct in the CSR field: company codes, trade association codes, multi-stakeholder codes, model codes and inter-governmental codes.[75] In addition to this a compendium of CSR instruments identifies reporting guidelines, state CSR laws and government initiatives, issue-based principles, conventions and standards focused around environment and sustainable development, labour, human rights, gender, corporate governance, money-laundering and anti-corruption.[76]

Santos captures something of this diversity in his work where he discusses the globalisation of legal relations and depicts the contrary tensions that all work

71 See G Teubner. 'Global Bukowina: Legal Pluralism in the World Society' in G Teubner (ed.), *Global Law Without the State* (Dartmouth, Aldershot 1997) 3–28

72 K Von Benda-Beckmann, 'Globalisation and Legal Pluralism' (2002) 4 *International Law Forum du droit international* 19–25

73 R Fowler, 'International Standards for Transnational Corporations' (1995) 25 *Environmental Law* 1–30, 3; P T Muchlinski, *Multinational Enterprises and the Law* (2nd ed., Oxford University Press, Oxford 2007); C D Wallace, *The Multinational Enterprise and Legal Control: Host State Sovereignty in an Era of Economic Globalisation* (Martinus Nijhoff, The Hague 2002); O Amao, 'Mandating Corporate Social Responsibility: Trends in Nigeria' (2008) 6(1) *Journal of Commonwealth Law and Legal Education* 75–95, 75

74 See A C Cutler, *Private Power and Global Authority – Transnational Merchant Law in the Global Political Economy* (Cambridge University Press, Cambridge 2003) 196

75 R Jenkins, 'Corporate Codes of Conduct: Self-Regulation in a Global Economy' *Technology, Business and Society Programme* Paper No. 2 (United Nations Research Institute for Social Development, Geneva 2001)

76 *Compendium of Ethics Codes and Instruments of Corporate Responsibility* (compiled as a companion to W Cragg (ed.), *Ethics Codes, Corporation and the Challenge of Globalisation* (Edward Elgar, Cheltenham 2005)

the legal field: *lex mecantoria*, law of regional integration, transnational factors causing changes in state law, migration laws, laws of groups within the state (indigenous peoples, grass-root movements, NGOs and so on), cosmopolitan law.[77]

The challenge has been the ways of conceiving and addressing these emerging non-state law and regulation.[78] These attempts to conceive of law at a pluralistic and broad level have been termed 'legal pluralism'[79] and it draws upon previous traditions from legal anthropology which examined customary laws, religious law and local laws.[80] Scholars point out that 'transnational law' in itself does not create legal pluralism but adds to pre-existing constellations of legal pluralism.[81]

These theories and debates which were founded on issues arising from legal anthropology have moved to examination of the pluralistic nature of law in modern societies.[82] Legal pluralism stands in contradiction to legal centralism, it disputes the focus on state law stressing that law is itself constituted by virtue of social relations.[83]

Within this field, several theorists have raised debates specifically relevant to the applicability of law to global concepts. Teubner examines the 'Global Bukowina'.[84] He analyses the possibility of the emergence of global law without the state by pointing out that 'it is not only the economy, but various sectors of the world society that are developing global law of their own'.[85] He puts forward his view of legal pluralism as involving 'a multiplicity of diverse communicative processes that observe social action under the binary code of legal/illegal'.[86] This perspective leads to a broader conception of law delinked from the state.

In line with this delinked or decentred perspective, De Sousa Santos defines law as 'a body of regularised procedures and normative standards, considered justiciable in any given group, which contributes to the creation and prevention of disputes and to their settlement through an argumentative discourse, coupled

77 B De Sousa Santos, *Towards a New Legal Common Sense: Law, Science and Politics in Paradigmatic Transition* (Routledge, New York 1995) Chapter 5

78 See Twining (n. 39) for a discussion of the implications of globalisation on legal theory. See also Tamanaha 2001 (n. 48); G Teubner (ed.) (n. 71); B De Sousa Santos (ed.), *Law and Globalisation from Below: Towards a Cosmopolitan Legality* (Cambridge University Press, Cambridge 2005)

79 This has been described as a 'central theme in the re-conceptualisation of the law/society relation'. S E Merry 'Legal Pluralism' (1988) 22(5) *Law and Society Review* 869–896, 869. This is often contrasted with legal centralism, see Galligan (n. 51)

80 Benda-Beckmann (n. 72) 19; Llewellyn would be placed in the earlier era of legal anthropology

81 Ibid.

82 S E Merry, 'Culture, Power and the Discourse of Law' (1992) 37 *New York Law School Law Review* 209–226

83 Merry, ibid. 209. See also Griffiths (n. 54)

84 Teubner (n. 71)

85 Ibid. 3

86 Teubner (n. 71) 14–15

with threat of force'.[87] This would allow for a pluralistic application of law which does not exclude the state but includes other groups.[88]

Law within CSR is more readily identifiable when linked with pluralistic perspectives of law amenable to globalisation. This perspective can operate at different levels: local, national and multi- or transnational. It is more amenable to pluralistic examples of law. Therefore the conceptions of law that are relevant are conceptions which examine law from a more flexible perspective. The focus is on how law can be conceived from a global standpoint while allowing the flexibility to engage actively with both state and non-state law.

The question is therefore one of legal conceptions relevant to global concepts like CSR. Twining in his work on general jurisprudence points out three conceptions of law which may be relevant to globalisation: those of Hart, Tamanaha and Llewellyn.[89]

Twining finds that Hart's conception of law through Tamanaha's modification can accommodate other forms of law outside state law. Tamanaha modifies Hart's conception by restating his law as '*whatever people identify and treat through their social practices as law (or reicht or droit etc)*'.[90] In Tamanaha's opinion a state of legal pluralism 'exists whenever more than one kind of law is recognised through the social practices of a group in a given social arena'.[91] This restatement emphasises Hart's rule of recognition but it does not provide a useful outline or criterion for examining such legal perspectives in context. In different contexts within globalisation CSR is giving rise to rules, procedures and mechanisms which may not yet be recognised as law in the social practices of a group but may however be performing law-like functions and fulfilling the roles of law.

What is relevant in such a scenario is a definition that can present a working framework of enquiry in order to discover what the law is, how it is performed or carried out and whether it could be carried out differently. In this vein, issues of legal format are less relevant to the answers being sought to problems posed, as they are emerging from global perspectives where the 'living law' scenario is evident.[92] The issue is not really one of 'form', rather it is one of fulfilling vital

87 B De Sousa Santos, *Towards a New Legal Common Sense: Law, Science and Politics in Paradigmatic Transition* (Routledge, New York 1995) 428–429

88 Another such analysis is carried out by Muchlinski, where he examines particular 'proto-legal' phenomena exploring the possibility of viewing the multinational enterprises as producers of a kind of transnational law. P T Muchlinski '"Global Bukowina" Examined: Viewing the Multinational Enterprise as a Transnational Law-making Community' in G Teubner, *Global Law Without a State* (Dartmouth, Aldershot 1997) 79–108

89 Twining 2009 (n. 39) Chapter 4

90 Tamanaha 2001 (n. 48) 194

91 Ibid. There is a similarity in logic between this assertion and Galligan's defence of legal centralism where he states that independence and autonomy of rule-based associations 'occur within the jurisdiction of state law and in relationship with it' therefore basing the recognition in state law. Galligan (n. 51) 177

92 Living law from the perspective of E Ehrlich, 'Montesquieu and Sociological Jurisprudence' 29 *Harvard Law Review* 582–600, 584; law in practice, where the rules that matter may not be the formalised rules or even where no formalised rules exist

roles. This is what recommends the examination of Llewellyn's law-jobs because it provides such a working framework of enquiry. It can outline roles that are geared towards frameworks for accountability and legitimacy within CSR.

Llewellyn developed the law-jobs theory to solve his particular research problem which was to enable him to study the law of the Indigenous American Indian groups.[93] However, in doing so he developed a theory which could provide a working framework of enquiry applicable to the discovery of law's role in contemporary group scenarios. This could be intra-group[94] or inter-group.[95] It is a flexible theory which does not have its own content but rather can be applied to various groupings, group rules and interrelationships emerging, even on a global scale.

This law-jobs perspective asks for the identification of the doing of the five law-jobs and shifts the question of law from 'format' to 'role'. The five law-jobs are: the disposition of trouble cases; the preventative channelling and the reorientation of conduct and expectations so as to avoid trouble; the allocation of authority and the arrangement of procedures which legitimise action as authoritative; the net organisation of the group or society as a whole so as to provide direction and incentive and the use of the juristic method.[96]

In this book the law-jobs theory will serve as an analytical tool that redefines our approach to what is termed law within CSR and thus broadens the basis of engagement of law with CSR. The aim of Chapter 6 is to highlight the potential of taking a 'law-jobs' legal approach within the field of CSR.

Twining affirms the utility of Llewellyn's law-jobs theory when he states that 'as a heuristic device it provides a useable framework and a set of questions that can be asked'.[97] Furthermore Harden and Lewis point out that the law-jobs theory allows for the identification of various mechanisms as legal and this serves as a precursor to questions of effectiveness and accountability. So in advocating the utility of the law-jobs theory, they point out that 'questions of how well they function, how publicly visible they are and whose interests they serve are of course crucial questions of legitimacy – but unless we identify such mechanisms as "legal" we have no initial purchase even to raise questions of legitimacy'.[98] This means

93 Twining 2009 (n. 39) 106

94 For example, in examining the use of contractual control in global supply chains. See D McBarnet and M Kurkchiyan, 'Corporate Social Responsibility through Contractual Control? Global Supply Chains and "Other Regulation"' in D McBarnet, A Voiculescu and T Campbell (eds), *The New Corporate Accountability: Corporate Social Responsibility and the Law* (Cambridge University Press, Cambridge 2007) 59–92

95 For example when examining interactions between transnational corporations and society through regulation, especially codes of conduct and reporting. A Wawryk, 'Regulating Transnational Corporations through Corporate Codes of Conduct' in J G Frynas and S Pegg, *Transnational Corporations and Human Rights* (Palgrave Macmillan, Basingstoke 2003) 53–78

96 K N Llewellyn, 'The Normative, the Legal and the Law Jobs: The Problem of the Juristic Method' (1940) 49 *Yale Law Journal* 1355–1400

97 Twining 2009 (n. 39) 104, footnote 75

98 I Harden and N Lewis, *The Noble Lie: The British Constitution and the Rule of Law* (Hutchison London 1986) 67

that for CSR unless its mechanisms are identified as valid legal subjects as well, there may be no basis on which legal scholars can raise questions of legitimacy and accountability. For practical purposes a CSR instrument such as a code should first be highlighted as fulfilling a law-job role and then it can be assessed for its adequacy in achieving such a role and so on.

Another major advantage of the law-jobs approach is the transferability of the framework because it emphasises the 'legal quality' on the basis of role and not form. Therefore diversity of regimes is still possible as McCoubrey highlights when she states that 'granted the diversity of municipal societies, such a functional criterion seems far more soundly based than a demand for institutional convergence with particular forms of Western Urban Industrial societies'.[99]

By analysing CSR using the law-jobs theory it is possible to take a non-traditional approach in contrast to the traditional legal approaches in corporate law. It is thus possible to discover potential roles that the law can play in augmenting CSR's legitimising function. In one sense, the situation with global concepts such as CSR can be likened to a situation where law and the governance of several issues is at an embryonic stage because authority over decision-making and rule-making are not clearly allocated. Identifying something as law or law-like in this most basic form serves a very useful function because it forces us to examine actions within concepts such as CSR for development and for novel ways of handling issues which are encountered in inter-group societal relationships.

Llewellyn reiterates this position (in relation to one of the law-jobs – allocating the 'say') when he states that 'the case is clearest when no one has any idea whose say is to go and both what we think of as law and what we think of as governance is only in embryo, as in primitively emergent leadership (in our case, it is rather inapplicable) . . .'.[100] Although Llewellyn speaks of 'primitive' societies[101] in this phrase, he could actually be describing modern global society where there are gaps, especially in international governance of MNCs in the CSR area. Consequently the theory becomes a heuristic device for the analysis of the ability of law within CSR to do certain functions necessary for the accountable coexistence of business and society. This will also allow for the suggestion of a diversity of legal methods for doing the law-jobs within the CSR arena.

It is important that law retains a dynamic and relevant nature in the CSR discourse to engage with the legitimacy exemplar. Twining points out that:

> the law-jobs theory is a valuable and underused tool as a starting- point for analysing and comparing the internal ordering of groups and organisations . . .

99 H McCoubrey, 'Natural Law, Religion and the Development of International Law' in M W Janis and C Evans (eds), *Religion and International Law* (Kluwer/Martinus Nijhoff, Netherlands 1999) 177–190, 178

100 Llewellyn (n. 96) 1384

101 Ibid. 1360 states that by (mine) 'primitive' he means 'without need for organs of expression or for careful deliberation (not) . . . outmoded or displaced in any modern or sophisticated culture'

> it can easily accommodate notions of normative and legal pluralism, non-state law and different levels of global, transnational and local relations and so can provide a basis for dealing with issues raised by globalisation and interdependence.[102]

These contemporary issues within CSR have made it untenable for solely traditional perspectives of law to remain entirely relevant to newer phenomena such as CSR without the inclusion of broader visions of law. The argument is that contemporary issues have opened up novel analysis about the way law is conceived and therefore the law must now be conceived through this pluralistic lens.

4.3.3 Hard and soft laws

This section deals with another relevant distinction between the type of laws found in legal literature: the distinction between 'hard laws' and 'soft laws'. This is also linked to questions of format and the new constellations of law which are found in global affairs. This distinction is also a subject of major interest in European community law and international law because the rise in soft law is linked to the context of globalisation. It is also increasingly utilised in transnational and regional law.[103]

Kirton and Trebilcock suggest that 'it is thus hardly surprising that the world has increasingly turned to soft law as solutions for the hard choices it confronts'[104] because, at the globalised level, legal relations are flexible and less rigid. This has given rise to a variety of powerful actors and institutions which have rule-making capability in response to challenges which they face.[105] Furthermore, in the face of global challenges such as those posed by the misuse of corporate power, the legal response from international law has been rather muted reflecting the high level of compromise now present at that level.[106]

This situation must also be coupled with the point that responsibility for hard legalisation at an international level is still in the hands of state governments and there has been an increasing reluctance to adopt a hard legalistic approach because

102 Twining 2009 (n. 39) 115. However Twining also points out that this inter-dependence is a relative matter. W Twining, *Globalisation and Legal Scholarship*, Montesquieu Lecture, Tilburg University 2009

103 S Picciotto, *Regulating Global Corporate Capitalism* (Cambridge University Press, Cmabridge 2011)

104 J J Kirton and M J Trebilcock, 'Hard Choices and Soft Law in Sustainable Global Governance' in J J Kirton and M J Trebilcock (eds), *Hard Choices, Soft Law: Voluntary Standards in Global Trade, Environment and Social Governance* (Ashgate, Aldershot 2004) 3–32, 4

105 K W Abbot and D Snidal, 'Hard and Soft Law in International Governance' (2000) 54(3) *International Organisations* 421–456, 423

106 C May, *Global Corporate Power* (Lynne Rienner, Boulder, CO 2006)

of the ideological move towards capitalism and a free market in many states.[107] This ideology is pro-market and pro-private enterprise and this is what MNCs symbolise. This 'liberal international order' has driven the adoption of different approaches to governance by states.[108]

'Hard laws' can be defined as 'legally binding obligations that are precise (or can be made precise through adjudication or the issuance of detailed regulations) and that delegate authority for interpreting and implementing that law'.[109] This is similar to the traditional view of law expressed earlier and they are easily identifiable in the traditional sense as laws. On the other hand, soft laws can be defined as 'rules of conduct which in principle have no legally binding force but which nevertheless may have practical effects'.[110] Soft law has therefore be viewed as a practical response to hard choices faced by real-life actors.[111] Alternatively it can be viewed more cynically as playing into the hands of capitalist power, because its non-binding nature can be exploited.[112] Nevertheless there is a sense in which these views may be focusing on the wrong issues: laws whether soft or hard are made in reaction to a problem or an issue and therefore are made to fulfil a role. The crucial question should be: does the given law fulfil that role?

There are two key instruments of soft law. They are voluntary standards and informal institutions at international, transnational and national levels.[113] This also raises the question of whether soft laws are a developmental stage before hard laws can be introduced or whether they are laws in their own right. This is because soft laws often lack the binding force or enforcement of hard law. There is no definitive answer to this question, rather it is apparent that soft law is more reactive when dealing with the uncertainty of societal problems. This is particularly the case 'when it initiates processes that allow actors to learn about the impact of

107 C Brummer, *Soft Law and the Global Financial System* (Cambridge University Press, Cambridge 2011); C Redgwell, 'International Soft Law and Globalisation' in B Barton, L K Barrera-Hernández, A R Lucas and A Rønne (eds), *Regulating Energy and Natural Resources* (Oxford University Press, Oxford 2006) 89–106. In a sense this is the outworking of the ideological shift which lends power to corporations.

108 Ikenberry identifies some aspects that have featured as part of this liberal international order and they include: open markets, international institutions, cooperative security, democratic community, progressive change, collective problem solving and the rule of law. See G J Ikenberry, 'Liberal Internationalism 3.0: America and the Dilemmas of Liberal World Order' (2009) 7(1) *Perspectives on Politics* 71–87. There are ancillary questions about this being an outworking of power in the form of ideological influence. The focus has been on enabling private corporate actors to self-govern (self-regulation)

109 Abbot and Snidal (n. 105) 421

110 F Snyder, 'The Effectiveness of EC Law' in T Daintith (ed.), *Implementing EC Law in the UK* (Chancery, London 1995)

111 Kirton and Trebilcock (n. 104)

112 This is because soft law is quite fluid and therefore can lack legitimacy and accountability. The variety of codes can disguise inaction or dictate the agenda on the terms of rule-making institutions. See A C Cutler, *Private Power and Global Authority – Transnational Merchant Law in the Global Political Economy* (Cambridge University Press, Cambridge 2003) 23

113 Kirton and Trebilcock (n. 104) 4

agreements over time'[114] and when it facilitates dialogue, compromise and mutually beneficial cooperation between actors with different degrees of power.[115]

Soft laws can be correctly characterised as laws when linked to notions of legal pluralism and decentred perspectives of laws. Robillant agrees with this view and identifies that the genealogies of soft law lie in the notions of social law and legal pluralism that have come to pervade debates over globalisation of law and harmonisation of European law.[116] It is a way of reconceptualising law to recognise rule-making activity with significant impact which does not fall within the traditional view of law. Soft laws are attempts to reconceptualise law in a way that is relevant to the issues and concepts emerging or gaining ground as a result of globalisation.

Yet soft law faces some genuine challenges which include a lack of accountability, strong surveillance and enforcement.[117] It also introduces uncertainty because there are often various voluntary standards.[118] This is what strengthens calls for hard laws to complement soft laws.[119] Nevertheless the characterisation of laws as 'soft' or 'hard' represents an attempt to capture the variety of rule-making that is taking place in global affairs. Soft laws are often introduced in response to urgent social action.

As De Sousa Santos concludes, the 'differences in labelling and content notwithstanding, these studies broadly share a diagnosis and a proposal for the solution of the regulatory dilemmas posed by globalisation'.[120] He identifies three fundamentally different legal spaces and their correspondent legality 'local, national and world' but he sounds a note of warning that it is futile to attempt to distinguish these spaces by what they regulate, 'as they regulate or seem to regulate the same social action'.[121]

It is therefore possible to perceive law not just from its labelling or content (that is its 'form') but rather from its role in society: for example, its role in regulating and attempting to control a given behaviour.

Picciotto points out that 'the question is not whether hard and soft law are mutually exclusive but how they can best be combined to produce effective

114 Abbot and Snidal (n. 105) 423
115 Ibid.
116 A D Robillant, 'Genealogies of Soft Law' (2006) 54(3) *American Journal of Comparative Law* 499–554, 501
117 Kirton and Trebilcock (n. 104) 6
118 Kirton and Trebilcock (n 104) 6
119 D M Trubek, M P Cottrell and M Nance, 'Soft Law, Hard Law and European Integration: Towards a Theory of Hybridity'(2005) *University of Wisconsin Legal Studies Research Paper* No. 1002
120 B De Sousa Santos, 'Law, Politics and the Subaltern in Counter-hegemonic Globalisation' in B De Sousa Santos and C A Rodriguez-Garavito, *Law and Globalisation from Below – Towards a Cosmopolitan Legality* (Cambridge University Press, Cambridge, 2005) 1–26, 6
121 B De Sousa Santos, 'Law: A Map of Misreading: Towards a Postmodern Conception of Law' (1987) 14(3) *Journal of Law and Society* 279–302, 287

regulations'.[122] It is thus possible to apply all the relevant kinds of rules to achieve the given role and then to modify the rules where the role is not being effectively carried out. The next section will examine the linkage between law and regulation as relevant to this perspective.

4.4 Law and regulation

There is often extensive reference to law and regulation in legal literature. This section indicates how this applies to our legal analysis. This is because yet again the relationship between these two concepts, 'law' and 'regulation', depends on the definition applied to each.[123] Black points out that 'decentred analysis of regulation will have clear similarities with decentred or pluralistic conceptions of law than with centred conceptions'.[124]

Regulation can be viewed in several ways. Baldwin and Cave give a list of three senses in which regulation can be understood: first, in a narrow sense, as a specific set of commands involving binding rules given for a specific purpose and applied by a given body.[125] In this sense it is similar to Selznick's definition of regulation as 'sustained and focused control exercised by a public agency over activities valued by a community . . .'.[126] Here regulation is perceived as an instrument of traditional prescriptive law and one of the means through which law can achieve its objectives.

The second sense of regulation given by Baldwin and Cave involves that of deliberate state influence where regulation refers to the variant forms of regulation that the state may use to influence and control social behaviour. This is a slightly wider sense of regulation as it covers state action that may be command-based or economic-based. Command-based is the term used when binding rules are implemented and economic-based when economic measures or incentives are applied.

However, this definition could also be read to include perceptions of state regulation from subject-specific aspects. For example, regulation as seen from an economist's perspective could emphasise rules relevant to the correction of market failure.[127] In relation to this Ogus points out that economic analysis attempts to identify the failure of the market which justifies intervention and select the method of intervention that would correct the failure at least cost.[128] These theories,

122 Picciotto (n. 103) 204

123 J Black, 'Critical Reflections on Regulation', Discussion Paper 4 January 2002, Centre for Analysis of Risk and Regulation, London School of Economics < http://www.lse.ac.uk/collections/CARR/pdf/DPs/Disspaper4.pdf > accessed 10 March 2010

124 Ibid. 22

125 R Baldwin and M Cave, *Understanding Regulation Theory, Strategy and Practice* (Oxford University Press, Oxford 1999) 2

126 P Selznick, 'Focusing Organisational Research on Regulation' in R Noll (ed.), *Regulatory Policy and the Social Sciences* (University of California Press, Berkeley, CA 1985) 363

127 Ibid.

128 A Ogus, *Regulation: Legal Form and Economic Theory* (Clarendon Press, Oxford 1994)

collectively referred to as 'economic theory of regulation', utilise different perspectives and tools to justify regulation and its implications. These theories include both public and private interest theories.[129]

Law in this arena of economic theory may at first sight appear limited, especially if it is merely perceived as an instrument of regulation, but this is not the case as it can also be reconceived as creating a facilitative framework which allows for the use of economic incentives.[130] This perception is compatible with the idea of meta-regulation where law would allow the recognition of 'some governance mechanisms that we might not have traditionally thought of as law, could in fact be thought of as law in an extended sense and evaluated according to criteria of legality'.[131] Morgan and Yeung also highlight 'the law's instrumental role in shaping social behaviour as well as the way in which the law may give expression to particular values'.[132]

They point out that in regulation law may have two roles: facilitative and expressive. Their given example is that of a community that decides to maintain the quality of its waterways. It may do so through prohibitory orders or through tradeable permits for dumping. In their opinion the law is involved in both: in one sense as a threat and, in the other, in facilitating the interaction between the state and the market.[133] This can be exemplified through some emerging CSR practice such as in Denmark where legislation has been passed mandating the publication of CSR policies where the corporation has one.[134] The choice to have a policy remains voluntary but once that decision is made, then publication of this policy is mandatory.

Finally, regulation in the third sense involves a broad conception to include all forms of social control or influence.[135] This would include regulation at an international, national or local level as well as regulation by the state or other actors. It would also include self-regulation.[136] Self-regulation embraces a wide range

129 Ibid.

130 B Morgan and K. Yeung, *An Introduction to Law and Regulation Text and Materials* (Cambridge University Press, Cambridge 2007)

131 C Parker, 'Meta-regulation: Legal Accountability for Corporate Social Responsibility' in D McBarnet, A Voiculescu and T Campbell (eds), *The New Corporate Accountability: Corporate Social Responsibility and the Law* (Cambridge University Press, Cambridge 2007) 207–240, 213

132 Morgan and Yeung (n. 130) 5

133 Ibid.

134 'Law on CSR Reporting', Danish Commerce and Companies Agency website < http://csrgov.dk/legislation > accessed 9 October 2016

135 Baldwin and Cave (n. 125) 2

136 See ibid. 125. See also A Ogus, 'Rethinking Self-regulation' in R Baldwin, C Scott and C Hood, *A Reader on Regulation* (Oxford University Press, Oxford 1998) 374–388; J Black, 'Constitutionalising Self-regulation (1996) 59(1) *Modern Law Review* 24–55. More relevant to the global context, see R Jenkins, 'Corporate Codes of Conduct: Self-regulation in a Global Economy' *Technology, Business and Society Programme* Paper No. 2 (United Nations Research Institute for Social Development, Geneva 2001)

within regulation and may apply to a range of institutional arrangements.[137] Ogus points out that such arrangements may vary in the degree of autonomy, legal force and monopolistic power.[138] Black examines four types of self-regulation:[139]: mandated self-regulation, sanctioned self-regulation, coerced self-regulation and voluntary self-regulation. She defines self-regulation as 'the situation of a group of persons or bodies, acting together, performing a regulatory function in respect of themselves and others who accept their authority'.[140]

This third sense of regulation is the most relevant for this book and our contextual definition of law from a law-jobs problem solving perspective because this refers to all types of instruments that can be harnessed to achieve the law-jobs. In this sense 'regulation can be described to include all forms of social control available to harness a wide range of actors in addressing a particular set of problems'.[141] This third definition of regulation can therefore be referred to as 'decentred regulation' and be non-specific as to the position of state actors as drivers of regulation. It has been noted that this resonates with issues arising from globalisation. Black has further refined this definition of regulation in an essentialist sense to mean:

> the sustained and focused attempt to alter the behaviour of others according to defined standards or purposes with the intention of producing a broadly identified outcome or outcomes, which may involve mechanisms of standard-setting, information-gathering and behaviour-modification.[142]

Defined in this way regulation becomes the means of achieving the law-job outcomes through a variety of identified mechanisms which could include variant regulatory instruments, soft laws and hard laws. In other words regulation is a 'law-tool' in the Llewellyn sense. Such dynamism is necessary for an extended and relevant role for law within CSR regulation and globalisation. It opens up the possibility for various permutations of law, regulation and CSR. The next section analyses contestations of law within the current CSR context to indicate how these debates about law develops its role within the CSR concept.

4.5 Law within the CSR context

This section outlines the current perceptions and contestations about law in the CSR context. The current CSR context is dominated by norms, codes,

137 Regulation within CSR will cover the use of corporate codes of conduct. See Jenkins ibid.

138 A Ogus, 'Re-thinking Self-regulation' (1995) 15(1) *Oxford Journal of Legal Studies* 97–108, 99–100

139 J Black, 'Constitutionalising Self-regulation' (1996) 59(1) *Modern Law Review* 24–55, 27

140 Ibid.

141 N Gunnigham and P Grabovsky, *Smart Regulation* (Oxford University Press, Oxford 1999) 4

142 Black (n. 123) 20

standards and guidelines. These include general global initiatives like the UN Global Compact, the ISO 26000, and the OECD Guidelines for Multinational Enterprises. Other global initiatives focus on specific aspects of CSR such as human rights: Universal Declaration on Human Rights, Voluntary Principles on Security and Human Rights, UN Guiding Principles on Business and Human Rights; labour: ILO Tripartite Declaration on Multinational Enterprises, ILO Declaration on Fundamental Principles and Rights at Work; and the environment: Rio Declaration on Environment and Development; anti-corruption: UN Convention against Corruption and the Extractive Industries Transparencies Initiative. There are also various company codes, framework agreements and reporting standards created by a variety of actors.[143]

Yet the starting point when examining a plethora of popular definitions of CSR is often that they appear to exclude law from the purview of CSR purporting that CSR is either beyond law or voluntary.[144] In spite of this it is certain that CSR at its core addresses issues arising from the relationship between corporations and society and that law is undeniably important in this sphere.[145] Sabapathy points out that 'irrespective of the explicit interest of law in framing corporate responsibility, the two are always and necessarily intertwined'.[146] The stumbling block has been that CSR is occasionally perceived as intrinsically voluntary, while law has been perceived as mandatory rules,[147] though it is important to stress that such simple categorisation is problematic at various levels. The way law is defined

143 For a comprehensive list see D Leipziger, *The Corporate Responsibility Code Book* ((3rd ed., Greenleaf, Sheffield 2015)

144 Some examples include: CSR defined as 'the firm's consideration of and response to, issues beyond the narrow economic and technical and legal requirements of the firm to accomplish social benefits . . .' K C Davis 'The Case For and Against Business Assumption of Social Responsibilities' (1973) *Academy of Management Journal* 312–322, 312; 'Actions that Appear to Further Some Social Good Beyond the Interests of the Firm and that which is Required by Law' A McWilliams and D Siegel 'Corporate Social Responsibility: A Theory of Firm Perspective' (2001) 26(1) *Academy of Management Review* 117 -127, 117; 'A Concept Whereby Companies Integrate Social and Environmental Concerns in Their Business Operations and in Their Interactions with Their Stakeholders on a Voluntary Basis' European Commission Green Paper 2001 *Promoting a European Framework for Corporate Social Responsibility.* The European Commission (EC) redefined this in 2011 to accept that CSR is the 'responsibility of enterprises for their impacts on society.' EC, *A Renewed Strategy 2011–14 for CSR* Brussels Com (2011) 681 Final

145 H Ward, 'Corporate Social Responsibility in Law and Policy' in N Boeger, R Murray and C Villiers (eds), *Perspectives of Corporate Social Responsibility* (Edward Elgar, Cheltenham 2008). See also the influential definition of CSR by Carroll pointing out that the legal is an aspect of CSR: A Carroll, 'Corporate Social Responsibility – Evolution of a Definitional Construct' (1999) 38(3) *Business and Society* 268–295

146 J Sabapathy, 'In the Dark All Cats are Grey: Corporate Responsibility and Legal Responsibility' in S Tully (ed.), *Research Handbook on Corporate Legal Responsibility* (Edward Elgar, Cheltenham 2007) 235–253.

147 This is entrenched in the positivist view of law especially with regard to narrowing law to state law or regarding state law as central and core. See Galligan (n. 51) 177–178

influences the perception of the intensity of the relationship between the two concepts but even at the most superficial level, where law is viewed in terms of formal state law backed by state authority, there is still a relationship.

First, because CSR is not inextricably linked to voluntary formats, the choice of a voluntary instrument as a means of achieving CSR objectives is not intrinsic to CSR as a concept. This is because, on the one hand, several aspects of CSR are not voluntary, as one writer put it, 'many CSR-related issues are already closely regulated';[148] this will include health, safety and environmental regulations which are subject to differing levels of regulation across different countries and then on the other hand, it is important that the concept of CSR should be divorced from the means of regulating to achieve it.

The choice of voluntary instruments for regulation to achieve CSR should not be seen either as a defining feature of CSR or a defining feature of law's relationship with CSR. Within this area of regulation, one agrees with Zerk when she points out that the 'voluntary versus mandatory debate reflects an overly simplistic view of what law is and how it guides human behaviour'.[149] Rather it is preferable to acknowledge that changing priorities and demands in society may lead to certain CSR issues and concerns being regulated in a voluntary, mandatory or hybrid regulatory fashion. A good example would be the environmental and social issues which may impact on climate change such as air pollution from vehicles where a range of measures are used as regulation across different countries.[150]

Werther and Chandler assert that this ongoing redefinition and evolution of societal expectation causes the CSR response to evolve and, in time, these expectations may evolve from a discretionary to a mandatory requirement.[151] There is also the distinct possibility that a hybrid system of regulation may emerge where voluntary action is carried out within an enabling framework. This does not define law's relationship with CSR; it only reflects the chosen methods of demanding social responsibility.

Second, even where the choice of CSR regulation remains to use voluntary instruments, that is not tantamount to excluding law. The law can and should be more broadly defined to include not only mandatory legal rules but rules more generally. This is especially relevant in a transnational context. Rules in this sense will cover 'general norms mandating or guiding conduct or action in a given type of situation'.[152] This would include soft laws (described earlier).

148 J A Zerk, *Multinationals and Corporate Social Responsibility Limitations and Opportunities in International Law* (Cambridge University Press, Cambridge 2006) 34

149 Ibid. 34–35

150 W B Werther and D B Chandler, *Strategic Corporate Social Responsibility: Stakeholders in a Global Environment* (Sage, Thousand Oaks, CA 2006) 13

151 Ibid.

152 W Twining and D Miers, *How to Do Things with Rules* (Cambridge University Press, Cambridge 1999) 123

Although law will not cover every rule as moral rules do not always coincide with legal rules, it has a paramount role in the creation of specific legal regulatory rules or a broader facilitative framework for other forms of regulation.[153] This perspective entails examining legal theory for a broad conception of law that captures this broader role of law. This conception would provide for the dynamism of law and its applicability to contemporary phenomena like CSR. Twining points out that:

> a broad vision of legal theory helps us see our subject whole, to locate law in a map of all learning, to spot gaps, biases and imbalances in contemporary treatments, and to identify questions or lines of enquiry that have been more or less marginalized in our legal culture.[154]

He also aptly captures the challenge that faces law as one of adaptability and relevance to issues on a transnational level.[155] These features of adaptability and relevance are most pertinent for our purposes because of the complexity of action taking place in the transnational arena.

Finally, where CSR is proclaimed as actions taken beyond the law, the relationship between law and CSR has been referred to as 'paradoxical'[156] as the term is used even where CSR is seen as beyond the law, it does not operate outside the law. Parker poses the question: 'How is it possible for the law to make companies accountable for going beyond the law?'[157] In the way already described, it is questionable that CSR is going 'beyond the law' but even where this is accepted the answer depends on how the law is conceived. Law, which is broadly conceived, appears most relevant in this category. In response to this question Parker suggests the potential of 'meta-regulation' as reflecting law which seeks:

> to hold businesses accountable for taking their responsibilities seriously by using various mechanisms to encourage or enforce businesses to put in place internal governance structures, management practices and corporate cultures aimed at achieving responsible outcome.[158]

This is a response which mirrors the practical aspect of a wider conception of law's role. This is because it echoes law's wider role in creating a facilitative framework for other types of normative activity. Yet it is still focused on form rather our suggested approach will involve a redefining of how law is conceived. This conception draws attention to the cognisance of law's potential role in a

153 Morgan and Yeung (n. 130)
154 W Twining (ed.), *Legal Theory and Common Law* (Basil Blackwell, Oxford 1986) 6
155 Twining 2009 (n. 39) 117
156 Parker (n. 131)
157 Ibid.
158 Parker (n. 156)

changing world.[159] A conception of law which would be focused on the doing of the relevant jobs which law can perform within CSR.

Therefore, despite the contestations on the role of law within CSR, it is possible for law to respond from the traditional perspective that is state law centred and hard law based or it can respond from a pluralistic perspective geared towards the doing of the law-jobs. The next two chapters examine these contrasting perspectives to show the potential contribution law can make to the core of CSR. Law has the ability both to frame and express power and to attempt to control power. This reflects what Cotterrell identifies as a necessary complexity and occasional contradiction which law must have as it seeks to deal with its complex relationship with power.[160]

4.6 Conclusion

The chapter explored what law could mean in the context of legitimacy and the drive for CSR. It identified a traditional perspective which is state-centred and a non-traditional perspective which includes pluralistic sources. It argued that to capture the potential role of law it is necessary to take a pluralistic view of law amenable to the concepts arising from globalisation. This view of law is not only capable of identifying the wider role for law but also of stimulating and framing the roles of law. This is necessary because at the core of CSR is the drive for the legitimacy of corporate power. This is an area where the law in both its traditional and non-traditional sense has a major role to play.

The complexity of the area of CSR entails demands from different levels and across a wide range of issues which requires flexibility and dynamism. Therefore when examining global concepts such as CSR, the role of law and regulation should be viewed from a perspective that is able to capture broader aspects of what the law can do. A conception of law should allow for the inclusion of both state law and non-state law and the evolution of new legal tools and mechanisms as well as the application of old ones where necessary.

The task identified as legitimating corporate power within CSR through legal approaches can now be examined through the traditional and the non-traditional lens. The next two chapters will juxtapose attempts to respond to these demands from a traditional law perspective (corporate law) with the new proposal to examine a broader perspective of law's role through legal theory (Llewellyn's law-jobs). These are not mutually exclusive but the newer approach will permit the framing of law within CSR under a broad view that will allow the use of varied law tools (traditional and non-traditional).

159 For support for this perspective, see Twining 2009 (n. 39)
160 Cotterrell (n. 31)

5 Why not corporate law?

> Different theoretical conceptions of the company have been intimately embroiled in the effort of company law to justify the vesting of substantial power in corporate management.[1]

5.1 Introduction

Corporate law as the law of corporations is often seen as the natural home for addressing questions about the relationship between law and CSR. This is why some scholars advocate having CSR issues integrated into this basic state legal framework, thus creating an identifiable framework from which CSR initiatives would flow.

Ward puts it thus:

> The argument here would be that sustainable development (and/or other values associated with CSR) should be integrated within the basic legal framework, governing the formation and functioning of business enterprises – not exclusively as an 'add-on' in the form of environmental, labour or anti-corruption legislation – to name a few examples.[2]

Frynas also suggests that:

> Policy makers should make a concerted effort to re-write company law and other regulatory instruments to increase the power of 'non-traditional stakeholders' and to require companies to become more transparent about

1 M Stokes, 'Company Law and Legal Theory' in W Twining (ed.), *Legal Theory and Common Law* (Blackwell, Oxford 1986) 155–183, 161

2 H Ward, 'Corporate Social Responsibility in Law and Policy' in N Boeger, R Murray and C Villiers, *Perspectives on Corporate Social Responsibility* (Edward Elgar, Cheltenham 2008) 8–38, 21

> all of their activities. Corporate governance reforms will help companies to make better social and environmental choices in front of shareholders.[3]

Furthermore corporate law represents a peculiar platform because it is the identifiable state legal framework that is common to most states in the world.[4]

This chapter examines corporate law's potential to drive this wider CSR agenda within corporate law. It demonstrates that whereas corporate law as a substantive body of law can handle the issue of corporate legitimacy relevant to CSR, it only chooses to partially address this issue. This is because, over time, corporate law has developed a focus on the utility aspect of legitimacy, where such utility is often narrowly interpreted as profit-maximisation.

Hurst points to this twofold division of the drive for legitimacy within corporate law, as the division between the drive for utility and the drive for responsibility.[5] In the US historical corporate context, he remarks that 'utility and responsibility as legitimizers were ideas which materially affected our public policy . . . yet utility tended to become an end in itself'.[6] This emphasis on utility within corporate law underscores law's role in entrenching legally protected corporate power and offering a structure for the aggregation of power but failing to respond to problems of the responsibility aspect of corporate legitimacy, especially responsibility to non-shareholders. This aspect has therefore had to develop outside the context of corporate law. This mirrors the division discussed previously between law that empowers versus law that controls. There is a definite tilt in corporate law towards law that empowers and this is done on the basis of a utility argument. There is also a limited control element but this has a narrow internal focus (control and responsibility towards the company (shareholders)).

The wide acceptance of this legal structure implies that there is a reluctance to change. Hurst maintains that:

> so long as dominant opinion continues to accept the large business as a legitimate constituent element in social power, the division of function between corporation law and regulatory law bearing on corporation's behaviour and impact rather than on their internal governance seems likely to remain.[7]

Yet it must be stated that it is not corporate law which is intrinsically unable to reform itself, it is the nature of corporate law as location for power contests

3 J G Frynas, *Beyond Corporate Social Responsibility* (Cambridge University Press, Cambridge, 2009) 175–176

4 I Seidl-Hohenveldern, *Corporations in and under International Law* (Grotius Publications Limited, Cambridge 1987) 1

5 J W Hurst, *The Legitimacy of Business in the Law of the United States 1780–1970* (University of Virginia Press, Charlottesville 1970)

6 Ibid. 58

7 Hurst (n. 5) 111

(hence its political nature) that detracts from the willingness to reform. Ireland instructively points out that:

> the corporate legal form as presently constituted is not an economic necessity but a political construct developed to further the interests of particular groups . . . as political constructs, the corporate legal form and its constituent elements – separate legal personality, limited liability and so on – should be subjected to critical analysis.[8]

In this analysis of corporate law as potential legitimiser of corporate power and thus home for CSR, the initial examination is one of corporate legal theory and corporate governance theory. This is because corporate theories have been influential in the attitude of law towards the corporation. It has also been crucial in the attempt by law to create justification for corporate power by ensuring that there is an existing framework of checks and balances.[9]

The present focus on utility in corporate law has emerged from the choice of a corporate legal theory that privileges private ownership in furtherance of a contractual vision of the corporation. The corporate governance theories and models within corporate law are examined because they are the specific aspect within corporate law which can be extended to both the organisation of the corporation's affairs and the relationship of the corporation to society.[10]

Then the chapter examines an example of state corporate law reform. The chosen example is UK company law because it has gone through what has been described as a 'landmark review of corporate law'.[11] This is because it engaged in a long review and reform process which resulted in the UK company law reform

8 P Ireland, 'Limited Liability, Shareholder Rights and the Problem of Corporate Irresponsibility' (2010) 34 *Cambridge Journal of Economics* 837–856, 838–839

9 D Millon, 'The Theories of Corporation' (1990) 2 *Duke Law Journal* 201–262, 'at any point in time particular theories are perceived to justify particular legal rules or at a more general level, a particular approach to the regulation of business activity' 204. See also M J Horwitz, 'Santa Clara Revisited: The Development of Corporate Theory' (1985–1986) 88(2) *West Virginia Law Review* 173–224. 175–176 reprinted in W J Samuels and A S Miller, *Corporations and Society: Power and Responsibility* (Greenwood Press Inc., Westport, CT 1987)13–64. Horwitz argues that the natural entity theory, for instance, has had a major influence in legitimising big business

10 See S Bottomley, 'From Contractualism to Constitutionalism: A Framework for Corporate Governance' (1997) 19(3) *Sydney Law Review* 277–313, also cited in B. Sheehy, 'Scrooge –The Reluctant Stakeholder: Theoretical Problems in the Shareholder-stakeholder Debate' (2005) 14(1) *Miami Business Law Review* 193–241. Sheehy, ibid., surmising that essentially four questions have been addressed under corporate governance: What is the entity being governed? By whom should the entity be governed? What is the best way to govern the entity? And in whose interests should the entity be governed?

11 B Horrigan, *Corporate Social Responsibility in the 21st Century: Debates, Models and Practices Across Government, Law and Business* (Edward Elgar, Cheltenham 2010) 141

and has been seen as the best demonstration of corporate law's response to pressure for change.[12]

As Horrigan points out, 'corporate law's conception of corporate responsibility and governance is also facing twenty-first century pressures (from within and without) to re-fashion itself, in ways that extend beyond simple perfecting the alignment between company, board and share-holder interests'.[13] This aspect of the analysis will look at the issues of shareholder primacy and director's duties, effective monitoring structure (corporate governance) and the limitations of this approach to broader issues of CSR.

The indications are that corporate law in this traditional form has the potential to contribute to the legitimacy of power but the limitations in the substantive content, existing framework and focus mean that the utility element of legitimacy is emphasised rather than the wider responsibility element.

The results of the UK corporate reform process indicate that the potential for this focus to change is minimal so law's response to demands for CSR will need to come from outside corporate law. This leaves room for an alternative approach from the non-traditional perspective of the law-jobs which will avoid issues of form altogether.

5.2 Corporate legal theory

Corporate legal theory has a history that is intertwined with the history of corporations and questions about their true nature. It is important to note that there is extensive literature on the theories covered in this chapter.[14] Nevertheless the issues involved are still far from settled and the actions of corporations always trigger fresh arguments. This could be simply because the nature of corporations is contestable or because we need to continuously re-examine these theories as we apply them to a changing and dynamic world.

12 Ward (n. 2). Ward points out that in the UK 'the discussion on the proper conceptual framework for linking company law with the pursuit of corporate responsibility took place between 1998 and 2006 in the context of the UK Company Law Reform Process' p. 21

13 Horrigan (n. 11) 10

14 Millon (n. 9); F Hallis, *Corporate Personality: A Study of Jurisprudence* (Oxford University Press, Oxford 1930); F M Maitland, *Introduction to Gierke's Political Theories in the Middle Ages* (Cambridge University Press, Cambridge 1900); A W Machen Jr, 'Corporate Personality (1911) 24(4) *Harvard Law Review* 253–267, P Vinogrdoff, 'Juridical Persons' (1924) 24(6) *Columbia Law Review* 594–604; J Dewey, 'The Historic Background of Corporate Legal Personality' (1926) 35(6) *Yale Law Journal* 655–673; S A Schane, 'The Corporation is a Person: The Language of a Legal Fiction' (1987) 61(3) *Tulane Law Review* 563–609; K Iwai, 'Persons, Things and Corporations, the Corporate Personality Controversy and Comparative Corporate Governance' (1999) 47(4) *American Journal of Comparative Law* 538–632. For corporate governance theories – the literature is listed within this book in later footnotes but an essential starting point remains A A Berle and G C Means, *The Modern Corporation and Private Property* (with a new introduction by M Weidenbaum and M Jensen) (Transaction Publishers, New Brunswick, NJ 1991 (originally published 1932))

Sommer suggests that 'our complicated political and economic society is constantly compelling us to re-examine the assumptions and the rules that guided us in the past to determine their relevance to what we confront today'.[15] As newer and wider forms of corporate power emerge from continued globalisation, the debates are renewed, hopefully with new insights and solutions relevant for the age.

There is a specific body of legal and economic theory built around arguments about the nature of the corporation which influences the direction of analysis about the methods of controlling corporations and corporate power. Horrigan affirms that 'corporate theorizing is the bedrock of normative justifications that inform corporate law making, law reform and practice'.[16] Recurring through the body of legal theory within corporate law is the question of who is the corporation for and, by implication, how should it be controlled? The answers are never static as these theories must be re-examined and applied to changes in political and economic realities.

The aim of such a re-examination is to prompt new perspectives and solutions. The manner in which such theories are interpreted and adapted inadvertently affects the approach adopted to deal with corporations, if only to be able to exclude certain solutions as tried and tested or irrelevant. Also corporations themselves by their actions and effects cause us to review our views and interpretations of them.[17] For instance, this premise allows for the argument that where it is found that corporations are entirely private in origin and consistent with the principles of contract and private property, then the focus must be inwards at internal regulatory measures and governance that satisfy 'the private owners'.

However one must bear in mind that this analysis is taking place against a background established in the previous chapter of the immense power of multinational corporations to affect societal interests. It seeks redress for the exercise of observable or potential corporate power in today's globalised society. This is a wider perspective relevant to a global but uneven world. Multinational corporations do not have legal status in and of themselves as 'multinational corporations',[18] therefore this study must begin with an examination of the legal theory behind the formation of the simple corporation.

The most common form or structure for large business such as multinational corporations is the public corporation (or company) limited by shares. This is because it offers the four most attractive features,[19] that is: (a) corporate legal

15 A A Sommer, Jr, 'Whom should the Corporation Serve? The Berle-Dodd Debate Re-visited Sixty Years Later' (1991) 16 *Delaware Journal of Corporate Law* 33–53

16 Horrigan (n. 11) 76

17 Sommer (n. 15) where he surmises that legal theory shapes social practice and practice informs theory at the same time

18 This was discussed in Chapter 4. See also P T Muchlinski, *Multinational Enterprises and the Law* (Blackwell Publishing, Oxford 1999) 111

19 This is as listed by Dean Robert Clark of the Harvard Law School in R A G Monks and N Minow, *Corporate Governance* (3rd ed., Blackwell, Oxford 2004) 11

personality; (b) limited liability for investors; (c) centralised management; (d) free transferability of interests. The corporation may then offer shares to the public and may then register to be quoted on the stock exchange market.[20] The latter three attributes are derived from the first attribute, which is corporate legal personality.

An understanding of corporate legal personality as it has evolved is central to comprehension of why the corporate form can give rise to such power as it possesses today and how its governance models have evolved. The origin and nature of the corporation has been a source of seemingly endless dispute.[21] There is an astonishing wealth of material on the controversy over the exact jurisprudential nature and origin of the corporation.[22]

The source of this dispute over the role of corporations can even be traced further back to two competing notions about the human individual or, as Allen put it, 'what it means to be human being in society';[23] are men individual beings or are they social beings? Allen finds that the first view of men as individual beings with individual rights has its roots in the works of Hobbes, Locke and Smith, further shaped by Bentham and Mills and then developed in Herbert Spencer's work.[24] This view is of 'the social world populated by individuals

20 Hansmaan and Kraakman list the five essential features of business corporations in major commercial jurisdictions as: separate legal personality, limited liability, shared corporate ownership, delegated management under a board structure and transferability of shares. H Hansmann and R H Kraakman, 'The End of the History of Corporate Law' in J Gordon and M Roe (eds), *Convergence and Persistence in Corporate Governance* (Cambridge University Press, Cambridge 2004) 33–68, 34

21 M Radin, 'The Endless Problem of Corporate Personality' (1932) 32 *Columbia Law Review* 643–667

22 A sample can be found in the works of Hallis (n. 14), Dewey (n. 14), Iwai (n. 14) and G Teubner, 'Enterprise Corporatism, New Industrial Policy and the "Essence" of the Legal Person' (1988) 36 *American Journal of Comparative Law* 130–155

23 W T Allen, 'Contracts and Communities in Corporation Law' (1993) 50 *Washington & Lee Law Review* 1395–1407

24 Ibid.; sometimes referred to as social contractarians, Hobbes and Locke believed in a social contract – 'the idea that only with his consent can a person be subjected to the political power of another'. See R Wacks, *Understanding Jurisprudence* (Oxford University Press, New York 2005) 20. Hobbes (1651) described life as 'solitary, poor, nasty, brutish and short' and advocated that persons will only pursue their own self-interests. For his most popular work see T Hobbes, *Leviathan*, M Oakeshott (ed.) (Basil Blackwell, Oxford 1960). Locke (1689), though influenced by Hobbes, rejected the nasty, brutish and short premise and promoted the right of oppressed people to resist tyranny and a man's right to property. For his work read J Locke, *Two Treatises of Government*, P Laslett (ed.) (Cambridge University Press, Cambridge 1964). Adam Smith (1776), the economist, in line with Locke, viewed property as a natural right and its protection as a law of nature. See A Smith *An Inquiry into the Nature and Causes of the Wealth of Nations*, M Cannan (ed.) (5th ed., Methuen & Co Ltd, London 1904) Book I, Chapter X, Pt II. Bentham and Mills are both utilitarians who are concerned are concerned with (among other things) the impact of judges' actions, laws and institutions on *individuals*. For a helpful discussion on this subject see N E Simmonds, *Central Issues in Jurisprudence: Justice, Law and Rights* (3rd ed., Sweet & Maxwell, London 2008). Herbert

rationally . . . pursuing their own vision of the good life'.[25] In his view, which he refers to as the liberal-utilitarian model, property law and contract law are of the greatest importance for human welfare.

However, the second view, which designates men as social beings, is aptly called the social model. This model perceives the world as 'populated by persons of limited rationality who lead lives embedded in a social context in a community'.[26] It also perceives only limited usefulness in contract and property law, reasserting that their utility rests on the basis of shared norms including fairness and trust. They are prepared to tolerate vagueness in rules in order to achieve a fair outcome. This debate follows through into disputes about the personality of the corporation.

Corporate personality is an attribute of the corporation common to most legal systems of the world.[27] In the case of *Barcelona Traction, Light and Power Company Ltd.*, the International Court of Justice observed that:

> seen in historical perspective, the corporate personality represents a development brought about by new and expanding requirements in the economic field, an entity which in particular allows of operation in circumstances which exceed the normal capacity of individuals. As such it has become a powerful factor in the economic life of nations. Of this, municipal law has had to take due account, hence the increasing volume of rules governing the creation and operation of corporate entities, endowed with a specific status. These entities have rights and obligations peculiar to themselves.[28]

Nevertheless the exact meaning of the nature of corporate personality and its consequential implications remain the source of incessant contention. The basic contention has been: does the personality of the corporation arise simply because individuals exercise their fundamental contractual rights or is it because society permits this socially desirable form of business?

It now appears settled that the corporation is recognised as a separate legal personality, and that, as a consequence of such separate legal personality, it is possible to have corporations with limited liability.[29] This limited liability in the case of multinational corporations, or 'groups of companies', implies that the

Spencer, a social Darwinist, was also of the view that society was evolving to increase the freedom of individuals so that government intervention ought to be minimal in social and political life. See H Spencer, 'Progress: Its Law & Causes' (1857) 67 *Westminster Review* 445–465

25 Allen (n. 23) 1396

26 Allen (n. 23) 1397. This model is championed by Emile Durkheim. For Durkheim's work see E Durkheim, *The Division of Labour in Society*, trans. George Simpson (Collier-Macmillan, London 1964)

27 Seidl-Hohenveldern (n. 4) 1

28 Judgement of 5 February 1970. ICJ Reports 1970 p. 3, p. 34, para. 39

29 The 'corporate personality' or 'separate legal personality', as it is called, is one of the few legal concepts common to most countries of the world

liability of the parent corporation is the same as that of a 'person' investing, limited to the amount left unpaid on the shares.[30] The interpretation of the exact nature of the concept of separate legal personality is at the root of problems regarding how the law views controls of corporate power. The disputes put in a different guise have simply been about the question, what is a corporation? Is it really a group of individuals taking on a fictional personality or is it a group of individuals forming a thing that takes on its own realness, distinct from its creators? These are questions about the nature of the corporation. There are also questions about its origin, is it formed just because individuals get together and draw up a contract or is it formed only by government recognition or concession?

Each of these answers has a defining role in what the purpose of the corporation is. If the corporation is merely a group of individuals contracting together, then it follows that it exists just for their own interests; but if the corporation needs recognition from society, then it exists for societal interests as well. These theories tend to be absolute which in practice is never the case, but still inherent in these theories are the fundamental principles which will help us unravel particular issues and adopt applicable and appropriate answers.

Bratton Jr notes that:

> theorists aspire to provide objective answers to all questions and their theories tend to pose clear-cut, determinant aspirations . . . legal decision-makers

30 In *Re Southard Ltd.* Per Templeman LJ (1979) 3 All ER 556, (1979) 1 WLR 1198 'English company law possesses some curious features, which may generate curious results. A parent company may spawn a number of subsidiary companies, all controlled directly or indirectly by the shareholders of the parent company. If one of the subsidiary companies, to change the metaphor, turns out to be the runt of the litter and declines into solvency to the dismay of its creditors, the parent company and the other subsidiary companies may prosper to the joy of the shareholders without any liability for the debts of the insolvent subsidiary. It is not surprising that when a subsidiary collapses, the unsecured creditors wish the finances of the company and its relationship with other members of the group to be so narrowly examined to ensure no assets of the subsidiary company have leaked away, that no liability of the subsidiary company ought to be laid at the door of other members of the group and that no indemnity from or right of action against any other company or against any individual is by some mischance overlooked'

Pettet notes that not all countries follow this approach notably Germany. Since 1965 West Germany has had special rules governing groups of companies the 'Konzernrecht' in which the parent company may become liable for 'the losses of the subsidiary in certain circumstances', B Pettet, *Company Law* (2nd ed., Pearson Education Limited, Harlow 2005) 38. See also C Alting, 'Piercing the Corporate Veil in American and German Law-Liability of Individuals and Entities; A Comparative View' (1994–1995) 2(5) *Tulsa Journal of Comparative & International Law* 187, who states that 'the United States legal doctrine of corporate veil refers to the common concept of limited corporate liability under which the shareholders of a corporate entity are not personally liable for the entity's debts and obligations. See, for example, Revised Model Business Corp. Act ss 6.22, 2.02(b)(2)(v) (1994). See also Del. Code Ann. tit. 8, s. 102(b)(6) (1992); C S Krendl and J R Krendl, 'Piercing the Corporate Veil: Focusing the Inquiry' (1978) 55(1) *Denver Law Journal* 1–60

share the theorist's aspirations but in the end tend to mediate between alternatives.[31]

For the most part, debates about these theories have been used for opposing and sometimes conflicting ends[32] but this does not detract from the value that has been derived from such theories over the years. As Millon argues, it can be ascertained that in specific settings in history, legal theory has been used to influence the direction of legal understanding.[33] Historically human pursuit can be carried out in collective and collaborative ventures. The corporation is not peculiar simply because it is a kind of collective venture. These collective forms of business organisation have existed for a long time. There is evidence of a long-distance partnership contract known as *naruqqum* used in conducting long-distance caravan trade in the Old Assyrian state in about the nineteenth century BC.[34]

The ancient Romans set up a number of partnerships for their maritime trade and these and other forms of collective business appear common to the pre-modern commercial worlds.[35] It appears to be the case that 'men are social beings' in the sense that no large business undertaking is carried out without social cooperation.[36] However the peculiarity begins with the conception of the corporation as a separate legal person imbued with limited liability.[37] Thus theories about the nature and origin of the corporation are vital to understanding corporate law's approach to the issue of CSR.

5.3 Theories about the nature and origin of the corporation

The origin of the corporation is linked (at least in the Anglo-American tradition) to the tradition of concessions by the crown in the form of charters or grants creating a body separate. This right, first extended to religious orders, local authorities and guild of merchants, evolved to a point where incorporation by registration was introduced in England in 1844.[38] In the United States until

31 W W Bratton, 'Public Values, Private Business and US Corporate Fiduciary Law' in J McCahery, S Picciotto and C Scott (eds), *Corporate Control and Accountability: Changing Structures and the Dynamics of Regulation* (Clarendon Press, Oxford 1993) 23

32 Dewey (n. 14) 671

33 Millon (n. 9). See also Horwitz (n. 9)

34 Iwai (n. 14) 583

35 Ibid.

36 Vinogradoff (n. 14). He was quoting Aristotle

37 Villiers describes the combination of the separate legal personality and limited liability as a 'lethal cocktail' for attempts to pursue parent corporations for liability of the subsidiaries, p. 95. C Villiers, 'Corporate Law, Corporate Power and Corporate Social Responsibility' in N Boeger, R Murray and C Villiers (eds), *Perspectives on Corporate Social Responsibility* (Edward Elgar, Cheltenham 2008) 85–112

38 Joint Stock Companies Act 1844; Limited liability was introduced by the Limited Liability Act 1855

the nineteenth century, incorporation for private business objectives was rare. Corporations were usually charitable or municipal corporations as well as privately owned banks, insurance companies or public utilities.[39]

With the expansion of communication networks and travel creating new markets, the scale and scope of business increased.[40] In one sense the transition from earlier forms of the collaborative business organisation to the multinational corporation seems to have come initially via the Dutch and English trading companies of the sixteenth and seventeenth century chartered by government in long-distance trade and colonial management.[41] However, in a more direct sense, the origin of multinational corporations is placed firmly within the mid-late nineteenth century with the renewed boost of international commerce and links.[42]

The features of corporate personality and limited liability, with the ability of the corporation to own shares in other corporations, has been a major trigger for the continued growth and popularity of the modern corporate form. These modern corporate forms of business organisation have then grown in structural complexity.[43]

The theories that attempt to explain the nature and origin of corporations (fiction theory, real entity theory, concession theory and contract theory) are important when one seeks to understand fully what the corporate form is and how it has been shaped by the thinking and practice of the time.

In this work, Pettet's distinction between theories that refer to the nature of the corporation such as the fiction theory and the real entity theory and theories that refer to the origin of the corporation such as the concession or contract theories has been of value in clarifying the use of the arguments within this context.[44] However, the theories are not incompatible and various writers have

39 Millon (n. 9)

40 A D Chandler, *Scale and Scope: The Dynamics of Industrial Capitalism* (Belknap/Harvard University Press, Cambridge, MA 1990)

41 A M Carlos and S Nicholas, 'Giants of an Earlier Capitalism: The Chartered Trading Companies as Modern Multinationals' (1988) 62(3) *Business History Review* 398–419

42 P Hertner and G Jones, *Multinationals: Theory and History* (Gower, Aldershot 1986)

43 There are also other economic factors. Professor Leslie Hannah is of the view that the availability of the joint stock limited liability company is a necessary precondition to the widespread adoption of modern industrial organisation. L Hannah, 'Mergers, Cartels and Concentration: Legal Factors in US and European Experience' in N Horn and J Kocka (eds), *Law in the Formation of Big Enterprises in the 19th and 20th Centuries* (Vandenhoeck & Ruprecht, Göttingen 1979) 306–315. In 1888 New Jersey in America was the first American state to adopt statute which allowed corporations to own shares in other corporations, creating the concept of a holding corporation. Muchlinski (n. 18) 40

44 In the main, a threefold distinction is commonly used between fictional theory, contract theory and the real entity theory. See P I Blumberg, 'The Corporate Entity in an Era of Multinational Corporation' (1990) 15(2) *Delaware Journal of Corporate Law* 283–376, putting forward a strong case for the selective utilisation of enterprise law (piercing the veil in groups of corporations) to supplement application of entity law on a case by case basis. This threefold distinction is not sacrosanct as other writers use different titles. For example, fiction/corporate realism/corporate nominalism – Iwai ibid.); creature/group/person –

linked them in a number of ways in past writings[45] but the analysis reveals how they have been used to justify different approaches within corporate law.

5.3.1 The fiction theory

The fiction theory is a theory about the nature of the corporation which can be traced to the nineteenth century, particularly in France and Germany where there was deep interest in the metaphysical nature of the corporation.[46] The proponents of this theory firmly asserted that the corporation is a legal fiction, existing only in law. Von Savigny, who is seen as the main proponent of the fiction theory, was a German Romanist who saw the corporation as an 'artificial subject admitted by means of pure fiction'.[47] This theory asserts that the corporation is a legal fiction only existing in law. Schane, as a proponent, points out that although a human being as a conscious and willing entity possesses inalienable rights and individuals may enter into association, the resulting group does not have independent existence of its own except in the contemplation of the law (as a *persona ficta*).[48]

This view had been prominent for many years and was expressed as early as the seventeenth century by Coke[49] and in later years by Kyd[50] and Blackstone.[51] This view also held sway in the United States in the early nineteenth century. This is evidenced by Chief Justice Marshall's statement that:

> a corporation is an artificial being, invisible, intangible, and existing only in the contemplation of the law. Being the mere creature of law, it possesses only those properties which the charter of its creation confers upon it, either expressly or as incidental to its very existence.'[52]

Schane 'The Corporation is a Person: The Language of Legal Fiction' (1987) 61 *Tulane Law Review* 563–595. See Pettet (n. 30) 48; Iwai (n. 14); Schane (n. 14)

45 Dewey (n. 14) argues that each theory has been used to serve opposing ends. See Pettet ibid.; see also B Pettet, 'Limited Liability: A Principle for the 21st Century?' (1995) 48(2) *Current Legal Problems* 125–159

46 Schane (n. 14)

47 See *Jurial Relations or the Roman Law of Persons as Subjects of Jurial Relations* being a translation of the second book of *Savigny's System of Modern Roman Law* (ed.) W H Rattigan (Wiley and Sons, London 1884) 181 and 204

48 Schane (n. 14)

49 Schane (n. 14) 563–564 notes an earlier pronouncement in the rolls of parliament for as early as 1444. This citation is recorded under the entry 'person' in 7 *Oxford English Dictionary* 724 (1961). See also *Case of Sutton's Hosp.*, 10 Coke 23a, 30b-32b, 77 Eng Rep. 960, 970–973 (1612) – Corporation is 'invisible, immortal and rests only in intendment and consideration of the law'

50 S Kyd, *A Treatise on the Law of Corporations* (1793) 69–70, 103

51 W Blackstone, *Commentaries on the Laws of England* (1st ed., 1765) 475–476

52 *Trustees of Dartmouth College v Woodward* (1819) (17 US) 4 Wheat 518, 636

This concept also has close links with the concession theory of the corporation and this is because in its period of popularity, prior to the mid-nineteenth century, charters and grants were the prevalent form of creating a corporation. In propounding this theory Savigny believed in the necessity of state sanction for the creation of every legal person. Therefore the legal fiction was viewed as a privileged legal creation of the state, with the state able to control and regulate the corporation.

Nevertheless the fiction theory has more recently been used as a theory of the nature of corporation without its corollary state/concession theory. This is because it simply envisages a legal fictional person created by law. Indeed recent agency theorists, Jensen and Meckling, who see the corporation as a nexus of contracts, have also used this theory as justification for their arguments. They define a 'corporate firm as simply legal fiction which serves as a nexus for a set of contracting relations among individuals.'[53] This means the emphasis can shift from the 'law' aspect of the theory to the 'fiction' aspect. This is why this theory is also linked to the aggregate or group theory which emphasises the real persons behind the fiction.[54] Its main advocates were Jhering in Germany and Vareilles-Sommières in France.[55] They saw the corporation as a label for identifying members of the group and felt that the corporation was really a group of individuals who contracted for its formation.[56] This is the reasoning behind Morawetz's characterisation of the group theory as stating that the rights and duties of the corporation are analogous to the rights and duties of its members. He states that:

> Although a corporation is frequently spoken of as a person or unit . . . the existence of the corporation independently of its shareholders is a fiction; and the rights and duties of an incorporated association are, in reality, the rights and duties of the persons who compose it, not an imaginary being.[57]

The theoretical conception of the corporation as a legal fiction has been used to justify the property rights of the shareholders who lie behind such a fiction and to insist that the corporation is really for its shareholders. However, this throws up the conundrum of the rule of limited liability.[58] Limited liability does

53 M Jensen and W Meckling, 'The Theory of the Firm: Managerial Behaviour, Agency Costs and Ownership Structures' (1976) 3 *Journal of Financial Economics* 305–360, 310

54 This appears to have drawn on Roman legal theory surrounding the Roman association *societas*, which had legal personality. A Dignam and J Lowry *Company Law* (4th ed., Oxford University Press, Oxford 2006) 354

55 De Vareilles-Sommières, *Les Personnes Morales* (1902) in Machen (n. 14) 257–258. A W Machen, 'Corporate Personality' (1911) 24 *Harvard Law Review* 253–267, 257–258

56 Ibid.

57 V Morawetz, *A Treatise on the Law of Private Corporations* (2nd ed., 1886)

58 Ireland refers to this as 'the no-obligation, no-responsibility, no-liability nature of corporate shares' and this 'permits their owners or their institutional representatives to enjoy income rights without needing to worry . . . they are not legally responsible for corporate malfeasance

not flow automatically from the rights and duties of the persons who compose the corporation, rather it appears to be a privilege derived as a consequence of incorporation. There must be a justification for limiting the liability of the members because if the corporation were to be regarded as merely individuals coming together under the corporate name, they would be fully liable for debts of that corporation under contract law.

For, as Chief Justice Taney points out, if they were simply members carrying out business under a corporate name and entitled to the privileges of contract, they would be liable under these contracts for the whole extent of its property and for the debts of the corporation like a mere partnership in business corporation.[59] The counter-position must therefore be that although it is a legal fiction when it is incorporated, yet by virtue of law it is endowed with several attributes as a result of it is given a strange realness and power.

This is the sense in which we speak of how corporations pervade our lives and acquire responsibility for providing several necessary public and private goods and impacting on services. This perception of impact helps extend notions of criminality to corporate action, where punishment is sought for 'corporate' crimes and criminal conduct.[60] This notion is captured in the alternative view of the corporation as a real entity.

5.3.2 The real entity theory

The real entity theory is a competing theory about the nature of the corporation which, in contrast to the fiction theory, views the corporation as a real and living entity. This theory is generally regarded as the work of the nineteenth-century German realist, Gierke.[61] He saw the corporations as a living organism with a separate existence and life of its own, distinct for that of its shareholders. He pointed to the notion of human nature to form groups and that such groups when formed acquire a life of their own.[62]

In the United States, the important turning point for the corporation towards the real entity theory came with the decision in the case of *Santa Clara County v Southern Pacific Railroad* in 1886,[63] which declared the corporation a person for the purposes of the Fourteenth Amendment. The court decided that the provision

and in the event of failure only their initial investments are at risk'. P Ireland, 'Limited Liability, Shareholder Rights and the Problem of Corporate Irresponsibility' (2010) 34 *Cambridge Journal of Economics* 837–856, 845

59 *Bank of Augusta v Earle* 38 U.S. (13 Pet.) 519, 586 (1839) cited in Horwitz (n. 9)

60 Legislation on corporate crimes such as the UK Corporate Homicide and Corporate Manslaughter Act 2007, UK Bribery Act 2010

61 Maitland (n. 14) xviii-xliii

62 Schane (n. 14)

63 (1886) 118 U.S. 394 although Horwitz (n. 9) argues to the contrary that the Santa Clara case has only been adapted to suit this view and that they were influenced by thinking on shareholder property rights

in the Fourteenth Amendment to the constitution which forbids the state to deny to any person within its jurisdiction equal protection applies to corporations. By implication, this equates the corporation with a real person, therefore having rights and by implication duties and responsibilities.[64]

In England the contrast in legal thinking between fiction and real entity theory can be illustrated by these two contrasting legal observations. Edward, First Baron Thurlow and Lord Chancellor of England in the eighteenth century remarking: 'Did you ever expect a corporation to have a conscience, when it has no soul to be damned and no body to be kicked?'[65]

As opposed to the statement of Denning LJ in 1957 that:

> A company may in many ways be likened to a human body. It has a brain and a nerve centre which controls what it does. It also has hands which hold the tools and act in accordance with the directions from the centre. Some of the people in the company are mere servants or agents who are nothing more than the hands to do the work and cannot be said to represent the mind or will. Others are directors and managers who represent the directing mind and will of the company and control what it does. The state of mind of the managers is the state of mind of the company and is treated by the law as such.[66]

Notwithstanding the slight absurdity of equating the corporation to a real entity, there is an element of practicality which has contributed to this being a theory that recognises the practical influence of the expansion of business. This is a distinct legal personality which can be seen in a natural or artificial way. Machen argues for a distinction between the entity and the recognition of the entity as a person. He perceptively notes that 'a corporation exists as an objectively real entity which any well-developed child or normal man must perceive: the law merely recognises and gives legal effect to the existence of this entity'. [67]

Regardless of whether this distinction is accepted, it is the recognition of the real entity nature by the law that has been the justifiable basis for allowing corporation as persons to own shares in other corporations, paving the way for larger groups of corporations such as MNCs. This principle of a separate legal person famously enunciated in *Salomon v Salomon* where Lord MacNaghten expounded that 'the company is at law a different person altogether from the subscribers to the memorandum'.[68]

This personhood extends to MNCs in beneficial ways as parent corporations can hold shares in subsidiaries just as a separate person can.[69] This has resulted in

64 Millon (n. 9)
65 Cited in Monks and Minow (n. 19) 31
66 *Bolton Engineering v Graham* (1957) 1 QB 159, 172
67 Machen (n. 14) 256
68 (1897) AC 22 (HL)
69 Ireland (n. 8)

peculiar distinctions in law with sometimes surprising results. For example, in the US case of *People's Pleasure Park Co. v Rohleder*,[70] where the court found that covenants restricting transfer of land to 'colored persons' in the early twentieth century did not apply to a company whose entire shareholders were African American. It found that the corporation was legally distinct and separate and could hold land in its own name.

However, this theory which allows for extension of rights to the separate legal personality of the corporation can by analogy be extended to that of responsibilities. This will permit a personality that is capable of demanding rights but also of acquiring responsibilities. This view can be gleaned from Lord Halsbury's statement in *Salomon v Salomon* that 'once the company is legally incorporated it must be treated like any other independent person with its rights and liabilities appropriate to itself.' [71]

There is also a direct analogy between this reasoning of corporations as distinct legal persons and cajoling the corporations to become better 'citizens'.[72] Therefore, as Millon identifies, the entity theory could be used as a theoretical basis for a form of corporate social responsibility.[73] He relies on Dodd's analysis to indicate that a corporation as its own entity can owe responsibilities to society.

Notwithstanding this there is still some doubt as to how far this analogy can be extended. Keay offers an alternative conception of an entity maximisation and sustainability model based on the company being regarded as a distinct legal entity and argues for a core objective of the corporation that is centred on maximising the entity for its sustainable survival.[74] This is a reflection of a self-interested entity. Self-interest and social responsibility are not easy bedfellows. Nevertheless the question of what range of interests this entity should have is intermingled with questions of its origin.

5.3.3 Concession theory

The concession theory pertains to the origin of the corporation. It perceives the source of the corporation's legal personality as emerging from the state. This proposition may have arisen in response to the state's desire to regulate groups within it, thereby creating a validation process through a grant system or registration system. The state through this process grants the corporate status and its advantages to groups who wish to carry on certain business.

70 61 SE 794 (Va 1908) Case in Virginia USA, Facts given in L E Talbot, *Critical Company Law* (Routledge, Abingdon 2008)
71 (1897) AC 22
72 J Androif and M McIntosh (eds), *Perspectives on Corporate Citizenship* (Greenleaf Publishing, Sheffield 2001)
73 Millon (n. 9) 219
74 A Keay, 'Ascertaining the Corporate Objective: An Entity Maximisation and Sustainability Model' (2008) 71(5) *Modern Law Review* 663–698, 665

On initial consideration this theory appears outmoded, better suited to the times when the state was directly involved in grants by royal charter and so on.

However, on deeper contemplation, there is an important fact which rings true in this theory which some now see as defunct, which is that corporate personality can only be acceptable where the society sees fit to give and recognise it. The idea of corporate personality and limited liability has been politically and legally constructed on the premise of the utility of the corporation.[75] The recognition of corporate personality and limited liability is accorded by state law.

It is not inherent in any group to be a body corporate except it complies with outlined steps (albeit simple steps) listed in statute. These steps may have been modified and eased to enable the growth of entrepreneurship and commerce (hence emphasising the utility aspect of corporate legitimacy) but they still remain a privilege accorded to a group in society by government.

If the government is taken to be the expression of the people through a democratic process,[76] Dodd's expression that corporations exist because they are beneficial to society is fulfilled.[77] Although the trend may be to ease restrictions, there is no denying the inherent power of society through government or other means to regulate, monitor or change the conditions and basis under which such corporate status should be acquired and how it should operate.[78]

This is exemplified in the UK by the extensive company law review process that culminated in the Companies Act 2006. There will always be a prescription of legal formalities for registering corporations and even where people come together to do business, they are not automatically recognised as corporations because they think they are. It is preferable to assert to assert that:

> A business corporation is able to act as an independent owner of its own property capable of making a contractual relation directly with others, not because the inside shareholders will it to be so, but because, and in so far as, the outside parties recognise it to be so. Such social recognition is indispensable and the law formalizes and reinforces the social recognition in the form of legal personality.[79]

This possibility of the formalisation of social recognition is what pushes Blumberg to request the recognition of the new reality of the MNC in law with

75 Millon (n. 9). This is seen as defunct because of the change in corporate formation and the death of the *ultra vires* rule

76 This is not always the case but issues of public governance are outside the scope of this work. For an overview of current and new thinking in this area, see J Lenoble and M Maesschalck, *Democracy, Law and Governance* (Ashgate, Farnham 2010)

77 E M Dodd, 'For Whom are Corporate Managers Trustees?' (1932) 45 *Harvard Law Review* 1145–1163

78 Horrigan (n. 11)

79 Iwai (n. 14)

an enterprise personality model.[80] This model, he suggests, will recognise the modern enterprise and go beyond the limited entity legal personality now present in national legal systems. He points out that over the last hundred years in which the law has eased permissions of the formation of groups the reality that has emerged is that some large corporations operate under common control as a multinational enterprise.[81] Nonetheless there is reluctance to recognise such an entity because of the decreasing emphasis on the role of the state which is linked to the predominant neo-liberal legal order and the emphasis on privatisation and deregulation.[82] This reasoning is also what drives the alternative contract theory on the origin of the corporation.

5.3.4 Contract theory

The contract theory is also about origin of the corporation. It views the origin of the corporation as rooted in contract. This is more attuned to the individualistic view of the human person and his inherent right to enter into contracts which has thrived in the current liberal legal order. The contract theory views the corporation as based on private contract, therefore the role of the state is limited to enforcing contracts.[83] The focus is on freedom of contract and the freedom to structure contracts between private persons.[84] More recently this theory has been refreshed not just as contract but as a 'nexus of contracts' and this revival is most evident in the development of economic theories of the corporation.[85] The proponents of this theory restate the corporation as a complex set of explicit and implicit contracts. For example, Easterbrook and Fishcel state that:

> The corporate structure is a set of contracts through which managers and certain other participants exercise a great deal of discretion that is 'reviewed' by interactions with other self-interested actors. The interaction often occurs in markets and we shall sometimes call the pressures these interactions produce 'market forces'.[86]

80 P I Blumberg, 'The Corporate Entity in an Era of Multinational Corporations' 15(2) *Delaware Journal of Corporate Law* 283–276
81 Ibid.
82 G J Ikenberry, 'Liberal Internationalism 3.0: America and the Dilemmas of Liberal World Order' (2009) 7(1) *Perspectives on Politics* 71–87
83 H N Butler, 'Contractual Theory of the Corporation' 11(4) *George Mason University Law Review* 99–123
84 Ibid. 100
85 See works such as R H Coase, 'The Nature of a Firm' (1937) 4 *Economica* 13–16, M Jensen and W Meckling 'Theory of the Firm: Managerial Behaviour, Agency Costs and Ownership Structure' (1976) 3 Journal of Financial Economics 305–360, 310, O E Williamson, 'Corporate Governance' (1984) 93 *Yale Law Journal* 1197–1230
86 F H Easterbrook and D R Fischel, 'The Corporate Contract' (1989) 89 *Columbia Law Review* 1416–1448, 1418

The underlying basis of the contract theory is that the individuals who make up the corporation contract to do so and, in essence, the corporation is a contract agreed among its members. In deference to the incomplete picture this paints, the nexus of contracts theorists simply add more layers of contracts which define the role of owners and the managers seen as their agents. This theory underlies most of the current writing about the corporation, however, in spite of its success, it is disputable that the corporation as a legal person can be reduced to a bundle of contracts. Yet this has been useful to justify the limited focus on the internal participants.

Nevertheless Parkinson points out that even where one accepts the contractual basis of corporations, this does not absolve corporate law from the issue of state intervention especially where such corporate power is contrary to public or societal interest. However he recognises that the concentration of power in private hands has come partly as a result of their existence. [87]

It has become one of the main vehicles of capitalism and forms the basis for corporate governance models in Anglo-American states.[88] The contractual theoretical underpinnings of corporate governance are the reason for the limited focus on issues of CSR within corporate law. Its impact is also significant globally as the evidence of convergence of corporate governance models increases.[89]

Overall the nature of these well-established disputes about corporations is that they help us understand perhaps the 'fluctuating reality of corporations'.[90] Teubner suggests that the social reality of the legal person can be found in the collectivity of the socially binding self-description of an organised action system of cyclical linkage of identity and action. He cites Weber as perhaps justified in treating collectivities as ideas in the heads of judges and yet assigning them a powerful and decisive influence on the course of action of real people.[91]

Therefore corporation can be perceived as creature of law yet real and powerful. Perhaps the idea of the corporation as real helps enhance its power but, more importantly, it makes it possible to assert that there are two sides to this coin, that is, that the corporation is a creature of law and therefore can be regulated by law even though within the corporation there lies a contractual arrangement for its members.

However, it is apparent that the influence and interpretations of these theories is what drives the direction of the governing of the corporation and the range of interests which the corporation will take into account. These are key issues for the

87 J E Parkinson, *Corporate Power and Responsibility: Issues in the Theory of Company Law* (Clarendon Press, Oxford 1995) 30

88 Butler (n. 83)

89 Hansmann and Kraakman (n. 20)

90 See G Teubner, 'Enterprise Corporatism: New Industrial Policy and the "Essence" of the Legal Person' (1988) 36 *American Journal of Comparative Law* 130, 138 citing Weber, *Economy and Society* (1978) 13. This is also examined in Blumberg (n. 80)

91 Teubner, ibid.

legitimacy and accountability of corporate power which CSR will require, if it is to fall within the corporate law framework.

5.4 Corporate governance models and theories

Corporate governance theories are derived from theories of corporate personality. It has been pointed out that 'the problems of "corporate" governance are literally the problems of governing the "corporate" form of business firms'.[92] Corporate governance debates also reflect the lack of clarity over the corporate objective and this lack of clarity is predicated on debates about the nature and origin of the corporation.[93] These include questions such as: Is the corporation ultimately for its owners and their profit or is it for society and its benefit?

These questions relate to the purpose of the corporation as well as to issues of control or governing and in whose interest. Therefore corporate governance covers how a corporation is run and how it behaves.[94] The problem of control becomes even more extended in large MNCs where the managers are distinct from the owners and there is a lack of control because ownership is dispersed and weak.

This problem was identified as early as 1838 in the work of Adam Smith where he identified a problem with joint stock companies having managers of other people's money and questioned the vigilance with which they would watch over it.[95] However, it is given a full analysis in the seminal work of Berle and Means.[96] Although the focus of the analysis is on large corporations in the United States, it is a problem that can be extended to large MNCs around the world.[97] Though it is doubtful whether there is such pronounced separation between ownership and control in states such as France, Germany, Japan and South Korea

92 K Iwai 'What is a Corporation? – The Corporate Personality Controversy and the Fiduciary Principle in Corporate Governance' in F Cafaggi, A Nicita and U Pagano (eds), *Legal Orderings and Economic Institutions* (Routledge, London 2007) 243–267

93 Jensen asserts that 'current global governance debate is a remarkable division of opinion about the fundamental purpose of the corporation. M C Jensen, 'Value Maximisation, Stakeholder Theory and the Corporate Objective Function' (2001) 4 *Journal of Applied Corporate Finance* 8–21, 8. Keay points out that establishing the objective of the corporation is critical to the formulation of its governance mechanisms. A Keay, 'Ascertaining the Corporate Objective: An Entity Maximisation and Sustainability Model' (2008) 71(5) *Modern Law Review* 663–698, 665

94 Horrigan (n. 11) 69

95 M Blowfield and A Murray *Corporate Responsibility: A Critical Introduction* (Oxford University Press, Oxford 2008) 41

96 A A Berle and G C Means, *The Modern Corporation and Private Property* (with a new introduction by M. Weidenbaum and M. Jensen) (Transaction Publishers, New Brunswick, NJ 1991 (originally published in 1932))

97 M S Mizruchi, 'Berle and Means Revisited: The Governance and Power of Large U.S Corporations' (2004) 33 *Theory and Society* 579–613

where ownership is not so dispersed, corporate governance issues are still relevant as they raise questions of how these variant corporate organisations are governed.[98]

There are two major types of corporate governance systems in capitalist states globally, namely the shareholder and the block-holder systems,[99] but there are forceful arguments for the emergence of a convergence of both systems on a system of corporate governance that prioritises the shareholder.[100] The shareholder model in practice in the United States and the UK is characterised by dispersed equity holding, delegation to management to run the corporation, supervision via single supervisory boards, deep trading markets and market regulations and the possibility of hostile takeovers.[101]

Block-holder or stakeholder models are of two major variants, the first kind is that found in Germany characterised by large banks as main investors[102] and a two-tier supervisory board structure and employees represented on the boards in line with the co-determination principle.[103] The second kind is peculiar to Japan and involves a network of cross-shareholdings resulting in a very complex network of interwoven groups. Iwai states that Japan has six major corporate groups – Mitsubishi, Mitsui, Sumitomo, Fuyo (Fuji), Sanwa and Dauchi-Kangin (DK). Each group is clustered around a main bank and extended over the whole industry[104] connected through intricate cross-shareholdings.[105] By virtue of anti-monopoly laws the shares held by the banks in each corporation cannot surpass 5 per cent but these networks of cross-shareholdings and lunch-club meetings of presidents of members of each group result in a substantial element of internal monitoring and control.[106]

98 This was highlighted by the work of R La Porta, F Lopez-de-Silanes and A Shleifer, 'Corporate Ownership around the World' (1999) 54(2) *Journal of Finance* 471–517, which found that the most common ownership around the globe is family or controlling shareholders

99 W W Bratton and J A McCahery 'Barriers to Global Cross-Reference' in J. McCahery (ed.) *Corporate Governance Regimes: Convergence and Diversity* (Oxford University Press, New York 2002). This may mask national differences

100 The most forceful advocates are H Hansmann and R Kraakman, 'The End of History for Corporate Law" in J N Gordon and M J Roe (eds), *Convergence and Persistence in Corporate Governance* (Cambridge University Press, Cambridge 2004)

101 See Bratton and McCahery (n. 99) 26–27 where they make a comparison of the elements of market and block-holder systems

102 Although La Porta *et al.* in their study find that other countries in Europe and the world are dominated by family or even state-owned corporations. See La Porta (n. 98)

103 V D Dinh, 'Codetermination and Corporate Governance in a Multinational Business Enterprise' (1999) 24 *Journal of Corporate Law* 975–999

104 Ramsweyer gives the example of Mitsui group which includes two banks, two insurance companies, a trading company, a construction firm, a paper company, an oil company, a steel company, Toshiba, Toyota and a real estate firm. See M. Ramsweyer, 'Cross-shareholdings in Japanese Keiretsu' in J McCahery (ed.), *Corporate Governance Regimes: Convergence and Diversity* (Oxford University Press, New York 2002)

105 Iwai (n. 92)

106 Ibid.

However, there are theoretical issues at the heart of the analysis of Berle and Means which are now relevant to virtually all industrialised capitalist nations regardless of the extent to which they have experienced a separation of ownership from control.[107] These issues go beyond a mere lack of accountability to shareholders and a loss of control to point out questions of accountability to society in general.

As Mizruchi put it:

> Berle & Means concern about separation of ownership from control was not only about managers' lack of accountability to investors. It was also a concern about managers' lack of accountability to society in general. Berle and Means thus wrote of a small group, sitting at the head of enormous organizations with the power to build, and destroy communities, to generate great productivity and wealth but also to control the distribution of that wealth, without regard to those who elected them (stockholders) or those who depended on them (the larger public).[108]

Although this assertion of Berle and Means's concern for the accountability to the public is somewhat expanded, Mizruchi raises a valid point about the applicability of Berle and Means's governance issues to countries beyond their scope of study, which was the United States.

This tentative conclusion of Berle and Means's work[109] that the loss of control by shareholders may have resulted in a surrendering of rights, that the corporation be operated in their sole interests and opened up the way firm wider claims, that demand that the corporation should serve all society is the basis for a lot of debate within corporate governance. It is not as far-reaching as Dodd's assertions that society's interests are paramount in the first instance because it only acknowledges that there has been significant change in the history of the corporation and that the shareholder-oriented model based on the contract theory is failing to capture this change.

Therefore it is possible to derive two theoretical implications from the Berle and Means conclusion. On the one hand, theories repudiating the loss of control by shareholding and re-emphasising mechanisms to achieve shareholder primacy through the agent-principal framework (agency theory)[110] or, on the other hand, those theories taking on the larger challenge of positing an opening up of corporations to wider interests by attempting the challenge to fashion out a more representative system (stakeholder theories).[111] As a result of this separation,

107 Mizruchi (n. 97) 580
108 Ibid. 581
109 Berle and Means (n. 96) 312
110 Jensen and Meckling (n. 85)
111 T Donaldson and L Preston, 'The Stakeholder Theory of the Corporation: Concepts, Evidence and Implications' (1995) 20 *Academy of Management Review* 65–91

in their own work Berle and Means suggest 'a purely neutral technocracy balancing a variety of claims by various groups in the community and assigning to each a portion of income stream on the basis of public policy rather than private cupidity'.[112] The theories will be analysed in further detail as they are riddled with questions of accountability to diverse interests. The examination will be to observe the potential range of interests and this will help arrive at conclusions on how relevant corporate governance theories can be to the newer set of legitimacy problems posed within CSR.

5.4.1 Separation of ownership from control

This theory of separation of ownership from control is sometimes called 'managerialism'. It originated from the seminal work of Berle and Means titled "The Modern Corporation and Private Property" published in 1932.[113] The work examined large corporations in the United States but has since then become of significance to large MNCs more generally. Its most enduring theme is that of the concentration of power within the 'managerial'[114] class of the large corporation and the consequent separation of ownership from control in the large modern corporation.[115]

Berle and Means studied 200 of the largest US non-financial corporations in 1929 and found that 44 per cent by number and 58 per cent by wealth were management-controlled.[116] Management-controlled was their description of corporations where the control lay not with the shareholders but with the management because it had become virtually a self-perpetuating body because ownership was sufficiently and significantly sub-divided.[117]

This was only part of the full picture. They discovered that on full examination of the five major types of control examined, that is, control through almost complete ownership, majority control, control through a legal device (such as pyramiding, a special class of voting stock or voting trust), minority control and management control, 65 per cent of the corporations and 80 per cent of their

112 Berle and Means (n. 96)

113 Berle and Means (n. 96) originally published in 1932 by Harcourt, Brace & World, Inc.

114 Interestingly they defined management as including both the senior officers of the corporation and the board of directors; this is dissimilar to contemporary usage of the word which refers to senior officers of the corporation only. Berle and Means, ibid. 196, 'Management may be defined as that body of men who in law, have formally assumed the duties of exercising domination over the corporate business and assets . . . under the American system of law, managers consist of a board of directors and the senior officers of the corporation'.

115 There are several themes raised by Berle and Means in their book because it was written at the height of the Great Depression in the United States

116 Berle and Means (n. 96) 109

117 Berle and Means (n. 96) 81

combined wealth were controlled by management or by a legal device involving a small proportion of ownership.[118]

This had resulted from a dispersal of stock ownership which had resulted in passive property ownership. They found several changes in the manner of property ownership,[119] key for them were: the changes from an active to a passive agent;[120] the separation of the spiritual values that formerly went with ownership; the value of wealth was no longer dependent on personal efforts; the value of wealth fluctuates and was constantly appraised; individual wealth had become liquid through organised markets; wealth was less in a form that can be employed directly by owner and the stockholders were left with mere symbols of ownership while the power, the responsibility and the substance, integral to ownership was now transferred to a separate controlling group. These findings strengthened their conclusion that ownership and control had become separable factors.[121]

While there have been some criticism of the Berle and Means study, it has been fundamental to the development of corporate governance.[122] La Porta and others attempted to show that outside the United States and the UK, other developed countries had controlling or block shareholders such as the state or the family in their largest firms because there was poor shareholder protection.[123] However, this is not always relevant for MNCs which make full use of the equity markets in the UK and United States as well as other large world economies. The crucial issue is not the existence or non-existence of the separation but that the 'separation implies shortfalls of competence and responsibility'.[124]

An important factor is that the Berle and Means study deals with the corporation from essentially a property rights perspective. This is important because as noted earlier, there appears to be a basic theoretical divide in approaches to analysis of large corporations. The divide between the contractarians and the communitarians;[125] the divide between those who emphasise private property rights as justification for corporations and those who insist that corporations are in essence necessary to the extent that society deems it so. Berle and Means approach their analysis from the private property and contractual rights

118 Berle and Means (n. 96) 110. They concluded that 'only 11 percent of the companies and 6 percent of their wealth involved control by a group of individuals owning half or more of the stock interest outstanding'

119 Berle and Means (n. 96) 64–65

120 They note especially that in place of actual physical properties over which the owner could exercise direction and for which the owner is responsible, the owner now holds a piece of paper representing a set of rights and expectations with respect to an enterprise

121 In their words, 'formerly assumed to be merely a function of ownership, control now appears to be a separate and separable factor' Berle and Means (n. 96) 111

122 See Introduction by Murray L. Weidenbaum and Mark Jensen in new republication of Berle and Means (n. 96)

123 La Porta *et al.* (n. 98)

124 W W Bratton, 'Berle and Means Re-considered at the Century's Turn' (2001) 26 *Journal of Corporate Law* 737–770

125 Allen (n. 23)

perspective, only allowing for the possibility of societal demands in the face of weakened passive property rights owners. This means that the Berle and Means analysis begins from a contractual theoretical standpoint.

In their study they trace the evolution of the modern corporate structure within American law from its starting point as inherited from English jurisprudence at the close of the eighteenth century. At this point they accept that the corporation was seen as a 'franchise' with its very existence conditional on a grant from the state. This grant set up a legal person distinct from its associates.[126] However, they note that at the same time the document of grant (that is, the charter or its more recent form, the certificate of incorporation) embodied the outline arrangement among associates and therefore was a result of threefold negotiations involving the state and the combined associates and between the associates as for themselves. Here they conclude it was recognised as a 'contract' and has been consistently dealt with as such under American law.[127] They remark that although the state enacted protections in the nineteenth century, many of these protections could have been qualified by contract.[128] However, the state's insistence on protecting and supervising the contract resulted, in their view, in a picture where a group of owners necessarily delegated certain powers of management, who were protected by a series of fixed rules under which the management had a relatively limited sphere (an owner-agent situation).

The breakdown in property rights comes into existence with the revolution of the general incorporation laws at the end of the nineteenth century and what they term 'the vanishing of the checks from the general incorporation laws', with all rigid requirements broken down, in effect leaving the originating group able to write its own contract on the broadest terms. Although every stockholder is bound by the contract, modifications and changes, in practice they never even

126 Berle and Means (n. 96) 120, 'The real privilege which the state grants is that of the corporate entity – the right to maintain business in its own name, to sue and be sued on its behalf irrespective of individuals, to have perpetual succession and from this flowed limited liability.' In their view limited liability was not a state granted privilege because a clause could be written into every contract by which the opposite party limited his right to recovery to the common fund

127 Berle and Means (n. 96) 121. 'The charter of a corporation having a capital stock is a contract between 3 parties and form the basis of 3 distinct contracts. The charter is a contract between the state and the corporation, between the corporation and the stockholders and between stockholders and the state' citing 2 Cook on Corporations, 5th edition, section 492 and I Clark and Marshall, ' Private Corporations' section 271f

128 They list the protections as: a. the enterprise was required to be defined and carefully limited in scope [*ultra-vires* doctrine]; b. contributions of capital were rigidly supervised – the corporation was not allowed to commence business until certain shares were paid up; c. a rigid capital structure was set up – with preferred and common stock. They also note common law added further safeguards a. residual control lay in the shareholder or in a specified proportion; b. shareholders had sole rights to invest new monies in the enterprise – foundations of the present 'law of pre-emptive rights'; c. in general dividends were permitted only out of surplus profits (ibid.)

see the documents giving management wide latitude to arrange participation in its own interests. This decline results in a position where they have surrendered a set of definite rights for indefinite expectations[129] and may thereby have surrendered the right that the corporation be run in their sole interest, probably opening up the claim that wider interests of the society be served.[130]

The Berle and Means proposition seen from this angle can give rise to any variant of two suggestions. First this proposition could mean that a strengthening of the role of shareholders could correct the imbalance in the power and control relationship and redress the problem of inadequate control of corporate power in the hands of managers. This has given rise to the agency theories which have fought to use market and structural mechanisms that reinstate shareholder primacy or. in contrast, where there continues to remain a separation of ownership and management interests then these wider claims may have validity and this is the ground occupied by the stakeholder theories.

Although the argument appears to be shareholder versus other stakeholders, the implication from the conception of separation of ownership and control is that these other interests only gain legitimacy when there is passive property ownership. This is not a satisfactory basis for the question of corporate control. For the multinational corporate power under analysis has much wider implications for the exercise of power than for shareholders. It is very weak to base the possibility of wider societal claims (that the corporation be run in the best interest of society) on the very narrow basis of separation of ownership from control and the resulting passive property ownership. There is a wider legitimacy question which is not fully addressed by corporate governance.

Berle and Means are not totally unaware of this because they accept that:

> the rise of the modern corporation has brought a concentration of economic power which can compete on equal terms with the modern state – economic power versus political power each strong in its own fields, the state seeks in some respect to regulate the corporation while the corporation, steadily becoming more powerful makes every effort to avoid such regulation.[131]

129 By this they refer to the limited reliance on director's duties –a decent amount of attention to the business; fidelity to the interests of the corporation; at least reasonable business prudence see Berle and Means (n. 96) 197

130 Berle and Means (n. 96) This oft quoted statement is located in p.311. They state that 'the owners of private property by surrendering control and responsibility over the active property, have surrendered the right that the corporation should be operated in the sole interest – they have released the community from the obligation to protect them to the full extent implied in the doctrine of strict property rights. . .the control groups have cleared the way for claims of a group far wider than either the owners or the control. They have placed the community in a position to demand that the modern corporation serve not alone the owners or the control but all society'

131 Berle and Means (n. 96) 313

This is even more in the case at the present time. The difficulty has become how to demonstrate a legitimacy of corporate power to society beyond that owed to the shareholders.

This is captured in the stark contrast that still remains between the Berle and Means tentative possibility that separation of ownership and control may have opened up wider demands that the modern corporation serve society's interests and Dodd's bold statement that business is permitted and encouraged by law because it is of service to the community rather than because it is a source of profit to its owners.[132] This difference is crucial and is affecting our approach to regulation for social responsibility within corporate law.[133]

Yet within the scope that the Berle and Means debate affords, relevant theories have arisen which will be analysed. This is because corporate governance is still advocated as covering some wider ground. For instance, when it is defined as:

> the whole set of legal, cultural and institutional arrangements that determine what publicly traded corporations can do, who controls them, how that control is exercised and how risks and returns from the activities they undertake are allocated.[134]

5.4.2 Agency theory

Agency theory covers a body of work that follows on from the first implication of the Berle and Means separation of ownership from the control thesis which is that owner and control interests can be reconciled in this agency relationship. It has both law and economic origins. It is the focus of the work of Jensen and Meckling[135] and the later work of Fama and Jensen.[136] The focus is purely a (property rights) contractual view and follows logically from the Berle and Means statement of the problem.[137]

For agency theorists, the relationship between the stockholders and managers of the corporation fits the description of a pure agency, therefore the issues related to the separation of ownership from control are associated with the general

132 Dodd (n. 77)

133 Voluntary or mandatory

134 M M Blair, *Ownership and Control, Rethinking Corporate Governance for the Twenty-first Century* (Brookings Institution, Washington, DC 1995) 3, contrast this with the definition of corporate governance as 'the way suppliers of finance assure themselves of getting a return on their investment;. A Shleifer and R W Vishny, 'A Survey of Corporate Governance' (1997) 52(2) *Journal of Finance* 737–783

135 C Jensen and W H Meckling, 'Theory of the Firm: Managerial Behaviour, Agency Costs and Ownership Structure' (1976) 3 *Journal of Financial Economics* 305–360

136 E F Fama and M C Jensen, 'Separation of Ownership and Control' (1983) 26(2) *Journal of Law and Economics* 301–325

137 This covers even more recent areas of advocacy for institutional shareholders such as pension funds to become more active within corporations. Monks and Minow (n. 19) 13–194

problem of agency costs.[138] For Jensen and Meckling, the private corporation is seen simply as a legal fiction which serves as 'a nexus for contractual relationships and which is also characterised by the existence of divisible residual claims on assets and cash flows of the organisation, which can generally be sold without permission of other contracting individuals'.[139]

This notion of stockholders as residual risk bearers is introduced by Fama and Jensen,[140] who argue that the separation of decision and risk-bearing functions observed in large corporations is common and generally indicative of agency problems which arise because contracts are not costlessly written and enforced. Agency costs include the cost of structuring, monitoring and bonding a set of contracts among agents with conflicting interests.

Under the Fama and Jensen scheme, a modern multinational will be classed as an open corporation, in this sense the common residual claims of such organisations are unrestricted so that stockholders are not required to have any other role in the organisation and their residual claims are freely alienable. As a result of the unrestricted nature of the residual claims of open corporations, there is almost complete specialisation of decision-management and residual risk bearing.[141]

The solutions proffered to the problem of agency costs are extremely popular in current corporate governance circles, they include the use of the stock market as visible signals for implications of internal decisions for current and future cash flows; external monitoring through the takeover market and an expert board of directors with inside and outside 'independent' members who can effectively limit the decision discretion of management.[142] The focus is on controls that realign the interests of the managers (controllers) with the interests of the shareholders or stockholders (owners).

The agency theory is also closely related to a body of work classed as 'transaction cost economics'. This is mainly based on the economic analysis of Coase in 1937 where he examined the theory of the firm from within.[143] He saw the rationale for a firm (corporation) to be simply a means of saving market transaction costs. 'The operation of the market costs something and by forming an organisation and allowing some authority (an entrepreneur) to direct the resources, certain marketing costs are saved.'[144] For him the firm becomes bigger when additional

138 Jensen and Meckling (n. 135)

139 Ibid.

140 Fama and Jensen (n. 136). The residual risk – seen as the risk of the difference between the stochastic inflows of resources and the promised payments to agents – is borne by those who contract for the rights to net cash flows. The 'agents' are called residual risk bearers

141 Fama and Jensen (n. 136)

142 Fama and Jensen (n 136)

143 R H Coase, 'The Nature of the Firm' (1937) 4 *Economica* 386–405, 392. Prior to this neo-classical economists viewed the firm as a black box

144 Ibid. 392

transactions are organised by the entrepreneur.[145] The transactions they increase would tend to be of different kinds or in different places and this is the reason why efficiency seems to decrease as firms get larger. He therefore suggests that 'all changes which improve managerial technique will tend to increase the size of the firm'.[146]

Coase's work did not dwell on governance but the work of another proponent did. Williamson analysed transaction cost economics as assigning transactions to governance structures in such a way as to accomplish an economising result.[147] For him 'any issue that can be posed as a *contracting problem* is usefully addressed in *transaction cost economising* terms' (emphasis added).[148] In his analysis of corporate governance he studies a contractual schema couched in terms of relation to the corporation in node A, B or C position. He then argues that in certain relationships representations on the board are unnecessary. Stockholders are located in node B while the atypical lender is usually node C. Customers are mainly located in node A, workers with general knowledge and skills would fall into node A unless they had firm specific investment, suppliers usually in node C and community, a specially grafted node C protection.[149] He concludes that:

> Representation is unwarranted for constituencies at node A because of negligible exposure to their transaction-specific assets. Moreover their legitimate interests are adequately safeguarded through neo-classical market contracting. Such constituencies have neither informational nor decisional needs to be served through board membership. Constituencies located at node B have exposed assets and will charge a higher price unless safeguards can be devised therefore generalised safeguards through voting board memberships may be warranted and finally those constituencies located in node C have devised a structure of bilateral governance and do not need membership on the boards.[150]

This constitutes a highly fascinating economic analytical response to corporate governance but it indicates that both agency and transaction cost economics regard the voting of board members by shareholders and investors, the stock markets for the public and the specialised contracting for lenders and suppliers as equivalent instruments of control which render direct representation of stakeholders on boards unnecessary. The attractiveness of these theories lies in the rather simplistic analysis of relationships within the corporation in terms of

145 Coase (n. 143) 393

146 Coase (n. 143) 397. This he actually states in terms of invention to bring the factors of production closer together such as telephone, telegraph and so on

147 O Williamson, 'Corporate Governance' (1984) 93 (7) *YaleLaw Journal* 1197–1230, 1203

148 Ibid.

149 Williamson (n. 147)

150 See Williamson (n. 147) 1205–1215

contracts, it appears faultless in the picture it paints and is immensely popular. The problem, however, is not that of a wrong picture but rather an incomplete one. The push for responsibility is coming from society because of the impact that corporate power is having and the focus of this theory is internal and self-interested. The safeguards need to be re-examined and alternative structures suggested.

5.4.3 Stakeholder theories

In contrast to the position of the agency theory the stakeholder theories cover a body of work that attempts to capture the idea that a corporation should have *some* social purpose beyond maximising returns to shareholders. In spite of the significant amount of literature on this subject, the theory is not as bold or revolutionary as it first appears.[151] Elhauge suggests that:

> Managerial discretion to sacrifice profits is both inevitable and affirmatively desirable [however] one cannot expect too much from such discretion. Corporate managers may rarely choose to sacrifice profits given product market competition, future job prospects, stock options and other rewards for making corporate profits. It may also be true that shareholders would rarely allow (or to only a limited degree) allow managers to pursue unprofitable public interest objectives.[152]

This theory follows from the second implication that may be made from the Berle and Means theory: the possibility of the consideration of other interests in the face of continued separation of ownership from control. This theme is reflected in the view of the corporation as an institutional arrangement for governing relationships between all parties that contribute firm-specific assets.[153] This self-imposed limitation on stakeholder theories to try to fashion a workable mechanism of control in all affected parties' interests from within the corporation has been its undoing. It has become largely an exercise to appeal to the corporate conscience.[154]

151 Such list of articles would include Blair (n. 134); M M Blair and L A Stout, 'A Team Production Theory of Company Law' (1999) 24 *Journal of Corporate Law* 751–806; K E Goodpaster, 'Business Ethics and the Stakeholder Analysis' (1991) 1(1) *Business Ethics Quarterly* 53–73; M Jensen, 'Value Maximisation, Stakeholder Theory and the Corporate Objective Function' (2001) 7 *European Financial Management* 297–317; T Donaldson and L Preston, 'The Stakeholder Theory of the Corporation: Concepts, Evidence and Implications' (1995) 20 *Academy of Management Review* 65–91

152 E Elhauge, 'Sacrificing Corporate Profits in the Public Interest' (2005) 80(3) *New York University Law Review* 733–869, 868

153 T Clarke, *Introduction to Theories of Corporate Governance: The Philosophical Foundations of Corporate Governance* (Routledge, London 2004) 11 (quoting Blair)

154 To adopt a 'real entity' phraseology

This is evident in such statements by stakeholder advocates accepting that clearly trying to run corporations in the interest of "society at large" . . . is an impossible end and in practice a vacuous objective'.[155] However, there are different strands of the stakeholder arguments: one strand sees stakeholder theories in terms of a manager's discretion to sacrifice shareholders' interests in the short-term for other vital interests that may be justified in the shareholders' long term interests.[156]

Other strands are more practically focused on conceiving a workable model that shifts management control from a shareholder to a stakeholder focus. An example of this is the Blair and Stout team-production theory,[157] which conceives of a model where rational individuals who hope to profit from team production overcome shirking and rent-seeking by opting out of an internal governance structure and opt instead for a 'mediating hierarchy' solution which requires that the team members give up important rights (including property rights over the team's joint outputs and over team inputs such as financial capital and firm-specific human capital) to a legal entity created by an act of incorporation so corporate assets belong to the corporation itself.

The Blair and Stout position of the stakeholder theory is distinctly appealing to a communitarian spirit that may lie within this 'contractual entity' and perhaps finds legal ground in the interpretation of director's duties as being owed to the corporation.[158] It is undoubtedly reflective of co-determination in Germany and the 'collective' focus of Japan but in no way implies direct liability to society.[159]

155 Blair (n. 134) 14. She, however, adds that the least we can hope for is that the goals of the corporation are in the interests of the larger society

156 W T Allen, 'Our Schizophrenic Conception of the Business Corporation' states 'that the long term/short term distinction preserves a form of stock-holder oriented property theory while permitting in fact a considerable degree of behaviour consistent with the view that sees public corporations as owing social responsibilities . . .', The only problem with this is that it is subject to managerial discretion and the company's behest hence entirely voluntary and arbitrary

157 Blair (n. 134), Blair and Stout (n. 151)

158 See *Re Smith and Fawcett Limited (*1942) where Lord Greene said that 'directors must exercise their discretion bona fide in what they consider – not what the court may consider – is in the interests of the company'. Statute expressly preserves this consideration of other interests in s. 306, 309 Company Act 1985 United Kingdom. In the United States there is a raft of other constituency statutes – see Blair ibid. – but this only serves to deepen and preserve managerial discretionary power. Indeed in this sense a duty is owed to everyone and yet the corporation is unaccountable to everyone

159 Clarke sees this conception of the corporation as a set of relationships rather than a series of transactions in which managers adopt an inclusive concern for all stakeholders as much closer to established European and Asian business values. Clarke (n. 153). There are two major types of corporate system in capitalist states globally, namely the shareholder and the block-holder systems, although this may mask national differences. Bratton and McCahery (n. 99) 23–55. Yet there are forceful arguments for the emergence of a convergence on a system of corporate governance that prioritises the shareholder. Hansmann and Kraakman (n. 100) The OECD Corporate Governance Code also emphasises shareholder primacy with the discretion to consider other interests

Indeed Clarke points out that the stakeholder theory represents an important step towards corporate citizenship as a mature appreciation by the corporation of its rights and responsibilities.[160] This could form a persuasive basis for acknowledging other interests.

In spite of the excellent aspects of this theory, there is a flaw. The focus of the stakeholder theory is ultimately internal to the corporation; it exemplifies corporate response to other stakeholders and therefore largely depends on identifying actors which have a stake in the corporation. There is a more compelling case for identified, efficient and enforceable solutions to the problem posed by large multinational corporate power. These solutions are required by wider society though it may be desirable to have this reflected in corporate law, it seems corporate law has become more oriented towards its own internal focus on corporations. It reflects the utilitarian perspective that privileges what is good for business and then uses this as a starting point.

The desire to see corporate governance 'as the design of institutions that induce or force management to internalise the welfare of stakeholders'[161] is still some way off, there needs to be a radical rethink of corporate law and structures for this to be done in a fundamental way. It may be necessary for CSR which has a more urgent agenda to explore a wider framework of its own.

However, this challenge to integrate external facing concerns within company law was addressed in the recent reform of the UK company law. This reform has been referred to as the best example of an attempt to face the contemporary challenges.[162] The next section analyses this reform as an example to further illustrate the potential and limitations of this traditional corporate law approach to embracing notions of responsibility and accountability to society as an aspect of corporate legitimacy and control.

5.5 UK corporate law reform as an example

In 1998 the UK embarked on a fundamental review of its company law which culminated in the Companies Act 2006. The incentive for this move was stated as follows:

> The last significant review of company law in the UK took place more than forty years ago. Since then, relevant statute and case law have changed, and there have been major developments in recognised 'best practice' in corporate governance, with the result that it is now difficult and time consuming for directors and other interested parties to discover exactly what the law relating to companies is.[163]

160 Clarke (n. 153)

161 J Tirole, 'Corporate Governance' (2001) 69(1) *Econometrica* 1–35

162 Horrigan (n. 11)

163 House of Commons Trade and Industry Committee *The White Paper in Modernising Company Law* Sixth Report of Sessions 2002–03 HC439 (Stationery Office, London 2003) 4

When the company law review was instituted, it was charged with a framework of company law that 'encouraged competitiveness as well as improving accountability'.[164] This reflects Hurst's assertion that the drive for utility and responsibility are the two elements of corporate legitimacy found within corporate law.[165]

The opportunity to broaden the agenda of CSR and debate issues proposed by the Company Law Review led to the formation of the non-governmental organisation Corporate Responsibility Coalition (CORE).[166] The aim was to use this as an opportunity to frame the debate of CSR within corporate law. The hope was perhaps to achieve a binding definition of corporate responsibility.[167] The resulting Companies Act 2006 came into force in stages with the final sections fully in force by 1 October 2009. While the resulting act was a much larger one, it did not radically depart from the agency theoretical view of the corporation. The relevant aspects which highlight some relevant changes made in the reform include: director's duties, company reporting and corporate governance structures.

5.5.1 Directors' duties

The notion of director's duties which was at the heart of the historical debate between Berle and Dodd was also an issue of substantial focus in the reform of UK corporate law.[168] The question of director's duties is at the heart of the debate in corporate law about the role of the corporation and the notion of control over the interests of affected parties. The purpose of the corporation (corporate objective) will affect the range of interests that the directors need to protect and the persons to whom the directors owe these duties.[169]

In the *ministerial Statements* about the bill prior to the passage of the Companies Act 2006, Darling (then Minister) notes that:

> For the first time, the Bill includes a statutory statement of directors' general duties. It provides a code of conduct that sets out how directors are expected to behave. That enshrines in statue what the law review called "enlightened shareholder value". It recognises that directors will be more likely to achieve long term sustainable success for the benefit of their shareholders if their companies pay attention to a wider range of matters . . . *Directors will be required to promote the success of the company in the collective best interest of the*

164 Company Law Review Consultative Meeting Note for Record, 21 July 1998, <www.dti.gov.uk> accessed 10 March 2010. See ibid. 5

165 Hurst (n. 5)

166 See J Sabapathy, 'In the Dark All Cats are Grey: Corporate Responsibility and Legal Responsibility' in S Tully (ed.), *Research Handbook on Corporate Legal Responsibility* (Edward Elgar, Cheltenham 2007) 235–253, 239

167 Ibid.

168 Horrigan (n. 11)

169 A Keay, 'Tackling the Issue of the Corporate Objective: An Analysis of the United Kingdom's "Enlightened Shareholder Value Approach"' (2007) 29 *Sydney Law Review* 577–612

> ***shareholders, but in doing so they will have to have regard to a wider range of factors, including the interests of employees and the environment.***[170]

This codification of director's or manager's fiduciary duties is contained in s. 170–177 but the relevant section which adopted this approach is s. 172 Companies Act 2006. This section states as follows:

> s. ***172 Duty to promote the success of the company***
>
> (1) A director of a company must act in the way he considers, in good faith, would be most likely to promote the success of the company for the benefit of its members as a whole, and in doing so have regard (amongst other matters) to—
>
> (a) the likely consequences of any decision in the long term,
> (b) the interests of the company's employees,
> (c) the need to foster the company's business relationships with suppliers, customers and others,
> (d) the impact of the company's operations on the community and the environment,
> (e) the desirability of the company maintaining a reputation for high standards of business conduct, and
> (f) the need to act fairly as between members of the company.
>
> (2) Where or to the extent that the purposes of the company consist of or include purposes other than the benefit of its members, subsection (1) has effect as if the reference to promoting the success of the company for the benefit of its members were to achieving those purposes.
> (3) The duty imposed by this section has effect subject to any enactment or rule of law requiring directors, in certain circumstances, to consider or act in the interests of creditors of the company.

This section has been heralded as innovative and novel because it incorporates elements of the stakeholder approach.[171] However, on closer scrutiny, it represents a mediated position quite similar to the position advocated by 'enlightened self-interest' models. This is an attempt to integrate wider considerations within a

170 Companies Act 2006 *Duties of Company Directors: Ministerial Statements* DTI June 2007 p. 7 (Alistair Darling, Commons Second Reading, 6 June 2006, column 12) <http://www.bis.gov.uk/files/file40139.pdf > accessed 10 March 2010 (emphasis added)

171 Horrigan (n. 11). There are similarities between this and the US non-shareholder constituency statutes which have also attracted some criticism. See S M Bainbridge, 'Interpreting Non-shareholder Constituency Statutes' (1992) 19(3) *Pepperdine Law Review* 971–1025; G Von Stange, 'Corporate Social Responsibility through Constituency Statutes: Legend or Lie? (1994) 11(2) *Hofstra Labor & Employment Law Journal* 461–497

shareholder wealth maximisation focused model. It does not alter the basic focus of the corporation from a contractual one. It is still self-interested.

Within the consultation document of the Company Law Steering Group another approach termed the 'pluralist approach' was considered. This pluralist approach would involve the notion that:

> company law should be modified to include other objectives so that a company is required to serve a wider range of interests not subordinate to, or as a means of achieving shareholder value (as envisaged in the enlightened shareholder view) but as valid in their own rights.[172]

This would have involved a radical rethink of directors' duties. It would have endorsed Dodd's view of the corporation owing duties and serving wider interests in society than that of shareholders as a fuller interpretation of the entity and modified concession theories of the corporation. However, this was not adopted.

Yet an extension of directors' duties in this way could have a significant point that would substantially alter the focus of corporations from a strict profit-making motive geared towards shareholders and increasing the immediate share price to other tangible goals which society deems fit for the corporation. Parkinson had pointed out that:

> broadening directors' discretion to permit them to depart from the requirements of profit maximisation would be a necessary adjustment to create an appropriate legal setting for changes in management behaviour that are the intended consequence of other methods of inducing responsibility. A reformed fiduciary duty might accordingly stipulate that the directors are under an obligation to conduct the business for profit, but that in so doing they must take account of affected interests (which might be specified).[173]

The 2006 Act endorsed this limited approach which it termed the 'enlightened shareholder value' approach. This approach adopts a shareholder focused model that allows for consideration of other factors which may affect that shareholder value in the long term. It permits the consideration of the interests of other 'stakeholders' but only as it affects shareholder value and 'the success of the company' (profit). Nevertheless it is evident from the ministerial statements about the bill that even this section could have multiple interpretations:

> There are two ways of looking at the statutory statement of directors' duties: on the one the hand it simply codifies the existing common law obligations

172 *Modern Company Law for a Competitive Economy The Strategic Framework* February 1999 <http://www.bis.gov.uk/files/file23279.pdf> accessed 10 December 2011, 37. This document expressly cites Blair (n. 134)

173 Parkinson (n. 87) 371

> of company directors; on the other – especially in section 172: the duty to act in the interests of the company – it marks a radical departure in articulating the connection between what is good for a company and what is good for society at large.[174]

The effect of this section on the use of corporate power in relation to interests in society will be explored in relevant legal cases that follow but it offers up an example of reform geared at extending directors' duties.

Arden LJ in *Rolls-Royce Plc v Unite the Union* pointed out in obiter while examining a provision under the Employment Age (Equality) Regulations and comparing to s. 172 Companies Act 2006 that:

> the reasonable employer . . . might well be expected to be motivated not simply by its narrow financial interest but also by enlightened self-interest and take into account the interests of employees generally as one of the factors to which it should have regard in determining the business need of the undertaking.[175]

The test for corporate law will also be in cross-national comparative reform and the willingness of other states to follow even this limited example. It creates a type of law-tool which can be applied in context.

In the 2008 report, the UN Secretary General's Special Representative on Business and Human Rights cites the new requirement under UK company law for directors to take account of such matters as community and environmental impact as an example of how countries might engage 'in re-defining fiduciary duties'.[176]

Nevertheless it is important to stress that for many analysts, this is a limited approach. Villiers points out that 'such provisions tend to increase the discretion of the directors and managers, thus giving them a potential defence against challenges from shareholders rather than protecting the non-shareholders'.[177] Other critics also remark on problems in corporate law's approach to corporate power and responsibility. They point out that in adopting a strict contractual approach to corporate personality which privileges shareholder interests, its fundamental structures permit irresponsibility.[178]

174 M Hodge, *Ministerial Statements* (n. 170) 1

175 (2009) EWCA Civ 387 para.169

176 <www2.ohchr.org/english/bodies/hrcouncil/docs/8session/A-HRC-8-5.doc> see p. 10. The Human Rights Council passed the *UN Guiding Principles on Business and Human Rights* in 2011 Resolution 17/4

177 Villiers (n. 37) 94

178 See P Ireland, 'Limited Liability, Shareholder Rights and the Problem of Corporate Irresponsibility' (2010) 34 *Cambridge Journal of Economics* 837–856, 848. Ireland states that 'The rigid application of the Salomon principle, coupled with de facto, no-liability shareholding, has thus greatly extended the scope for opportunistic behaviour, further

The necessity for shareholder focus is not integral to corporate law but has emerged due to political interests utilising influential theories. Hurst again indicates that it is the utilitarian emphasis which politics privileges that holds us back from the demand for corporate power to be structured so as to be responsible.[179] Therefore the mediated position of s. 172 is unsatisfactory because it does not address this core issue. It falls short of Dodd's more radical view that 'business is permitted and encouraged by law because it is of service to the community rather than because it is a source of profit to its owners;.[180] Ireland points out that:

> While the former entailed important changes to the way in which the corporation was conceptualised (and to the constitution of the corporate legal form), contemporary CSR, with its emphasis on voluntary self-regulation, leaves untouched the shareholder-oriented model of the corporation and the corporate legal form as presently constituted. It is hardly surprising that CSR has been so warmly embraced by so many corporations.[181]

These critics simply point to the theoretical debates at the heart of corporate legal theory stressing that the nature of corporate personality as a legal construct with the resultant attribute of limited liability has been explored and utilised in ways which privilege the utility aspect of legitimacy and inadvertently advance and strengthen corporate power, giving room for exploitation and irresponsible use of such power. While this section falls short of a radical rethink of the focus of corporate law, it leaves room for compelling evidence that the business-society balance is changing and that other factors affect corporate interests more palpably than would otherwise have been admitted in the traditional shareholder-focused corporate law.

5.5.2 Company reporting

The Companies Act also enshrines reporting as a method of evaluating the compliance with s. 172. This approach is adopted for large corporations. This requirement can be found in s. 414A-D the Companies Act 2006 (Strategic Report and Directors Report) Regulations 2013.

institutionalising corporate irresponsibility. It is not, perhaps, surprising that the leading legal academic Otto Kahn-Freund, writing in 1944 when group structures were beginning to proliferate, described Salomon and its rigid application by the courts as "calamitous".'

179 Hurst (n. 5) 59

180 Dodd (n. 77)

181 Ireland (n. 178) 853

414C Contents of strategic report

(1) The purpose of the strategic report is to inform members of the company and help them assess how the directors have performed their duty under section 172 (duty to promote the success of the company).

(2) The strategic report must contain—

(a) a fair review of the company's business, and
(b) a description of the principal risks and uncertainties facing the company.

(3) The review required is a balanced and comprehensive analysis of—

(a) the development and performance of the company's business during the financial year, and
(b) the position of the company's business at the end of that year, consistent with the size and complexity of the business.

(7) In the case of a quoted company the strategic report must, to the extent necessary for an understanding of the development, performance or position of the company's business, include—

(a) the main trends and factors likely to affect the future development, performance and position of the company's business, and
(b) information about—

(i) environmental matters (including the impact of the company's business on the environment),
(ii) the company's employees, and
(iii) social, community and human rights issues, including information about any policies of the company in relation to those matters and the effectiveness of those policies.

If the report does not contain information of each kind mentioned in paragraphs (b) (i), (ii) and (iii), it must state which of those kinds of information it does not contain.

The Operating and Financial Review (OFR) was initially advocated by the UK government.[182] The OFR was to be a detailed report within the annual report. This was to be a mandatory endorsed means of social and environmental reporting.[183] However, the government reversed the decision to make the OFR mandatory and instead adopted the business review approach stipulated in the originally enacted s. 417 Companies Act. for a business review. This approach has now been revised by the 2013 regulations for a strategic report. The UK

182 J Solomon, *Corporate Governance and Accountability* (Wiley, Chichester 2007) 169
183 Ibid.

government cites this as part of the state implementation of the 2011 UN Guiding Principles on Business and Human Rights.[184]

Yet the primary audience outlined in s. 414C is still the 'members of the company', the shareholders. Therefore the report is shaped to the perceptions of the shareholder and what projects the success of the company. The inclusion of social and environmental issues is only in so far as it affects 'the success of the company'.

Horrigan points out that the emphasis is on reporting how the company's internal and external affairs affect the company and its prospects for the future as distinct from reporting on how the company and its affairs affect and otherwise relate to the societal landscape around them.[185] Therefore the focus is internal and inward looking, not external and outward facing. Its focus is on how the corporation and its financial position is affected by social or community issues, environmental matters and employees.

In addition, there is a subjectivity in such reporting that may result in anomalies and partial disclosures as it rests with the directors to decide what amounts to 'an understanding of the development, performance or position of the company's business'.[186] The use of disclosure as a monitoring mechanism can shape corporate behaviour but there are other critical issues which may detract from its value. The intended users of these reports, the shareholders, may not use these reports in the intended fashion. There is evidence that the corporate annual reports are not effectively utilised by shareholders.[187] In addition, the large shareholders, institutional investors, have mainly chosen inaction on CSR issues. They have largely opted to remain guided by the economic incentive.[188] The drive for socially responsible investors is still in its infancy.[189]

Finally the subjective nature of the reporting may lead to it being selective or incomplete, so that information is judicious and tailored to audience. The emphasis of such reporting could then be on the public relations aspect, rather

184 HM Government *Good Business: Implementing the UN Guidelines on Business and Human Rights* May2016 <https://www.gov.uk/government/uploads/system/uploads/attachment_data/file/522805/Good_Business_Implementing_the_UN_Guiding_Principles_on_Business_and_Human_Rights_updated_May_2016.pdf> accessed 8 June 2016, p. 7. Solomon (n. 182) points out that the previous s. 417 was based on the EU Accounts Directive for the adoption of a member-wide business review. For the latest update see Directive 2014/95/ EU 22 October 2014 amending Directive 2013/34/EU as regards disclosure of non-financial and diversity information by certain large undertakings and groups

185 Horrigan (n. 11) 260

186 s. 414C (7) the Companies Act 2006 (Strategic Report and Directors Report) Regulations 2013. Although there is a guide in the sub-section.

187 C Villiers, *Corporate Reporting and Company Law* (Cambridge University Press, Cambridge 2006) 34

188 L Kurtz, 'Socially Responsible Investment and Shareholder Activism' in A Crane, A McWilliams, D Matten, J Moon and D Siegel (eds), *Oxford Handbook on CSR* (Oxford University Press, Oxford 2008) 249–280

189 Ibid.

than an integration of such considerations into the business model.[190] This section represents an innovative but limited response incorporated within corporate law.

5.5.3 Complementary corporate governance reform

Alongside the UK Company Review and the Companies Act 2006, the UK has a long and established history of corporate governance reform and is acknowledged as a world leader in this field.[191] However, corporate governance in this guise is also focused on structures and the narrow questions of internal control and the running of the company.[192] This may also be for reasons of convenience which privilege aspects of utility within legitimacy, aspects which are already accepted within the traditional model. Mitchell points out that this narrow focus has been more rewarding in terms of scholarly attention. He indicates that:

> unlike the CSR debate per se, the corporate governance debate does repay scholarly attention as a focus of social responsibility defined as it is by the traditional parameters of corporate law and articulated within a well-developed framework of fiduciary duties. Whereas CSR operates free-form and can seem either superfluous or threatening corporate governance issues operate within well-defined and accepted structures.[193]

However, that is not to say that even such narrow corporate governance is settled. It has external effects or, more aptly, it has been influenced by external events. It is caught in a cycle of reactionary reform prompted by external corporate financial scandals and crises which reflect the inadequacy of previous reform.

The OECD confirms that 'pressure on governments and on the business sector to improve corporate governance arrangements has arisen often in the context of the failure of large companies and particularly marked instances of corporate fraud'.[194]

190 Villiers (n. 187) 36; C Valor, 'Corporate Social Responsibility and Corporate Citizenship' (2005) 110(2) *Business and Society Review* 191; C Pedamon, 'Corporate Social Responsibility: A New Approach to Promoting Integrity and Responsibility' (2010) 31(6) *Company Lawyer* 172–180

191 Solomon (n. 182) 49

192 R Mullerat, *International Corporate Social Responsibility: The Role of Corporations in the Economic Order of the 21st Century* (Kluwer Law International, The Netherlands 2010) 49

193 L Mitchell, 'The Board as a Path toward Corporate Social Responsibility' in D McBarnet, A Voiculescu and T Campbell (eds), *The New Corporate Accountability: Corporate Social Responsibility and the Law* (Cambridge University Press, Cambridge 2007) 279–307, 279

194 OECD, *Corporate Governance: A Survey of OECD Countries'* (OECD, Paris 2004) 18. The recent G20/OECD Principles of Corporate Governance were endorsed in November 2015. 'The corporate governance framework should protect and facilitate the exercise of shareholders' rights and ensure the equitable treatment of all shareholders, including minority and foreign shareholders. All shareholders should have the opportunity to obtain effective redress for violation of their rights', p. 18

The Cadbury Report[195] which was the UK's first major attempt to 'formalise corporate governance best practice'[196] was commissioned after the collapse of Maxwell Publishing Group and the ensuing scandal after the death of its chairman and chief executive Robert Maxwell in 1991.[197]

This report investigated the three traditional aspects of control and ownership: the board of directors, the shareholders and the role of auditors. The FRC points out that:

> The Cadbury Report addressed issues such as the relationship between the chairman and chief executive, the role of non-executive directors and reporting on internal control and on the company's position. A requirement was added to the Listing Rules of the London Stock Exchange that companies should report whether they had followed the recommendations or, if not, explain why they had not done so (this is known as 'comply or explain').[198]

The next report, the Greenbury Report 1995, was in response to excessive executive remuneration and the ensuing scandals. The objective was to 'establish a balance between directors' salaries and their performance'.[199] The Hampel Report in 1998 dealt with both aspects as well and recommended a bringing together of the financial perspectives of corporate governance and the issues of directors' remuneration which led to the Combined Code 1998. This was followed by the Turnbull Report in 1999 which set out best practice of internal control systems for UK listed companies.[200]

The fall of Enron in the United States prompted a re-evaluation of the corporate governance system in the UK but this was not only a UK response. The OECD pointed out that the 'essential difference between now and the past is the international implications of the problems which have come to light in the US have been marked'.[201] In this case, questions of corporate governance were directly raised by the allegations of fraud and active cover up and dissimulation by management which precipitated the stunning collapse.[202]

195 Cadbury, *Report of the Committee on the Financial Aspects of Corporate Governance* (Gee Publishing, London 1992)

196 Solomon (n. 182) 49. The Financial Reporting Council (FRC) points out that 'the development of corporate governance in the UK has its roots in a series of corporate collapses and scandals in the late 1980s and early 1990s including the collapse of the BCCI bank and the Robert Maxwell pension funds scandals both in 1991'. FRC, *The UK Approach to Corporate Governance* November 2006, 3

197 OECD (n. 194) 19

198 FRC, *The UK Approach to Corporate Governance* November 2006, 3

199 Solomon (n. 182) 55

200 FRC (n. 198) 4

201 OECD (n. 194) 18

202 Ibid. 20

Nevertheless the focus of the Higgs Report that followed was on the role and effectiveness of NED recommending among other things that one non-executive director champion shareholder interests,[203] the recurring theme of the reports being a strengthening of the accepted model of owner-control analysis in corporate law (shareholder focus). This also led to the review of the Combined Code in 2003. The Financial Reporting Council (FRC) was confirmed as having responsibility for publishing and maintaining the code.[204]

The FRC, which is now the UK's independent regulator for promoting corporate governance and reporting to foster investment, adopts a 'comply or explain' approach which reflects a kind of policed voluntary approach for listed companies.[205] There were some associated reports in 2003 including the Smith Report on the role of the audit committee and the DTI commissioned Tyson Report on the recruitment and development of NEDs.[206]

In predictable fashion, the 2008 financial crisis in the banking industry prompted an independent review of corporate governance in the UK banking industry. The resulting Walker Report was published in 2009. This report led to a wider review by the FRC. In 2010 the FRC published the new UK Corporate Governance Code replacing the Combined Code. It also led to the formulation of a stewardship code for institutional investors.

The Code adopts the definition of corporate governance given by the Cadbury Report:

> Corporate governance is the system by which companies are directed and controlled. Boards of directors are responsible for the governance of their companies. The shareholders' role in governance is to appoint the directors and the auditors and to satisfy themselves that an appropriate governance structure is in place. The responsibilities of the board include setting the company's strategic aims, providing the leadership to put them into effect, supervising the management of the business and reporting to shareholders on their stewardship. The board's actions are subject to laws, regulations and the shareholders in general meeting.[207]

This area of corporate governance is very active. However, again, it is focused on narrow internal questions. It falls fully on the side of the contractual agency vision of control tackling questions of legitimacy from a limited internal focus

203 Solomon (n. 182) 61
204 FRC (n. 198) 4
205 FRC (n. 198)
206 Solomon (n. 182)
207 FRC, *UK Corporate Governance Code 2010* <http://www.frc.org.uk/corporate/ukcgcode.cfm> 1, accessed 10 December 2011. The most recent UK Corporate Governance Code is 2014, see <https://www.frc.org.uk/Our-Work/Publications/Corporate-Governance/UK-Corporate-Governance-Code-2014.pdf> accessed 8 June 2016

of reconciling the power of directors (managers) to shareholder interests. The frequency and reactionary nature of the changes leave room for questions on its effectiveness even at the narrow level but its failure from a CSR perspective is that it adopts an unadulterated shareholder and utility focus. It follows the ideology that ownership (shareholder) control and oversight is the primary requirement for governance and accountability. While this is an important aspect, it ignores wider questions such as the impact of corporate power, which as a result fall within CSR sphere.

5.6 Conclusion

Ensuring controls, accountability and the responsible use of corporate power is tantamount to devising the means by which such power is exercised legitimately. This is particularly important because liberal society requires the legitimate use of powers located within it for its proper functioning. The corporation is a very attractive form of business because it is a source of significant wealth but where it becomes a source of unaccountable power, this threatens the very existence of liberal society. It is therefore important to have constraints on the exercise of such power through adequate accountability and regulatory processes.

This chapter explored the traditional legal perspective of corporate law as a potential framework for the legitimacy of corporate power. At the outset it noted the desire expressed by several scholars that fundamental change in corporate law to signal wider responsibilities would create an inclusive framework for CSR. However, in exploring corporate theories and corporate governance theories that inform practice as well as recent reform in the UK it was discovered in this chapter that corporate law has imposed upon itself a narrow focus on the shareholder model.

The importance placed within corporate theory on privileging the contractual and fictional origins and nature of the corporation means that there is a dominance of the shareholder profit-making model. It strongly adopts a focus on the utility element of corporate legitimacy centred wholly on the success of the corporation. Hurst is right when he suggests that:

> Weakness in the demand for responsibility did not derive from the immediate context of that demand but from other undesirable by-products of our utilitarian emphasis. Power continually presented new temptations and shifted into new forms. To structure power for responsibility called for continuing close attention and an investment of resources of mind and energy which we begrudged. We begrudged the investment because we felt that it subtracted from our primary interest in the economy, which was the main area in which we pursued utility.[208]

208 Hurst (n. 5) 59

This focus on utility may be as a result of the nature of traditional state-centred law which is always striving for certainty and tangibility and, in some ways, equating that with effectiveness. This is a quest that the law never fully achieves, bearing in mind this is a dynamic ever-changing world. Legal scholars are often left in a mediated position, sometimes trying to fit traditional old concepts to newer problems and failing. Perhaps the law needs to evolve and proffer new and more adequate legal solutions to these newer problems. The conclusion seems to be that the core agenda of CSR cannot be suitably carried out within the current corporate law agenda.[209]

Yet the problem of the law's role in achieving the legitimacy of corporate power within CSR is still a crucial one and, as Villiers points out, CSR cannot be left in the hands of the corporation.[210] This points to the need for states, international organisations and civil society to explore other frameworks for responsibility. The theoretical underpinnings of corporate law reveal a reluctance to tackle the issues and contestation that have driven a utilitarian perspective and affected the content of corporate law. It also reveals the limitations of the substantive approach. The reform process takes time and is not the most efficient. The contestations often result in little change and show the inflexibility and reluctance to change sometimes evident in traditional law. It is also driven by the state and the issue of political will becomes paramount. However, as shown previously, the law can be viewed from a different perspective. This other approach would ensure that the wider CSR question is addressed by the law in a different way. It suggests a shift in focus from searching for legal legitimacy of CSR within traditional laws like corporate law to conceptualising new non-traditional legal approaches that focus on role-based definitions of legal quality, whilst driving for legitimacy in the form of responsibility.

These newer multi-stakeholder frameworks can still be developed within the law especially if a non-traditional pluralistic perspective is adopted. The next chapter proposes a legal theoretical approach that could lead to a framework for addressing CSR issues in a non-traditional way.

209 This ties in with the Hansmann and Kraakman pronouncement that: 'Asserting the primacy of shareholders interests does not imply the interests of stakeholders must and should go unprotected. It merely indicates that the most efficacious legal mechanism for protecting the interests of non-shareholders lie outside corporate law.' Hansmann and Kraakman (n. 100) 43

210 Villiers (n. 37) 87

6 Proposing a law-jobs approach

> All three questions – the identification of beneficiaries (fiduciary responsibility), the available mechanisms (corporate governance), the role of law – led to the same need for identifying the social functions of CSR in a broader context . . . *CSR then seems to be one of those decentralised integrative mechanisms* which place restrictions on economic action in the interest of other subsystems – trees and people included.[1]

6.1 Introduction

The law-jobs approach shifts our focus in discovering the potential of law's legitimating role to a pluralist legal viewpoint. It addresses law's ability to contribute to legitimising CSR in a pluralist way outside traditional substantive law structures such as corporate law. It examines CSR's legitimating core from a 'role-based' legal approach which is not based wholly on one form of law. This acknowledges the nature of CSR as a decentralised integrative device which is not anchored on substantive state law alone.[2]

It also responds to current demands that other non-state actors in society such as international institutions and civil society have a responsibility within the drive for legitimacy framework that is CSR to create the structural processes necessary to ensure legally and socially responsible behaviour by corporations.[3]

1 G Teubner, 'Corporate Fiduciary Duties and Their Beneficiaries: A Functional Approach to the Legal Institutionalisation of Corporate Responsibility' in K J Hopt and G Teubner (eds), *Corporate Governance and Directors Liabilities: Legal, Economic and Sociological Analyses of Corporate Social Responsibility* (De Gruyter, Berlin 1984) 149–177, 160 and 162 (words in brackets are mine, emphasis added)

2 Teubner, ibid., extensively analyses the implications of CSR as a decentralized integrative device

3 C Villiers, 'Corporate Law, Corporate Power and Corporate Social Responsibility' in N Boeger, R Murray and C Villiers (eds), *Perspectives on Corporate Social Responsibility* (Edward Elgar, Cheltenham 2008) 85–112, 87

This can be seen as a step away in the assessment of law within CSR from a traditional state-based substantive law perspective towards a more inclusive, dynamic and pluralistic role-based legal perspective. This approach utilises the term 'law' in the inclusive pluralist sense as earlier identified in Chapter 4. This application should result in a legal theoretical framework which would allow for examination of law's potential as a legitimiser at different levels and in different contexts. This could be local, national, cross-national or industry specific.

The legal theoretical approach chosen in this chapter to represent this non-traditional view is derived from Llewellyn's law-jobs theory. This theory embodies the flexibility and shift that is seen as necessary to gauge law's role in legitimising corporate power. This chapter uses the fivefold breakdown of Llewellyn's law-jobs[4] to examine the potential role of law within CSR. The five law-jobs are: the disposition of trouble cases; the preventative channelling and the reorientation of conduct and expectations so as to avoid trouble; the allocation of authority and the arrangement of procedures which legitimise action as authoritative; the net organisation of the group or society as a whole so as to provide direction and incentive and the use of the juristic method.[5] There are two aspects to this approach: a basic one which allows for an evaluation of how the jobs are done and an aspirational one, which allows for how the jobs could be done better.[6]

In other words, this chapter frames the law's legitimating role in CSR around Llewellyn's law-jobs. The aim is to illustrate that this can be a framework that promotes the use of varied tools, legal structures and processes utilising both traditional and non-traditional law and regulation towards the legitimacy objective.

The law-jobs legal theoretical approach is relevant for the question of assessing CSR's ability to be a legitimising force for corporate power and indicates the necessity of legal structures in the net organisation and evaluation of CSR. This approach underscores the importance of law as an aspect of legitimacy. The law, irrespective of form, can be a legitimising force especially where such rules are geared towards performing important legal roles within society. Therefore, such a framework should involve open and transparent application, with adequate provisions for re-evaluation. This approach may not find all the instruments in

4 K Llewellyn, 'The Normative, the Legal and the Law Jobs: The Problem of the Juristic Method (1940) 49 *Yale Law Journal* 1355–1400, 1373. There are actually four law-jobs and an advocated method of doing those jobs as a fifth

5 Llewellyn (n. 4) 1392. It must be noted that the juristic method is not a law-job *per se* but an advocated method for the evaluation, reform and upkeep of the law-jobs. It therefore in essence goes to the doing of the law-jobs

6 S Taekema, 'The Point of Law: The Interdependent Functionality of State and Non-state Regulation' in H Van Schooten and J Verschuuren (eds), *International Governance and Law: State Regulation and Non-state Law* (Edward Elgar, Cheltenham 2008) 56–73, 59. Llewellyn also noted that the law-jobs have a 'questing' aspect and a 'better' aspect, in other words, an aspect that simply enquires into how these jobs are done and another aspect that examines how they could be done better. Llewellyn (n. 4) 1375

one body of law, but it takes a holistic view of that context, searching for rules, standards or 'law tools' that could be used to fulfil these roles.

This chapter sets out its suggested approach and the applicability of law-jobs to CSR but it does not seek to demonstrate whether the law-jobs are currently done adequately or inadequately. It purely seeks to identify that such a perspective holds enormous potential for CSR. This leaves room for future research to assess and measure the doing of the law-jobs in given CSR contexts.

Consequently the next section outlines the background to Llewellyn's law-jobs theory. This is followed by an analysis of law-jobs potential application within CSR using Llewellyn's fivefold framework. Finally the conclusion draws out the unique potential which this shift in focus of perspective of law may afford the drive for legitimacy within CSR in general.

6.2 The law-jobs theoretical approach

The wider debates about law in Chapter 4 drew our attention to the limited nature in which traditional legal approaches relate to new phenomena. Law is often regarded in the formal sense of mandatory legal rules backed by sanctions and this has resulted in almost relegating the significance of law in the study of contemporary concepts arising against the background of globalisation such as CSR. However, the law or 'legal' does not consist of only formal legal rules, it can and should be perceived from the perspective of the role it fulfils in society. This is a view shared by the eminent jurisprudential scholar, Llewellyn.
He points out that:

> . . . the formal legal, the law stuff and the law ways, travel paths of their own once they specialise into recognisability, upon them in conflicting sense of particular parts and of the whole, play human interests and normative generalisations which are thrown and followed into the ring by men. All this takes shape, takes body under the eye, if it be set against those law-jobs whose sufficient doing goes to the very continued existence of society as society; of a group as a group.[7]

Llewellyn proposed the law-jobs approach as a process of stripping away to the bare bones and conceiving or discovering law from the point of the necessary roles that law can and does perform in society or groups.[8] This approach can also be adapted to allow the examination of the law-jobs within the corporate-society relationship. In particular providing a framework for analysing how these law-jobs could be performed to achieve CSR aims, this leaves open the opportunity for suggestions in future about how these law-jobs could be performed differently.

7 His position was that law or the legal must be set against law-jobs which are essential for the continued functioning of society as society. Llewellyn (n. 4) 1373
8 Ibid.

This approach endorses the view that where one finds (as is currently the case in CSR) a conundrum – the existence of significant societal problems and corresponding activity to demand the social responsibility of corporations – it may be necessary to take a basic skeletal view that seeks out relevant law and law tools for the roles which they can perform in context.

The law-jobs theory initially propounded by Llewellyn in the 1930s aimed to provide a framework for sociological enquiry in the law-ways of the Cheyenne.[9] Yet it finds relevance today because of its adaptability to the global questions asked of the law.[10] Twining points out the strengths of the law-jobs theory as its inherent simplicity and flexibility. He stresses that it brings together ideas about rules, processes, institutions, arenas, actors, decisions, techniques, coordination and conflict.[11]

The law-jobs theory can also be used in a sense which renders it devoid of empirical claims in itself and yet useful for analytical purposes.[12] The law-jobs perspective identifies law from a very crucial angle, which is that of its role, point and purpose but makes no empirical or wholly functionalist assumptions. It simply provides a tool that can be used to create a framework for analysis of concepts through a law-based lens.

However, there are certain limitations to the use of a law-jobs approach, some of which are acknowledged by Llewellyn himself. First, the proposition is that the law-jobs are performed by law but they are not exclusively jobs for law. There is interplay between law and other social disciplines. Llewellyn points out that:

> the legal cannot exhaust the whole nature of a culture . . . those same ways also involve governance, and can be studied with profit, from that angle alone . . . there is almost no part of culture which is not also legal in nature, (whatever else it is as well).[13]

This is the multidisciplinary dimension present in many phenomena on a global scale. Contemporary studies in CSR have multidisciplinary elements drawing on notions from various fields including the social sciences and law. They can be studied from a chosen perspective but not to the exclusion of all other perspectives, different perspectives may serve different purposes.

9 Ibid. 1355

10 W Twining, *General Jurisprudence: Understanding Law from a Global Perspective* (Cambridge University Press, Cambridge 2009); W Twining, *Globalisation and Legal Theory* (Cambridge University Press, Cambridge 2000)

11 Twining rightly points out that this inter-dependence is a relative matter. W Twining, *Globalisation and Legal Scholarship*, Montesquieu Lecture, Tilburg University 2009

12 Twining 2009 (n. 10) 107; CSR is already loaded with initiatives in various contexts – this will be a useful analytical tool to gauge for roles

13 Llewellyn (n. 4) 1377

Second, the only claim made with regard to these jobs is ***that law can and does do these jobs in society***. This is because some of these jobs are also pertinent issues in the social sciences. The validity of this approach is that it helps to identify law-like phenomena and to suggest novel ways of handling the development of these nascent forms of law within CSR. It also permits law to show its dynamism and relevance when faced with new challenges. Consequently, as Llewellyn puts it 'the social disciplines . . . discover that modern work in the legal field is not only a market for their product but a rich productive area'.[14]

Llewellyn points out these law-jobs apply to and get to the essence of any group; therefore the theory can be applied to units within society such as corporations and the local communities in which they operate and may be seen as a 'functional' approach, but it is important to highlight that this does not imply that law does these jobs best or even that these jobs are the exclusive preserve of law.[15] Llewellyn is merely pointing out that law does fulfil these roles in society, so seeking out how these jobs are done will lead to the discovery of law, law tools and rules relevant to that context.

This position is also defended by Ehrenberg,[16] who argues for methodological space for a functional theory of law that does not commit to a view about the value of that function for society, nor whether law is the best means of accomplishing it but rather provides a conceptual framework for understanding the nature of law. He points out that there is some agreement that law performs some social functions and that the disagreements often lies in the description of these social functions and the extent to which law is the best or only tool to be of use in these situations.[17]

It may be better to replace the word 'function' with 'role' or 'job' or even 'point' as suggested by Twining.[18] This is in an effort to get away from functionalist debates and focus on the utility of the emerging conceptual framework in analysing relevant phenomena.

6.3 Applying the law-jobs approach to corporate social responsibility

The next task is to discover if this can be a heuristic device for law within CSR. This section therefore adopts the fivefold law-jobs framework for CSR

14 Ibid. 1357

15 Twining 2009 (n. 10) for an analysis of such criticism. See K M Ehrenberg, 'Defending the Possibility of a Neutral Functional Theory of Law' (2009) 29(1) *Oxford Journal of Legal Studies* 91–113

16 Ehrenberg ibid.

17 Ibid. (n 15)

18 Twining 2009 (n, 10) 110

and examines how law tools in CSR respond to these five law-jobs. These law tools are used in the pluralistic sense to include law and regulation in the broad sense as earlier defined. Taekema points out that the law-jobs have two aspects – basic and aspirational – and that this twofold aspect permits analysis of the varied achievements of law-jobs.[19] Llewellyn himself points out that the law-jobs have a 'questing' aspect and a 'better' aspect, in other words, an aspect that simply enquires into how these jobs are done and another aspect that examines how they could be done better.[20] The focus here is on setting out an organising framework of how these jobs could be done in CSR, so it only tackles the 'questing' or basic aspect.

To perform the first 'law-job' the CSR law tool, instrument or mechanism has to play a role in the adjustment of trouble cases (disputes), in the sense of having the ability to eliminate conflict or grievance which has broken out. This ability must be such as to allow for the diffusion of tensions, trouble or potential trouble as well as to provide the means of resolving the trouble cases or CSR violations. This is a job traditionally carried out by the judiciary and the courts but the law-jobs mechanism can also be extended to dispute resolution mechanisms of other kinds. Therefore it could be seen as inclusive of judicial and non-judicial dispute resolutions. It could then be applied to dispute resolution in the corporate–community context at different levels or even among corporations. This use of alternative dispute resolution would also have to factor in resolution of deviant behaviour of corporations as well as grievances from different interest groups in society.

The next law-job which CSR law tools should do is the job of channelling people's attitudes and conduct preventively towards the corporation as well as channelling and reorientating the corporation's attitude towards society. In the sense not only of 'channelling overt behaviour, but also [of] channelling . . . expectations, norms and claims'.[21] This is an area of central concern already expressed through the proliferation of CSR codes and reports. Some of these codes and other forms of communication such as social and environmental reports attempt to put forward a new ideology for the corporation, defining what it sees as social issues within its sphere. They acquire the status of a law tool as they begin to guide the behaviour of both the corporation and society.

However, this law-job of channelling conduct in CSR is not exclusively focused on voluntary codes because substantive environmental, labour, human rights and health and safety laws would have an impact here. It is even probable that certain contexts may desire to draft laws with explicit focus on CSR. There are

19 Taekema (n. 5)
20 Llewellyn (n. 4) 1375
21 Llewellyn (n. 4)

examples in Indonesia, Mauritius, India and Denmark of law explicitly focused on CSR.[22] Some states like the UK and Nigeria have debated CSR bills.[23]

The third law-job is the allocation of authority and the arrangement of procedures which legitimise action as authoritative. This is a constitutive function and this refers to the role of allocation of power and to the indication of authoritative persons and procedures. In corporate and society relations, this deals with identifying the responsibility for the exercise of power by corporations, identifying forms, procedures and ideologies that limit or direct the exercise of power as well as specifying those responsible for CSR action, policies and procedures. It also involves the creation of processes that provide for consultation, participation and CSR rule creation. This law-job identifies the stakeholders and the rules of engagement. However, this role may be carried out at different levels, such as the company level, industry level or even state level. It is necessary that such procedures are identified and that they operate transparently and accountably.

In several ways, CSR action has involved an implicit acknowledgement of spheres of power and therefore the next logical step is the clear allocation of responsibility. Connolly points out that 'to acknowledge power over others is to implicate oneself in responsibility for certain events and to put oneself in a position where justification for the limits placed on others is expected'.[24] Llewellyn also points out that 'It is at this point that an imperative system and the net effect and intent of its authoritative staff make necessary contact with justification of themselves.'[25] For his purposes this was evident in his application of the juristic method and its institutions but for global society. In the context of CSR, the picture is more complex. It is an emerging picture where those who have the 'say', the states are no longer sole speakers or power holders and, therefore, new entities are emerging, large corporations, NGOs and so on.

In a law-job, CSR instruments should provide for responsibility for the exercise of procedures outlined within it. If it is a CSR law then it should spell out all relevant actors including departments with CSR responsibility, Corporations should provide clear lines of responsibility within their departments and the

22 Law No. 40 Limited Liability Company 2007 (Indonesia) and Government Regulation No. 47 of 2012 concerning Social and Environmental Responsibility of Limited Liability Companies (GR 47/2012) implementing legislation. Finance Bill (Mauritius) sub-part AD. S. 50k-l <http://www.nef.mu/csr/finance_bill.php> accessed 10 December 2011. Clause 135, Companies Act 2013 (India). The Danish Financial Statements Act ('Årsregnskabsloven'), cf. Consolidated Act No. 647of 15 June 2006, as amended by section 5 of Act No. 108 of 7 February 2007, section 63 of Act No. 468 of 17 June 2008 and Act No. 516 of 17 June 2008 <http://www.csrgov.dk> accessed 10 December 2011

23 UK CSR bill copy available online: <http://www.publications.parliament.uk/pa/cm200203/cmbills/129/03129.i.html > <http://www.publications.parliament.uk/pa/cm200203/cmbills/129/2003129.pdf > accessed 10 December 2011, Nigeria CSR bill available online: <http://www.femiamao.com/files/CSR_BILL.pdf > accessed 10 December 2011

24 W Connolly, *The Terms of Political Discourse* (3rd ed., Blackwell, Oxford 1993) 97

25 Llewellyn (n. 4) 1385

relevant non-governmental stakeholders and their responsibilities should also be clearly identified.

In examining this law-job Taekama admits that:

> the law-job of allocating authority is certainly not by definition the state's prerogative or task. Private institutions are quite capable of making such decisions under the right conditions: the institutions represent multiple interests, are open to public scrutiny and prevent self-interested and lax monitoring'.[26]

The key issue becomes whether CSR law tools developed by multi-stakeholders could be fulfilling that role of identifying and redefining who is responsible for what and how such responsibility should be exercised at both micro and macro levels. The role or job becomes one of identifying who has the say and authority and placing limits (explicit or tacitly) on the exercise of that power. These limits and the allocation of responsibility are the crux of legitimacy.

The fourth law-job of net organisation is a result of the previous three law-jobs and therefore it involves incentivising, integrating and directing society as a whole. CSR law tools should be able to play a pivotal role in providing direction and organisation on the issues arising from the relationship between society and business. CSR is already developing as a specialist area and may yet develop its own specialist area of law. The application of law-jobs theory to any existing CSR mechanisms permits analysis to consider what these mechanisms currently achieve as well as what they could potentially achieve.

Llewellyn stresses that the 'official-legal and the official political are not the only mechanisms for doing law-jobs':[27] the net organising framework could also be CSR law or instruments that allow for an overview. It is important that even where CSR law is not the framework for net organisation, the framework should involve a multi-stakeholder initiative that provides for public scrutiny and future reform. This overall framework should therefore occur in the given context.

Finally CSR should be able to evolve mechanisms that perform the evaluative role of the juristic method. For Llewellyn, these are the ways of handling 'legal tools for law job ends, and the on-going upkeep and improvement of both the tools and ways'.[28] In other words it is possible to decide on a method for achieving the law-jobs and then review the results to see if this method can be improved upon. The current way of carrying out the law-jobs may be ad hoc and informal but that is not the only way. This law-job could be done through monitoring and certification or through regulatory inspections. It embodies the review and reform element. The inter-linkages between the law-jobs mean that re-evaluation may cause changes in the style of the law mechanisms or tools used to channel behaviour, especially in the face of persistent irresponsibility.

26 Taekema (n. 5) 66
27 Llewellyn (n. 4) 1389
28 Ibid. 1392

The law-jobs framework is devoid of its own content, so the content can be analysed in context. In this sense it provides an invaluable heuristic device that also allows for re-evaluation, reform and reorganisation. Each of these law-jobs will be examined in more detail in the sections below.

6.3.1 The disposition of trouble cases

Llewellyn refers to the first of the law-jobs as the adjustment of the trouble-case that is, offense, grievance and dispute. This reference is a generic one that addresses the role of law or law-like phenomena in the handling of conflicts or grievances that arise in any social group. This often involves the creation of rules and legal institutions to handle such conflicts.

Within the CSR scenario, the major trigger for CSR has been public scandals about corporate action taken on social and environmental issues, therefore one of the objectives of CSR actions has been to create a means of managing and handling grievances. In our chosen example of the oil industry, the triggers for active engagement with CSR would include the Exxon Valdez oil spill off the coast of Alaska, the Shell Brent Spar incident with Greenpeace and the Shell and Ogoni social and human rights crisis in Nigeria.[29]

These problems have stemmed from environmental and social issues, where blame has been fully or partially apportioned to the MNCs. From a legal perspective, there have been two major developments: the attempted use of traditional dispute resolution through the courts in the home states of the MNCs and the development of non-judicial dispute resolution mechanisms. These are the specific developments which will be examined below.

6.3.1.1 Traditional dispute resolution (litigation)

On the one hand, there have been several attempts to use traditional legal instruments to seek redress from grievance. This has been done by recourse to courts in the home states of the MNCs, where liability is alleged to lie with the corporations for torts or wrongs, but there have been limitations with the use of this method. They can be found in the notion of the corporate veil and *forum non conveniens.*

In the case of the MNC, recourse to the parent company is severely restricted by the doctrine of corporate personality and limited liability.[30] These principles appear to cast a veil over the corporation and place the parent corporation in the position of a shareholder. However, the veil can be lifted where the parent corporation has sufficient involvement and control in the affairs of the subsidiary.

29 P Utting and K Ives, 'The Politics of Corporate Responsibility and the Oil Industry' (2006) 2(1) *St Anthony's International Review* 11–34

30 For a summary of problematic issues see P Muchlinski, 'Limited Liability and Multinational Enterprises: A Case for Reform?' (2010) *Cambridge Journal of Economics* 915–928

The position in the UK has been outlined in the case of *Lubbe v Cape Plc.*[31] Lord Bingham stated:

> The first segment concerns the responsibility of the defendant as a parent company for ensuring the observance of proper standards of health and safety by its overseas subsidiaries. Resolution of this issue will be likely to involve an inquiry into what part the defendant played in controlling the operations of the group, what its directors and employees knew or ought to have known, what action was taken and not taken, whether the defendant owed a duty of care to employees of group companies overseas and whether, if so, that duty was broken. Much of the evidence material to this inquiry would, in the ordinary way, be documentary and much of it would be found in the offices of the parent company, including minutes of meetings, reports by directors and employees on visits overseas and correspondence.[32]

This endorses the position that where sufficient involvement in the control of the subsidiary is indicated via shareholding, and also through other mechanisms of control which show significant involvement in the activities of the subsidiary, the lifting of the corporate veil is possible with the parent–subsidiary relationship.[33] The position in the United States is similar but, as Blumberg points out, the issue of control is crucial. Additionally in the United States, it is necessary to show that the parent corporation is using the subsidiary as a shelter to accomplish unjust, inequitable or fraudulent behaviour that has caused injury to the plaintiff (claimant).[34]

Nevertheless even where this link between the parent and subsidiary corporations is shown other jurisdictional limitations have come sharply into focus. One of these jurisdictional questions asks if the foreign forum is the proper forum for such litigation. This has become a significant limitation because, as Blumberg points out, 'jurisdiction continues to be one of the most litigated areas involving the clash of enterprise and entity'.[35]

In view of the nature of MNCs operating in multiple locations, the litigants have often sought to sue these MNCs in their home states. These attempts to access courts in the home states of the MNCs have met with limited success. One of the main obstacles has been the notion of '*forum non conveniens*' (FNC) prevalent in many common-law countries such as the United States and the UK

31 (2000) UKHL 41

32 Para. 20 This was couched in the language of assumption of responsibility in the case of Chandler v Cape plc (2012) EWCA Civ 525 but the effect is that of lifting the veil.

33 R Meeran, 'The Unveiling of Transnational Corporations: A Direct Approach' in M Addo (ed.), *Human Rights Standards and the Responsibility of Transnationals* (Kluwer International, The Hague 1999) 161–170

34 P I Blumberg, 'Accountability of Multinational Corporations: The Barriers Presented by the Corporate Juridical Entity' (2001) 24(3) *Hastings International and Comparative Law Review* 297–320

35 P I Blumberg, *The Multinational Challenge to Corporations* (Oxford University Press, Oxford 1993) 117

which are home states for a major portion of the large MNCs.[36] This FNC concept raises the question of whether there is a better and more convenient forum and often results in remitting the matter back to the courts of the state (country) where the alleged incident occurred.[37] This is often not desirable for the litigants as the incidents occur in developing countries, where the legal regime may lack adequate legal mechanisms, penalties or even political will and there may also be considerable limitations on the funding of such litigation on the part of the injured party which may be an individual or a community.[38]

In the UK, the doctrine of FNC is established by the case of *Spiliada Maritime Corporation v Cansulex.*[39] The Spiliada test involved two parts: it is for the defendant claiming there is an alternative forum to make out a case that the natural foreign form is better and then the plaintiff (claimant) can show special circumstances that substantial justice cannot be obtained there, to rebut this claim. However, the scope of this doctrine has been significantly eroded by the signing of the Brussels Convention.[40] The Civil Jurisdiction and Judgments Act (1982) as amended by the Civil Jurisdiction and Judgments Act (1991) which adopts this convention specifies in s. 49 that:

> Nothing in this Act shall prevent any court in the United Kingdom from staying, sisting, striking out or dismissing any proceedings before it, on the ground of *forum non conveniens* or otherwise, where to do so is not inconsistent with the 1968 Convention.

This EU position rather adopts the notion of '*Lis alibi pendens*' which is more prevalent in civil law countries which states that:

> (1) Where proceedings involving the same cause of action and between the same parties are brought in the courts of different Member States, any court other than the court first seised shall of its own motion stay its proceedings until such time as the jurisdiction of the court first seised is established.
> (2) Where the jurisdiction of the court first seised is established, any court other than the court first seised shall decline jurisdiction in favour of that court.[41]

36 Home countries for some of the largest MNCs such as Exxon and BP

37 *Spiliada Maritime Corporation v Cansulex Ltd* [1987] AC 460; *Adams v Cape Industries plc* [1990] Ch 433; *Lubbe v Cape Plc* (2000) UKHL 41. See also S Joseph, *Corporations and Transnational Human Rights Litigation* (Hart Publishing, Oxford 2004)

38 Joseph ibid. 11

39 (1972) 3WLR 972

40 This is affirmed by the case of the ECJ cases of *Group Josi Reinsurance Company SA v Compagnie d'Assurances Universal General Insurance Company* (2000) Case C-412/98 and *Owusu v Jackson* (2005) Case C-128/01

41 Article 27 of the Council Regulation (EC) No. 44/2001 of 22 December 2000 on jurisdiction and the recognition and enforcement of judgments in civil and commercial matters

The European Court of Justice in *Owusu v Jackson*[42] then interpreted the Brussels Convention in a way which effectively curtailed the use of FNC in the UK by holding that:

> the Brussels Convention precludes a court of a Contracting State from declining the jurisdiction conferred on it by Article 2 of that convention on the ground that a court of a non-Contracting State would be a more appropriate forum for the trial of the action even if the jurisdiction of no other Contracting State is in issue or the proceedings have no connecting factors to any other Contracting State.[43]

While this may end up creating a good weapon for litigation against MNCs domiciled in EU countries including the UK, it has been badly received in England. It was perceived as 'forcing litigation to take place in an inappropriate jurisdiction with greater inconvenience and expense'.[44] The courts have already begun limiting the impact of the case as it did not exclude the discretion of the courts to stay proceedings in favour of proceedings in a foreign forum.[45]

In the United States (which is the home of a significant number of MNCs) the instructive case on FNC is the case of *Piper Alpha v Reyno*.[46] This prescribes a more restricted approach on the basis of FNC. The courts at the outset determine whether there exists an alternative forum and then consider issues of private and public interest. The private interest factors include relative ease of access to evidence and all the other practical problems that make the trail expeditious and inexpensive. The public interest factor considers congestion of courts in the United States as against the courts in the alternative forum. Consequently the result is often that the US approach is more restrictive on the basis of FNC.

An instructive example is the Bhopal Union Carbide disaster of 1984 which was unsuccessfully litigated in the United States. The Bhopal gas plant, where the gas leak occurred, was operated by Union Carbide India Limited, a 51 per cent affiliate of the parent corporation, Union Carbide Corporation. The US courts concluded that India would be a better forum as it has a stronger regulatory interest.[47] The MNC Union Carbide Corporation paid a settlement figure to the Indian government in 1989 of about US$470 million[48] but it was only in 2010 that the Indian courts finally found some Indian ex-executives of Union Carbide

42 (2005) Case C-128/01; 2 WLR 942 (2005)

43 Para. 46

44 J Harris, 'The Brussels I Regulation and the Re-emergence of English Common Law' (2008) 4 *European Legal Forum* 181–189, 185

45 *Konkola Copper Mines plc v Coromin* (2005) 2 Lloyd's Rep. 555

46 (1981) 454 US 235

47 *In re Union Carbide Corporation Gas Plant Disaster at Bhopal, India*, 634 F. Supp. 842, 844 (SDNY, 1986), aff'd, 809 Fed. Rptr. 2d 195 (2nd Cir., 1987)

48 R A G Monks and N Minow, *Corporate Governance* (3rd ed., Blackwell, Oxford 2004) 19

liable for causing death by negligence and sentenced them to two years' imprisonment. This may not even spell the end of the matter as the Indian Supreme Court has been asked to reopen the case due to the leniency of the sentences.[49]

Nonetheless in the United States, another controversial traditional legal instrument that had emerged to attempt to give access to justice for the victims of wrongful corporate action is the *Alien Tort Statutes.*[50] The Act gives 'district courts the power to hear civil claims from foreign citizens for injuries caused by action in violation of the law of nations or a treaty of the USA'.[51] The term the 'law of nations' can be construed in several ways, for in a literal sense it refers to other sources of international law outside treaty law. However, this will include customary international law.

Joseph points out that 'generally it seems that the US courts are satisfied that Alien Torts Claims Act (ACTA) is activated if the human rights violation at issue breaches customary international law'.[52] This casts a wide net and therefore several issues may trigger ATS claims. They include torture, genocide, forced labour, peaceful assembly and association, freedom of political belief, opinion and expressions among others, although controversially environmental abuses may not ground a claim.[53]

An important ATS decision was made in the case of *Filartiga v Pena-Irala*[54] where the court accepted the extension of universally accepted norms of international human rights law (as a violation of international law) as constituting a violation of the domestic law of the United States. Since then there have been several attempts to litigate oil MNCs but very few have reached substantive hearing. Cases have been brought against oil MNCs for their actions in several countries. Examples include Shell in Nigeria,[55] Chevron in Nigeria,[56] Texaco in Ecuador[57] and Exxon Mobil in Aceh.[58]

In spite of FNC as a procedural obstacle, ATS remained a major factor as a potential avenue for litigation for human rights violation.[59] The US Supreme

49 <http://www.guardian.co.uk/environment/2010/aug/31/india-reopens-bhopal-case> accessed 10 September 2011

50 28 U S C § 1350. This includes the Aliens Torts Claims Act (ACTA) and the Torture Victim Prevention Act (TVPA). This ATCA was part of the Judiciary Act of 1789

51 Ch. 20, §9, 1 Stat. 73, 77 (1789)

52 Joseph (n. 36)

53 Ibid.

54 630 F.2d 876(2d Cir 1980)

55 *Wiwa v Shell Petroleum Development Co. 532 US 941(2001); Kiobel v Royal Dutch Petroleum* No. 06–4800-cv, 06–4876-cv, 2010WL 3611392 (2d Cir. Sept. 17, 2010)

56 *Bowoto v. Chevron Corp.,* No. 09–15641, 2010 WL 3516437 (9th Cir. Sept. 10, 2010)

57 *Aguinda v Texaco303 F.3d 470* (2d Cir 2002)

58 *Doe VIII v. Exxon Mobil Corp.,* No. 09–7125 (D.C. Cir. 2011)

59 One of the major procedural obstacles, however, is the FNC doctrine which allows the courts to dismiss the case if there is a more suitable alternative foreign forum.

Court in the case of *Sosa v Alvarez-Machian*[60] accepted the use of the Alien Tort Statute in application of ACTA to binding norms of customary international human rights law.[61] However, in September 2010 some doubt was reintroduced with the decision of the second circuit (appeals) US court in the case of *Kiobel v Royal Dutch Shell*[62] which found that the Aliens Torts Statute did not apply to corporations. The court's reasoning was that 'corporations are liable as juridical persons under domestic law, (but that) does not mean they are liable under international law'.[63] This position was then confirmed by the landmark 2013 US Supreme Court case which settled the question of extraterritorial corporate liability for human rights violations in the negative. Kiobel affirmed the presumption against extraterritorial application.[64]

Furthermore, even if the result of the litigation had been favourable, litigation is not always the best dispute resolution process as it can be a slow and drawn-out process. The 2013 US *Kiobel Case* referred to alleged violations of human rights by Shell Oil Corporation which occurred in the Niger-Delta region of Nigeria in the early 1990s.

6.3.1.2 Non-traditional dispute resolution

On the other hand, there is an increasing expansion of alternative dispute resolution and grievance mechanisms. Ruggie, in his role as the special representative of the Secretary General on issues of business and human rights has suggested that these mechanisms could be extended to address certain community–company disputes.[65] In his April 2008 Report, he outlined a three-part global framework

60 (2004) 542 U.S. 692

61 R G Steinhardt, 'Laying One Bankrupt Critique to Rest: *Sosa v Alvarez-Machain* and the Future of International Human Rights Litigation in U.S. Courts' (2004) 57(6) *Vanderbilt Law Review* 2241–2301

62 Nos 06–4800-cv, 06–4876-cv, 2010WL 3611392 (2d Cir. Sept. 17, 2010)

63 Ibid. See also C I Keitner, '*Kiobel v Royal Dutch Petroleum:* Another Round in the Fight over Corporate Liability under the Alien Tort Statute' 14(30) *American Society of International Law* (ASIL) Insight 30 September 2010. These are cases arising from alleged Shell complicity in the execution of the Nigerian 'Ogoni nine'

64 *Esther Kiobel (individually and on behalf of her husband) v Royal Dutch Petroleum Co. et al* 133 S. Ct. 1659. A substantial amount of *amicus curiae* had been filed for the case. These included legal scholars, universities, NGOs, corporations.

65 See J Ruggie, *Protect, Respect and Remedy: A Framework for Business and Human Rights,* Report of the Special Representative of the Secretary-General on the issue of human rights and transnational corporations and other business enterprises (April 2008) 22 <www2.ohchr.org/english/bodies/hrcouncil/docs/8session/A-HRC-8-5.doc> accessed 8 June 2016. He points out with regards to human rights, a major aspect of CSR, that 'effective grievance mechanisms play an important role . . . in the corporate responsibility to respect'. He adds that 'equally, the corporate responsibility to respect requires a means for those who believe they have been harmed to bring this to the attention of the company and seek remediation . . . providing access to remedy does not presume that all allegations

for allocating human rights responsibilities between states and business: '(a) [s]tates have the duty to protect individuals and communities from human rights abuses from all sources, including business; (b) business has the responsibility to respect human rights; and (c) those who suffer harm from business activities should have access to remedy, both judicial and non-judicial'.[66]

The reference to the non-judicial method of dispute resolution is an acknowledgement of another way of carrying out this law-job that is present within CSR. Some the existing CSR codes of conduct already contain provisions and standards which pertain to the handling of complaints and grievance mechanisms. A report by the CSR Initiative at Harvard University, examining how integrated conflict management programmes can be extended to external stakeholders such as the community, gives an overview of these mechanisms.[67]

This report from the CSR initiative maps out the grievance mechanisms that are in place in the business and human right area outside of the traditional legal mechanisms. This analysis of mechanisms was done with three key themes: institutional levels, key functions and types of processes. The different institutional levels analysed were company, industry, multi-industry, national, regional or international. The key functions referred to included standards, access, agents, process, enforcement, outcomes and transparency. The types of processes ranged from information facilitation, negotiation, mediation, conciliation, arbitration, investigation to, even, adjudication.

This investigation was novel in many ways but it underpins Llewellyn's point that law can be perceived from the perspective of the jobs. Although these activities are non-judicial, they are capable of handling a significant amount of grievance remediation in the absence of other effective remedies. It is, however, important that recognition of the capabilities of these frameworks must also be coupled with issues of accountability and legitimacy.

To understand how such a system works at the company level,[68] the report gives the example of the construction of the Baku-Tbilisi-Ceyhan (BTC) pipeline by an oil consortium led by BP. The process of grievance remediation on this project

represent real abuses of bona fide complaints'. This position is adopted in his Final Report 2011 A/HRC/17/31

66 Ibid.

67 C Rees and D Vermijis, 'Mapping Grievance Mechanisms in the Business and Human Rights Arena', *Corporate Social Responsibility Initiative Report* No. 28, Cambridge, MA, Harvard Kennedy School; Corporate Social Responsibility Initiative, Harvard Kennedy School of Government Governance and Accountability Program <http://www.hks.harvard.edu/m-rcbg/CSRI/prog_ga.html> accessed 25 October 2010. See also J Sherman, 'Embedding Rights Compatible Grievance Processes for External Stakeholders within Business Culture', *Corporate Social Responsibility Initiative Report* No. 36, Cambridge, MA, Harvard Kennedy School August 2009 p. 3; the BASES wiki platform (Business and Society Exploring Solutions – a dispute resolution community) <http://baseswiki.org/en/Main_Page> accessed 25 October 2010

68 See Rees and Vermijis, ibid. 10

allowed for affected individuals in the communities to register grievances with community liaison officers appointed by the company. The first level of dispute resolution would involve seeking a negotiated settlement within a short period of time. However, where this settlement could not be achieved directly or the matter related to a land dispute, compensation or other primary non-technical issue, then the matter could be taken to a local NGO, Center for Legal and Economic Education (CLEE), engaged by BP to provide a form of arbitration. This process did not exempt the right to redress in the courts where such rights exist. This was a rights-based approach, with rights derived from domestic law, or voluntary standards adopted by BTC including BP's code of conduct, standards of the IFC and the Voluntary Principles on Security and Human Rights. The process was published on the Web as a means of accountability and transparency. These mechanisms have evolved as a means of dealing with persistent problems that are thrown up by regulatory gaps.

Another example at a national level can be derived from the use of national contact points under the OECD Guidelines for Multinational Enterprises.[69] The Guidelines cover employment and industrial relations, human rights, environment, information disclosure, combating bribery, consumer interests, competition, taxation and science and technology.[70] The Guidelines have been highlighted as having one of the best coverage of CSR issues.[71]

The national contact points handle complaints against MNCs about violations of the guidelines. These violations must, however, have taken place in an OECD country or a non-OECD adhering country. Any 'interested party' has standing to bring a complaint, this covers a multitude of stakeholders such as individuals, communities, trade unions or other NGOs. It uses investigation, mediation and conciliation, which may result in remediation and conciliation. The national contact points can also produce a publicised statement with recommendations.

There is no formal appeals process, however OECD member states or OECD business or trade union advisory bodies (Business and Industry Advisory Committee (BIAC) and Trade Union Advisory Committee (TUAC)) can request the OECD Investment Committee's views on whether a national contact point (NCP) has correctly interpreted the Guidelines' text and implementation procedures.[72] However, there have been recommendations that this be extended to a larger role of specific recommendations.[73]

69 (2000) 40 ILM 237 (2001)
70 Ibid.
71 D Leipziger, *The Corporate Responsibility Code Book* (2nd ed., Greenleaf, Sheffield 2010) 55
72 BASES established as part of the Corporate Social Responsibility Initiative, Harvard Kennedy School of Government Governance and Accountability Program <http://baseswiki.org/en/OECD_National_Contact_Points,_General_Information> accessed 10 December 2011
73 OECD Watch 2008 review of NCP and the implementation of OECD Guidelines June 2008 <http://baseswiki.org/w/images/en/7/7d/OECD_Watch_2008_Review_of_National_

The OECD also reviews NCP as different states adopt varying mechanisms of compliance. This review allows for comparative analysis of mechanisms aimed at achieving the core criteria of visibility, accessibility, transparency and accountability, i.e. 'functional equivalence'.[74] The 2008 Review Report points out 'The flexibility embedded in the "functional equivalence" principle constitutes a recognition that the conditions and circumstances upon which various corporate responsibility actors operate may vary from one adherent country to another'.[75]

This analysis suggests that in enhancing a CSR legitimacy framework, this type of non-judicial mechanisms are newer regulatory tools which can be harnessed to do the law-jobs. These mechanisms are also the legitimate concern of law especially because they are an emerging type of law and dispute-resolving mechanism which may in future be more relevant to some communities than traditional legal instruments. Frameworks for non-judicial or alternative dispute mechanisms are often built in to CSR instruments. However, this area of non-judicial mechanisms and alternative dispute resolution is an underdeveloped area within CSR.

6.3.2 Channelling and rechannelling

The next law-job within this perspective of the CSR legitimacy framework is the channelling and rechannelling of behaviour. This refers to the channelling of overt behaviour as well as the channelling of expectations, norms and claims. In a traditional legal sense, this refers to law's ability to define expected conduct from actors within the applicable community through legislation and regulation. However, within CSR the most visible means of channelling conduct is through the use of non-traditional codes of conduct. This aspect therefore tackles the situation within CSR, where preventative channelling of corporate behaviour towards responsible action is desirable. This can be done in a traditional or non-traditional way.

6.3.2.1 Traditional

Some states have attempted to use traditional laws to reinforce the channelling of corporate behaviour but have been largely unsuccessful. Two examples are

Contact_Points_and_the_Implementation_of_the_OECD_Guidelines.pdf > accessed 10 December 2011

74 *Review of the NCP Performance: Key Findings of the Investment Committee: Background Paper for the OECD-ILO Conference on CSR* June 2008, OECD, Paris, p. 15 <http://www.oecd.org/dataoecd/34/15/40807797.pdf> accessed 10 December 2011

75 Ibid. The OECD also has annual reports on the guidelines which review the activity of the previous 12 months. The 2010 report is *OECD, Annual Report on the OECD Guidelines for Multinational Enterprises 2010: Corporate Responsibility: Reinforcing a Unique Instrument* (OECD, Paris 2010)

the 2003 UK Corporate Responsibility bill[76] and the 2008 Nigerian CSR bill.[77] There appears to be a lack of political will to regulate for CSR, especially with the ideological dominance of the voluntaristic perspective. Furthermore, the push for deregulation and the reduction of state capacity have dominated global discourse on the role of the state.[78]

Jenkins points out that although critics of this rather voluntaristic turn raise the objection that such regulation serves as a substitute for statutory legislation and at the same time legitimises the absence of statutory regulations by governments and international bodies but in the context of globalisation, he concedes there is at present no clear platform for re-regulation.[79]

Notwithstanding this, a new set of CSR regulation is emerging in developing countries that attempts to link CSR spending with developmental objectives. In Indonesia, a modification to their corporate law was made in 2007 to include a mandatory obligation for corporations in the field of and/or related to natural resources to carry out social and environmental responsibility (SER).[80] This obligation to carry out CSR is also extended to investors.[81] The Mauritius government has also instituted a legislation that mandates a 2 per cent of profits spend towards CSR programmes.[82] In 2014, India finally adopted CSR legislation[83] which mandated a 2 per cent spend of net profits in pursuance of CSR policies.

76 Copy available online: <http://www.publications.parliament.uk/pa/cm200203/cmbills/129/03129.i.html > <http://www.publications.parliament.uk/pa/cm200203/cmbills/129/2003129.pdf > accessed 10 December 2011

77 Copy available online: <http://www.femiamao.com/files/CSR_BILL.pdf> accessed 10 December 2011

78 World Bank World Development Report 1997, *The State in a Changing World* (World Bank/Oxford University Press, Washington, DC/New York 1997)

79 He focuses on labour but the same can be said for other aspects of CSR – social, human rights, environment. R Jenkins, R Pearson and G Seyfang, *Corporate Responsibility and Labour Rights – Codes of Conduct in the Global Economy* (Earthscan, London 2002) 5

80 Article 74 of Limited Liability Company Law 2007 Article 1 defines SER as 'the company's commitment to participate in sustainable economic development in order to improve the quality of life and beneficial environment both for the company itself, the local community and society in general'. This obligation for CSR is extended to investors see Article 5b of the Investors Investment Law No. 25 2007. See details in O Amao, *CSR, HR and Law: Multinational Corporations in Developing Countries* (Routledge, Abingdon 2011); see also P R Waagstein, 'The Mandatory Corporate Social Responsibility in India: Problems and Implications' (2011) 98(3) *Journal of Business Ethics* 455–466

81 Amao ibid.

82 Finance Bill sub-part AD. S. 50k-l <http://www.nef.mu/csr/finance_bill.php> accessed 10 December 2011. This CSR legislation was enacted in 2009, for more detail of the implications see R Pillay, *The Changing Nature of Corporate Social Responsibility: CSR and Development in Context – The Case of Mauritius* (Routledge, Abingdon 2015)

83 This was initially touted as a voluntary measure in an earlier Companies Bill 2011 <http://www.business-standard.com/india/news/2-csr-spend-not-mandatory-for-companies-moily/152054/on> accessed 12 March 2016, agreed in 2014 as s. 135 Companies Act 2013

There are also examples of regulation aimed at fostering and facilitating the voluntary framework; The Danish Financial Statement Act (as amended) mandating CSR reporting for its large corporations.[84] However, there is a limitation which is that it remains the prerogative of the corporations to decide if they want to engage with CSR. This Act specifies that:

> CSR shall mean businesses voluntarily include considerations for human rights, societal, environmental and climate conditions as well as combating corruption in their business strategy and corporate activities. Businesses without policies on social responsibility shall disclose this information in their management's review.[85]

This is not dissimilar to the reporting requirement of the UK Companies Act 2006.[86] It is too early to gauge the effectiveness of the use of legislation in CSR. There are already some criticisms of the form of CSR endorsed in the Mauritius and Indian law, as being a legislative endorsement of corporate philanthropy.[87]

6.3.2.2 Non-traditional

The more prevalent instruments within CSR for channelling conduct are the codes of conduct. Codes of conduct can be classified into five categories: company codes, trade association codes, multi-stakeholder codes, model codes and inter-governmental codes.[88] Codes of conduct have been defined as 'written policy or statement of principles intended to serve as a basis of commitment to a particular conduct'[89] and they have emerged to prescribe expected conduct or behaviour of corporations as well as to channel society's expectation of corporate action.

This has a twofold effect. First, affecting what society expects of corporations and, second, spelling out the change required in corporate attitudes and behaviour.

84 The Danish Financial Statements Act (*Årsregnskabsloven*), cf. Consolidated Act No. 647 of 15 June 2006, as amended by s. 5 of Act No. 108 of 7 February 2007, s. 63 of Act No. 468 of 17 June 2008 and Act No. 516 of 17 June 2008 <http://csrgov.dk/legislation> accessed 8 June 2016 – latest amendment implements the EU Directive 2014/95/EU on disclosure of non-financial information

85 S. 99(a) Danish Financial Statements Act

86 S. 414A-D Companies Act 2006 (Strategic Reports and Director's Report) Regulations 2013

87 Pillay (n. 81) and <http://www.theguardian.com/sustainable-business/india-csr-law-debate-business-ngo> accessed 29 May 2016

88 R Jenkins, 'Corporate Codes of Conduct: Self-Regulation in a Global Economy' *Technology, Business and Society Programme* Paper No. 2 (UNRISD, Geneva 2001)

89 L Dubin, 'The Direct Application of Human Rights Standards to and by Transnational Corporations' (1999) 61 *Review of the International Commission of Jurists* 35–66, 42 cited in A Wawryk, 'Regulating Transnational Corporations through Corporate Codes of Conduct' in J G Frynas and S Pegg, *Transnational Corporations and Human Rights* (Palgrave Macmillan, Basingstoke 2003) 53–78

CSR is not only the result of changes in societal expectation but also a result of the increasing acknowledgment that business significantly affects society. The codes of conduct are playing a legal role by prescribing areas of corporate responsibility and concern not defined in traditional law but now expected from corporations. They play an effective channelling role as they prescribe standards of accepted conduct in the relevant areas.

This is why Wawyck points out that a code of conduct should not only set out the principles to guide behaviour; it should also establish mechanisms for implementation, monitoring enforcement and review.[90] This can also be facilitated or reinforced by traditional legislation. An example of such innovative connections within codes can be seen in the extractive industries transparency initiative (EITI) which has created a global standard for transparency and publication of oil revenues between oil corporations and governments.

This can be reinforced in the adopting country by legislation.[91] Candidate countries within this initiative need to develop a work plan for implementation in consultation with stakeholders.

This notion of inter-relationship between self-regulatory instruments and law is not new. Galanter reminds us that:

> the drafting of the Uniform Commercial Code was a self-conscious attempt (by Karl Llewellyn) to synthesise formal law and commercial usage: the formal law would incorporate the best commercial practice and would in turn serve as a model for refinement and development of that practice. The code's broadly drafted rules would be accessible to businessmen and would provide a framework for self-regulation which would in turn furnish attentive courts with content for the code's categories. Thus the code would serve as a vehicle for business communities to evolve law for themselves in dialogues with courts operating not as interpreters of imposed law but as articulators and critics of business usage.[92]

In addition, the code of conduct can also offer up standards by which these companies can be held to account in a traditional legal sense.[93] An instructive case is the US case of *Kasky v Nike*.[94] The case captured the attention of many corporations as Microsoft, Exxon Mobil and Pfizer are among the corporations that filed *amicus curiae* briefs. The case hinged on the claims made by Nike in a series of publications about the labour conditions in overseas factories.

90 Wawryk ibid. 53
91 Nigeria passed the Nigerian Extractives Industries Transparency Act 2007
92 M Galanter, 'Justice in Many Rooms' (1981) 19 *Journal of Legal Pluralism* 1–47, 29–30
93 C Glinski, 'Corporate Codes of Conduct: Moral or Legal Obligation?' in D McBarnet, A Voiculescu and T Campbell (eds), *The New Corporate Accountability: Corporate Social Responsibility and the Law* (Cambridge University Press, Cambridge 2007) 119–147
94 *Kasky v Nike, Inc* 45 P 3d 243 (Cal. 2002)

Kasky alleged that these claims were misleading and sued under California's unfair competition and false advertising law. In 2002 Kasky won the case at the California Supreme Court but Nike appealed to the US Supreme Court. The US Supreme Court failed to give a definitive ruling and instead sent the case down to the trial court. The case was, however, settled without addressing the issue of whether Nike's assertions could be classed as political speech protected by the First Amendment or commercial speech which is less protected.

There are two vital points here. This case highlighted the potential for voluntary speech and assertions on social responsibility to have legal and financial consequences and also illustrated, rather disappointingly, that corporations were making assertions which could be open to attack as false, perhaps for marketing or branding reasons.

The potential of such statements to have a legal effect is not limited to the United States. Glinski also highlights this potential in German and EU law, especially where the objective is to increase one's sales.[95] She points out that German courts already have a body of case law on environmental advertising. Advertising would include longer texts such as codes of conduct and environmental reports. The European Commission Directive on unfair commercial practices requires firm commitments which can be verified with regard to commercial communication directly connected to the promotion, sale or supply of a product to consumers but this is not a right that can be derived by the consumer or individual. The Directive is for application within the Member State area and then these states provide mechanisms which may be through public authorities or consumer associations. However, the European Commission in its renewed Strategy for CSR 2011 confirmed that this issue of misleading marketing (green washing) will be addressed and in May 2016 the Commission adopted an updated version of the 2009 Guidance on the application of the Unfair Commercial Practices Directive. The Guidance confirms that CSR initiatives can qualify as commercial practice and will therefore have to abide by the rules under Article 6 of the Directive which covers any commercial practice which 'contains false information and is therefore untruthful'.[96]

Nevertheless the basic aspect of this law-job is that it transcends the traditional legal perspective and it allows for the examination of the accountability perspective from traditional and non-traditional perspectives. It permits codes of conduct as simple rules channelling conduct to be examined as legal instruments. It allows the examination of such instruments for standards and mechanisms for accountability within those standards. It also allows for complementary schemes where non-traditional standards can give rise to traditional legal consequences such as litigation or be reinforced by traditional legislation. It is also possible to

95 Glinski (n. 93) 126

96 <http://ec.europa.eu/justice/consumer-marketing/files/ucp_guidance_en.pdf> accessed 16 August 2016, pp. 59–64. European Commission, *EC: A Renewed Strategy 2011–14 for CSR Brussels Com* (2011) (681 final) p. 9

create effective and transparent reporting mechanisms complemented by legislation. Again form is less relevant, what is crucial is that conduct is channelled effectively.

Therefore, within the corporate and society relationship, where CSR performs this channelling and rechannelling function, it is doing a law-job. It can be examined from this perspective and this will allow for more innovative ways of channelling conduct.

6.3.3 The say

This aspect of the law-jobs is viewed as a constitutive function. It has been seen as 'the constitution of groups, concerning the establishment and allocation of authority . . . establishes the location of legitimate institutional power . . .'.[97] This is an aspect which needs to be discovered and developed within CSR. In prescribing the processes and procedures within CSR, the initiative and influence driving CSR appears to move from the corporations to co-opting NGOs. However, it is neither the preserve of corporations nor the preserve of states and non-governmental actors. It should be a multi-stakeholder process. This is why it has been suggested that:

> The law-job of allocating authority is certainly not by definition the state's prerogative or task. Private institutions are quite capable of making such decisions under the right conditions: the institutions represent multiple interests, be open to public scrutiny and prevent self-interested and lax monitoring.[98]

Llewellyn admits that this area more than any other points to the question of the allocation of power rather than rights.[99] It goes to the question of who defines the CSR rules. He prescribes that:

> to get these matters settled in advance and to get settled also what procedures must be done in order to legitimise a decision and give it standing and what limits are on any person's authority is a matter of peculiar importance.[100]

However, this law-job, especially in the CSR context, should not only be about choosing or allocating who has the say. It should also be about establishing mechanisms that allow for the decisions on 'who has the say'. This may be the sense in which structures are being advocated for taking cognisance of 'stakeholders' in decision-making with regards to CSR.[101]

97 M Feintuck and M Varney, *Media Regulation, Public Interest and the Law* (2nd ed., Edinburgh University Press, Edinburgh 2006) 34
98 Taekema (n. 5) 66–67
99 Llewellyn (n. 4) 1383
100 Ibid.
101 T Donaldson and L Preston, 'The Stakeholder Theory of the Corporation: Concepts, Evidence and Implications' (1995) 20(1) *Academy of Management Review* 65–91

In the EITI example above, one of the challenges has been multi-stakeholder groups defining the process in context, this has created flexibility but it is also flexible and each candidate country has to work out its own process towards achieving compliance with the general principles, although there is also an independent assessment which reviews the country's progress and delineates which steps should be taken to improve the process.[102] Through its renewed strategy the European Commission has created a multi-stakeholder forum on CSR, which meets around key milestones and has participants from a range of sectors. The forum also has a coordination committee which meets more regularly with the commission.[103]

The primary task of creating a CSR strategy and ensuring compliance with CSR procedures currently lies with CSR departments in corporations and their managers. CSR is becoming a distinct field with its own specialists charged with integrating CSR processes into management. Other key actors are the NGO involved in this aspect and the auditors who verify these processes. However, this raises larger questions of power, legitimacy and authority and redressing such relationships under the CSR framework.

A first step is to identify this as a key law-job within the relationship. The centrality of power to CSR means that the law-job of the say is very important. The ability to develop participative publicised processes that shape the direction and decision-making processes within CSR in a multi-stakeholder fashion is essential. This would imply the importance of principles of participation, transparency and publicity. The legal environment also has to be made conducive and facilitative to the organic development of the identified allocation of authority and responsibility.

These debates can be internal to the company where issues of employee participation in decision-making are raised[104] or external where issues of corporate power and its impact on social responsibility are addressed.[105] It is only with the recognition of the allocative function, that there can be a re-allocative function to change 'who has the say'. This law-job is at its most relevant where no one has any idea whose say is to go, as a legal perspective can and should begin to define, direct and limit the exercise of authority. It forms the basis of a relevant legal enquiry.

102 Rainbow Insight, *Evaluating the EITI's Impact on the Transparency of Natural Resource Revenues* 2009 <http://eiti.org/files/Rainbow%20Insight%20Report.pdf > accessed 10 December 2011

103 The last meeting took place in February 2015, see <http://ec.europa.eu/growth/industry/corporate-social-responsibility_en> accessed 16 August 2016

104 P Maclagan, 'Corporate Social Responsibility as a Participative Process' (1999) 8(1) *Business Ethics: A European Review* 43–49

105 D Lewis and S MacLeod, 'Transnational Corporations – Power, Responsibility and Influence' (2004) 4(1) *Global Social Policy* 77–98

6.3.4 Net drive

There are many drivers of CSR practice;[106] they include civil society, consumers, the investment climate or government and the workplace (internal company management or employees).[107] The civil society,[108] especially the NGOs, have played a major role in the promotion and popularisation of CSR.[109] NGOs, especially international NGOs, arose out of the desire to fill the regulatory gap or vacuum left by the uncoordinated regulation by states at both state and international level. They sought to forge alliances with local communities, employees and aggrieved persons in order to publicise their grievances on the global stage.[110] They excelled in the use of the media to disseminate information especially through the internet. This is demonstrated by the Greenpeace and Brent Spar campaign which galvanised the media and consumer focus on Shell and prompted a change of tactics by the oil corporation.[111]

These NGOs began to attack corporations directly because of a perceived inability to govern multinational corporate conduct at an international level. The effectiveness of the NGO attack on transnational corporations was greatly assisted by the speedy and widely available communication networks that now exist under globalisation. There is huge variation in tactics adopted by NGOs: with some NGOs adopting a cooperative stance and forming partnerships with corporations in carrying out and monitoring CSR activities, and others remaining critical and actively advocating for mandatory regulation with support for international

106 M Haigh and M T Jones, 'The Drivers of Corporate Social Responsibility: A Critical Review' (2006) 5(2) *Business Review Cambridge* 1–9, Haigh and Jones identify six sets of influences: 'internal pressures on business managers, pressure from business competitors, investors and consumers and regulatory pressures coming from governments and non-governmental organisations'

107 DFID, *DFID and Corporate Social Responsibility Issues Paper* <http://www.dfid.gov.uk/pubs/files/corporate-social-resp.pdf> accessed 10 December 2011. These are all factors counter-influenced by globalisation to varying degrees.

108 LSE Centre for Civil Society defines civil society as referring '*to the arena of un-coerced collective action around shared interests, purposes and values. In theory, its institutional forms are distinct from those of the state, family and market, though in practice, the boundaries between state, civil society, family and market are often complex, blurred and negotiated. Civil society commonly embraces a diversity of spaces, actors and institutional forms, varying in their degree of formality, autonomy and power. Civil societies are often populated by organisations such as registered charities, development non-governmental organisations, community groups, women's organisations, faith-based organisations, professional associations, trades unions, self-help groups, social movements, business associations, coalitions and advocacy group especially the non-governmental organisations.*' <http://www.lse.ac.uk/collections/CCS/what_is_civil_society.htm> last accessed 10 September 2010

109 A Lindblom, *Non-governmental Organisations in International Law* (Cambridge University Press, Cambridge 2006)

110 P Newell, 'Managing Multinationals: The Governance of Investment for the Environment' 13 *Journal of International Development* 907–919, 910

111 G Jordan, *Shell, Greenpeace and Brent Spar* (Palgrave Macmillan, New York 2001)

initiatives like the UN Norms on the Responsibilities of Transnational Corporations and Other Business Enterprises with Regard to Human Rights.[112] The key objective for them is a net drive for CSR on an international level.

The government can also be a driver of CSR either through its action or inaction: through its inaction or omission to provide regulation or laws regarding socially irresponsible conduct thus creating a vacuum which has to be filled by other actors or by actively encouraging CSR practice through the creation of codes and standards. The former course of action is evident in some developing countries where there is inadequate environmental, health safety and torts laws and a lack of enforcement juxtaposed with the pressing social needs of the local community which must be addressed by the corporation so as to create a stable and sustainable environment for it to carry out its operations.[113] Conversely, however, the government can positively drive the direction of CSR practice through policies, incentives and establishing frameworks and systems. Examples can be found in the UK.[114] This may arise as an additional scheme within an existing regulatory framework or as an alternative to direct regulation.

Another major driver of CSR is the consumer. In this sense it is as a result of the perceived consumer effect which may occur as a result of damage to corporate reputation and brand or as a result of adoption of responsible initiatives and strategies. It is often assumed that the result of the increased awareness is an increase in vulnerability of the corporations to consumers and consumer reaction.[115] Consumers may choose to reward a corporation positively by use of a particular brand seen as 'responsible' or negatively by the boycott of a brand seen as 'irresponsible'.

However, the specific reaction of consumers to corporate acts is not an exact science because, in deep similarity to any analysis of other aspects of human behaviour, the reaction of consumers to behaviour of corporations is largely unpredictable, varying across sectors and changes over time. The vulnerability of corporations in the retail sector may be different from the exposure of corporations in the manufacturing sector. Personal choices may also vary from boom periods in the economy to recession times. For example, the choice of buying

112 P Muchlinski 'Multinational Enterprises as Actors in International Law: Creating 'Soft Law' Obligations and 'Hard Law' Rights' in M Noortmann, C Ryngaert *Non-State Actor Dynamics in International Law* (Ashgate, Aldershot, 2010) 9–41, 20

113 W Visser 'Corporate social responsibility in developing countries' in in A Crane, A McWilliams and others (eds) *The Oxford Handbook of CSR* (Oxford University Press, New York 2008) 473–502

114 J Moon, *Government as a Driver of Corporate Social Responsibility: The UK in Comparative Perspective* (ICCSR Working Papers No. 20 Nottingham 2004) <https://www.nottingham.ac.uk/business/ICCSR/assets/researchpapers/20-2004.pdf> accessed 8 June 2016. See also s. 54 of the UK Modern Slavery Act 2015 which enforces voluntary disclosure of slavery and forced labour in supply chains

115 Y Fan, 'Ethical Branding and Corporate Reputation' (2005) 10(4) *Corporate Communications: An International Journal* 341–50

free trade products, or perhaps free range eggs, in everyday commodities may vary. Smith points out that:

> for any given company – or at any given issue, to take a campaign group perspective – the likelihood of corporate responsibility affecting consumer behaviour vary tremendously. Academic research findings of positive and negative ethical consumerism highlight the heterogeneity and complexity of consumer response.[116]

Occasionally classed in this group is a slightly different set of consumers. Such consumers are the investors who choose to invest on the basis of CSR. This refers to ethical or socially responsible investors who, in theory, seek to reward responsible behaviour by investing in corporations with a high ethical rating. Swanson points out that:

> Investors and the financial community care about these issues. Share value is much more than just the value of tangible assets. Reputation forms a large part of it, thus companies must respond to these challenges, if for no other reason than to protect their reputation and the financial implication this has.[117]

However, ethical investment forms only a small proportion of all investments[118] and this affects their ability to significantly affect the market in favour of social responsibility. Such ethical investment can take varied forms, which include negatively screening out corporations according to an ethical criteria or positively screening for corporations that adopt the best socially responsible performance or using rights as shareholders to encourage corporations to improve their performance.[119]

Finally managers are important in the implementation of CSR in practice. They have practical control of the resources and can determine the strategy of utilising such resources.[120] However, this raises a few problems, first most managers will examine CSR and its activities through economic notions of competitive advantage or an increase to the financial performance and it is far from certain that all CSR

116 N C Smith, 'Consumers as Drivers of CSR' in A Crane, A McWilliams, D Matten, J Moon and D Siegel (eds), *The Oxford Handbook of CSR* (Oxford University Press, New York 2008) 281–302

117 P I Swanson, 'CSR and the Oil Sector' (2002) 11(1) *CEPMLP Internet Journal* <http://www.dundee.ac.uk/cepmlp/journal/html/vol11/article11-1.html> accessed 10 September 2010

118 M Haigh and J Hazelton, 'Financial Markets: A Tool for Social Responsibility (2004) 52(1) *Journal of Business Ethics* 59–71

119 Ibid.

120 L Swanson, 'Top Managers as Drivers for Corporate Social Responsibility' in A Crane, A McWilliams, D Matten, J Moon and D Siegel (eds), *The Oxford Handbook of CSR* (Oxford University Press, New York 2008) 227–248

activities yield higher financial performance.[121] If, on the other hand, they simply drive for CSR on the basis of personal values certain agency issues may arise as they are deemed to be acting on behalf of the principal (the corporation) with its primary focus on its interests.[122]

The nature of CSR with its multiplicity of drivers in any given context means that the development of the net effect or overall picture is a crucial one. From a legal perspective this can be seen in the development and organisation of policies and laws pertaining to CSR. In a given context this could mean drafting an explicit CSR law or CSR policy which presents the overall picture of the interaction of CSR tools to achieve outlined aims or it could evolve in an organic way.[123]

Llewellyn makes an important point in this area which is relevant to newer concepts like CSR, he points out that 'in an aspect where from the overall picture not all traditional law is visible then that is a law choice at least . . .'.[124] It therefore becomes a legal choice to continue in CSR in a non-traditional format. It is pertinent at this point to reiterate that the history of CSR debates can be traced to the Berle-Dodd debate and the fundamental question of society's view of the role of the corporation.[125] This debate is valid for choices to be made in the doing of this law-job.

It affects the way in which CSR engages with law. This job also contains the overarching effect of 'goal orientation'. It indicates the direction that CSR is to take and that law has a role in shaping the future direction of CSR but this remains the law's choice. It can choose to engage more visibly in traditional forms or pluralistic forms. It can also choose to become more facilitative and less visible but that remains a law choice. It can choose to engage with CSR at different levels: local, national, regional or international but it can also engage in a variety of other ways. This choice for law is expressed through the law-makers who react to given contextual circumstances. However this law-job is what informs debates on the future of CSR, its role and its importance. It is a significant step to acknowledge that this is a relevant law-job, relevant to the essential function of CSR, which is

121 C A Adams, 'Internal Organizational Factors Influencing Corporate Social and Ethical Reporting: Beyond Current Theorising' (2002) 15(2) *Accounting, Auditing and Accountability* 223–250

122 J Salazar and B W Husted, 'Principals and Agents: Further Thoughts on the Friedmanite Critique of CSR' in A Crane, A McWilliams, D Matten, J Moon and D Siegel (eds), *The Oxford Handbook of CSR* (Oxford University Press, New York 2008) 137–155

123 The legal notion of written or unwritten constitutions comes to mind. For example, the EC Renewed Strategy (n. 96) seeks to promote its own international CSR policy while encouraging policies at the national, regional and local level with a peer review mechanism for national CSR policies. See EC Renewed Strategy (n. 96) 12

124 Llewellyn (n. 4) 1388

125 A A Berle Jr, 'Corporate Powers as Powers in Trust' (1931) 44 *Harvard Law Review* 1049–1074; E M Dodd, 'For Whom are Corporate Managers Trustees?' (1932) 45 *Harvard Law Review* 1145–1163; A A Berle Jr, 'For Whom Corporate Managers are Trustees: A Note' (1932) 45 *Harvard Law Review* 1365–1372

legitimising corporate power. This perspective adapted to a given context will allow for dialogue and goal orientation between the many identified drivers of CSR.

6.3.5 Juristic method

The juristic method may be best described as a law method. The first four law-jobs need doing and the juristic method refers to the chosen means to do the law-jobs. Llewellyn calls the problem of the juristic method, 'that of the ways of handling "legal" tools to law-job ends and of the on-going upkeep and improvement of both ways and tools'.[126] For him, as a legal realist, this points to the creation of institutional machinery. However, for CSR purposes, the focus is on the tools used to achieve law-jobs' objectives. The relevant point being that within CSR more legal tools may need to be examined or developed in line with the ongoing review and improvement which is required of both ways and tools.

With the doing of this law-job, it is important to acknowledge the context of CSR as a struggle for the legitimacy of corporate power, a site for hegemonic and counter-hegemonic struggles at various levels.[127] Therefore, the ongoing review of the ways of handling tools aimed at doing these law-jobs within the corporate-society relationship is of utmost importance.

Rajagopal points out that there is an increasing sensibility that law is a terrain of contestation between different actors including social movements and states and that a theory of law or adjudication that ignores this fact is inadequate.[128] It may be that there needs to be an established non-judicial remedial system as advocated by some researchers[129] but, on the other hand, it could also be that there is a need for the development of a relevant legal framework for CSR. However, it remains paramount that there should be ongoing improvement and a re-examination of the tools currently used in CSR. Where there is strong evidence that the juristic method used is not furthering the doing of the law-jobs, then this should become the basis for reform and improvement. That is to say, if law in CSR appears invisible or if the law-jobs are not being adequately handled,

126 Llewellyn (n. 4) 1392

127 B D Santos, *Towards a New Legal Common Sense: Law, Globalization and Emancipation* (Butterworths, London 2002), R Shamir, 'Corporate Social Responsibility: A Case of Hegemony and Counter-hegemony' in B De Sousa Santos and C A Rodriguez-Garavito (eds), *Law and Globalisation from Below – Towards a Cosmopolitan Legality* (Cambridge University Press, Cambridge 2005) 92–117, 95

128 B Rajagopal, 'Limits of Law in Counter-hegemonic Globalisation: The Indian Supreme Court and the Narmada Valley Struggle' in B De Sousa Santos and C A Rodriguez-Garavito (eds), *Law and Globalisation from Below – Towards a Cosmopolitan Legality* (Cambridge University Press, Cambridge 2005) 183–217, 183

129 Rees and Vermijis (n. 66)

rather than abandon CSR or assert law has little to do with CSR, it may be that some type of system reform is required.[130]

This often results in the pluralisation of normative opportunities and the earlier analysis of law and regulation is relevant in this regard. Law tools include the varied use of regulation for social control. This will permit the use of both traditional state law and non-state law to achieve law-job objectives. In other words regulation is a 'law tool' in the Llewellyn sense. It is not the only law tool as there can also be 'juristic' tools but for the use of non-state law extends to the examination of self-regulation and regulatory instruments proposed by international organisations, associations and corporations.

Such dynamism is necessary for law to have an extended and relevant role within CSR regulation and globalisation. It opens up the possibility for various permutations of law, regulation and CSR. The end result is uncertain and unpredictable but necessary in view of the changing and complex context of globalisation.[131]

6.4 Conclusion

The law-jobs approach creates a neutral framework which can be applied to different contexts to discover and examine how the role of law in legitimising corporate power is being performed. An adaptation of the law-jobs perspective can provide the legal theoretical basis that allows a broad overview of law's potential roles within CSR.

The chosen perspective of law-jobs presents a neutral legal perspective that allows flexibility in the form of law used but certainty about the roles it can play in corporate-society relationships. The law-jobs framework will therefore allow further analysis and research into areas of trouble disposition or dispute resolution in CSR, and highlight where there are existing instruments or new ones that need to be drafted, to handle the channelling or orientation of behaviour. The law-jobs perspective also engenders analysis and debate over the allocation of authority in matters pertaining to the relationships within CSR. It can provide an umbrella for the net direction which CSR so desperately needs. Finally it also provides for the examination and re-evaluation of law's tools for doing the jobs. This will lead to aspirational perspectives that raise questions of how they could be done better.

130 This is not the immediate goal of this book but reflects a suggestion borne out by the evaluation of the law-jobs. The new EC Renewed Strategy (n. 96) reflects this point.

131 'The pluralisation of normative opportunities for contestation, the outcomes of social movements' engagements with law are highly uncertain in terms of their impact either on law or on the movements themselves . . . the outcome of the dialectic between law and social movements seem to depend on a number of scripts that are both internal and external to law and seem to depend on particular local and national contexts. These scripts need to be unearthed and examined to properly appreciate the role of law . . .' Rajagopal (n. 128) 183

All of which is in line with first a 'questing' aspect and then a 'bettering' aspect. It paves the way for studies in context.

The law-jobs approach can provide a general universal CSR legal framework focused on the legitimacy objective which gains content and expression in context. This context can then be industry, geographic or even between specific parties in the corporate-society relationship.

7 Exemplifying a law-jobs approach – Shell in Nigeria

> No other single industry affected 20th Century civilisation more rapidly or more profoundly than the oil industry . . . throughout the 20th century – the most inventive hundred years that humanity has seen – oil was the great enabler, providing from one basic resource a rainbow range of products . . . fuels for heating, lighting and engine-power and lubricants . . . from textiles to the bases of perfumes.[1]

> Hydrocarbon contamination was found in water taken from 28 wells at 10 communities adjacent to the contamination site. At seven wells the samples were at least 1000 higher than the Nigerian drinking water standard of 3μg/l. Local communities are aware of the pollution and its dangers but state that they continue to use water for drinking, bathing, washing and cooking as they have no alternative . . . SPDC's own procedures have not been applied creating public safety issues.[2]

7.1 Introduction

The oil industry has a chequered social history.[3] Its history has been more global than most industries with a product essential to the contemporary way of life. The search for oil gave rise to some of the earliest MNCs as these corporations were from Europe and the United States seeking out oil reserves located in other areas of the world.[4] It has involved huge investment and intensive contact with the environment and local communities through exploration for oil. Oil as a

1 S Howarth, *A Century in Oil. The "Shell" Transport and Trading Company 1897–1997* (Weidenfeld & Nicolson, London 1997) 7

2 United Nations Environment Programme, *Environmental Assessment of Ogoniland Report* 2011 <http://www.unep.org/disastersandconflicts/CountryOperations/Nigeria/EnvironmentalAssessmentofOgonilandreport/tabid/54419/Default.aspx> accessed 16 August 2016, 11–12

3 Howarth (n. 1) 18 – 'in the 20th century, battles and even whole wars have been fought over the ownership of oil, and have been won or lost through possession or lack of it'

4 D Yergin, *The Prize: The Epic Quest for Oil, Money and Power* (New York, Free Press 2008)

product has also increased in importance over the years as more inventions in the developed world began to utilise oil as a source of energy.

Yet the industry, in the course of its oil business, has had issues with environmental pollution as a result of exploration, production and transportation activities. It has had health, safety and labour rights issues, conflicts with local communities for impacting on their human rights and several allegations of corrupt dealings with state governments in oil-rich countries.[5] These issues are all core areas of concern for CSR as they have a direct bearing on the relationship between society and the corporations, especially the accountability for power that their position affords the corporations.

Even the adoption of some CSR codes and practices in the oil industry was triggered by a series of 'critical incidents' arising from the aforementioned issues and the conflicts which they engendered.[6] Conflicts over these issues have focused society's attention on problems between the corporations active in this industry and the communities and other stakeholders present in the areas in which they operate. In this sense, the oil industry is the best choice for analysis as it represents the uneven effects of the global product of oil. It is also an industry that *prima facie* has attempted to engage with CSR demands.[7]

Shell in Nigeria has become synonymous with the CSR campaign both in Nigeria and globally. There have been a number of critical events, which forced the issue of CSR to the fore in the oil industry. First, the Exxon Valdez spill in 1989 highlighted the environmental effect of oil spills and then, more significantly, the dual problems of Shell with Brent Spar and Shell issues in Nigeria in 1995 publicised the explicit need for a holistic approach to CSR in the oil industry.[8]

5 S Pegg, 'World Leaders and Bottom Feeders: Divergent Strategies Toward Social Responsibility and Resources Extraction' in C May (ed.), *Global Corporate Power, Volume 15: International Political Economy Yearbook* (Lynne Rienner, Boulder, CO 2006) 249 -272; M Jungk, 'A Practical Guide to Addressing Human Rights Concerns for Companies Operating Abroad' in M K Addo (ed.), *Human Rights Standards and the Responsibility of Transnational Corporations* (Kluwer Law International, The Hague 1999) 171–186

6 P Watts, 'The International Petroleum Industry: Economic Actor or Social Activist?' in J Mitchell (ed.), *Companies in a World of Conflict* (London RIIA/Earthscan 1998) 23–31, discussing Shell Brent Spar and Shell Nigeria as critical incidents for Shell. He was the Group Managing Director of the Shell/Royal Dutch Group. There is a view that CSR in the oil industry can be seen as *'managing the relationship between actors (e.g. key stakeholders), activities (e.g. actions to handles critical incidents) and resources (e.g. internal ethical reporting')* (emphasis added). This rather pragmatic but narrow definition can be seen in T I Vaaland and M Heide, 'Managing Corporate Social Responsibility: Lessons from the Oil Industry'(2008) 13(2) *Corporate Communications: An International Journal* 212–225

7 P Utting and K Ives, 'The Politics of Corporate Responsibility and the Oil Industry' (2006) 2(1) *St Anthony's International Review* 11–34, 12

8 J G Frynas, *Beyond Corporate Social Responsibility: Oil Multinationals and Social Challenges* (Cambridge University Press, Cambridge 2009) 22

These two major critical incidents have influenced Shell's approach to CSR. In 1997, it presented the first Shell Sustainability Report titled *Profits and Principles – Does There Have to be a Choice?*[9] It set out the agenda very clearly:

> Clearly the forces of globalisation, rapid improvements in technology and dramatic changes in world order have caused considerable confusion over exactly what is and is not – expected of business. Should it play a bigger role in society, by providing infrastructure and social services where government does not and then face accusations that it is interfering or buying influence? Or should it concentrate on what it does best: serving its customer and getting best return for shareholders?[10]

These questions have not been effectively tackled, irrespective of all the action that has taken place since. This is because they are fundamental questions about the role and legitimacy of corporate power. It is difficult to delineate the exact scope of CSR. This is why it requires contextualisation and a continuous reassessment of tools, which can be provided by adopting the law-jobs approach.

In the report, Shell confirms the two events that caused the re-evaluation process to begin. Shell states that:

> we were all shaken by the tragic execution of Ken Saro-Wiwa and eight Ogonis by the Nigerian authorities; we were ill-prepared for the public reaction to plans to dispose of the Brent Spar off-shore storage buoy in deep water in the Atlantic.[11]

Brent Spar was a North Sea oil-storage and tanker-loading buoy operated by Shell. This facility was no longer in use and had to be decommissioned or disposed of. The options available to Shell were deep-sea disposal or onshore dismantling. Shell proposed deep-sea disposal. It had been granted a UK licence permitting such disposal. In 1995, Greenpeace activists occupied this facility in protest in a bid to stop such disposal; this sparked protests against Shell across Europe and resulted in a decline in sales. In the face of a huge onslaught of public outcry, falling share prices and consumer boycotts Shell decided to dismantle onshore. The figures given by Greenpeace on the amount of oil left on the spar were later proven to be inaccurate but Greenpeace maintained that 'the amount of oil left on the Brent spar was never central to the campaign'.[12] Shell then successfully

9 Shell Sustainability Report 1998 *Profits and Principles: : Does There Have to Be a Choice?* (Shell, London 1998)

10 Ibid. p. 4 (emphasis added)

11 Ibid. (emphasis added)

12 Greenpeace <http://www.greenpeace.org/australia/en/about/history/the-brent-spar> accessed 3 April 2016. See also P Owen and T Rice, *Decommissioning the Brent Spar* (Routledge (Spon Press), London 1999) 26

dismantled Brent spar onshore and it is now UK government policy and OSPAR Commission regulation to prohibit offshore dumping of such installations.[13]

Around the same period, Shell's operations in Nigeria were embroiled in human rights and environmental controversy.[14] Shell has been in Nigeria for over 70 years. It first gained an oil exploration licence as Shell D'Arcy in 1938 and discovered a commercial well in Oloibiri in 1956.[15] In the early 1990s Shell was accused of complicity in human rights abuses and environmental pollution. It had been severely criticised for its actions and inaction at crucial times during the crisis in the Niger delta leading up to the trial and execution of the 'Ogoni 9' under the then military dictator and president of Nigeria. Manby of the Human Rights Watch points out that international attention centred on Shell Nigeria for three major reasons:[16]

1. It was the biggest and longest-standing oil producer in Nigeria
2. Shell facilities were onshore and therefore directly exposed to community protests
3. It was the main target of the Movement for the Survival of Ogoni People (MOSOP), which accused the company of complicity in the alleged genocide of the Ogoni people.

Shell began a review of its actions and has been hailed for the strides it has made in CSR practice subsequently. However, its past actions have not been laid to rest. The Niger delta is still an area of great unrest, partly because of years of neglect and environmental pollution. For instance, the United Nations Environment Programme (UNEP) Environmental Assessment Report in 2011 pointed out that Shell's extraction in Ogoniland in Nigeria caused grave environmental harm with consequent impacts on health and well-being.[17] Shell's alleged complicity in the death of the 'Ogoni 9' and human rights violations has been the subject of litigation under the Aliens Tort Statute culminating in the US Supreme Court.[18]

13 E A Kirk, C Warbrick and G McGoldrick, 'OSPAR Decision 98/3 and the Dumping of Offshore Installations' (1999) 48(2) *International and Comparative Law Quarterly* 458–464

14 In 1995. See B Manby, *The Price of Oil: Corporate Responsibility and Human Rights Violations in Nigeria's Oil Producing Communities* (Human Rights Watch, New York 1999) 9

15 J G Frynas, *Oil in Nigeria: Conflict and Litigation between Oil Companies and Village Communities* (Lit Verlag, London 2000)

16 Manby (n. 14)

17 UNEP Report (n. 2)

18 *Kiobel v Royal Dutch Petroleum Co.* (2013)133 S. Ct. 1659. The case decided that there was a presumption of 'extraterritoriality', thus the substantive issues of complicity in human rights violations and extra-judicial killings remain unproven. For a synopsis of past cases see S Joseph, *Corporations and Transnational Human Rights Litigation* (Hart Publishing, Oxford 2004). For illuminating analysis post-Kiobel see C Kaeb and D Scheffer 'The Paradox of Kiobel in Europe' (2013) 107(4) *American Journal of International Law* 852–857; R McCorquodale, 'Waving not Drowning: Kiobel outside the United States' (2013) 107(4)

This chapter briefly analyses the context and examines the potential for applying the law-jobs approach.

7.2 Shell and the Nigerian context

In 1938, Shell D'Arcy was given an exploration licence for oil throughout Nigeria.[19] Shell and BP formed Shell D'Arcy to explore for oil in Nigeria.[20] The search for oil had moved global, to the Middle East, Persia and, later, Africa as demand for oil increased, through the wars and with the invention of cars and other modern amenities. Anglo-Persia (later British Petroleum (BP)) was formed to enable the search for oil in Persia and to fuel this demand for oil. The company was created in 1909 to explore oil discovered in Persia in 1908;[21] but received a huge investment boost from the British government in 1914 when Churchill, as first Lord of the Admiralty, became convinced that only a British-owned oil company would protect British interests and create a dedicated source of supply.[22] The French state invested in a similar manner in Total, which began in the Middle East (Iraq) in 1924 as the Compagnie Française des Pétroles (CFP).[23] The search for oil was fuelled by greater demand, more competition and the desire of states for dedicated sources of supply. In addition, advances in transportation had made it possible to explore farther regions and move the products to different markets.

In the industry, the product and markets were paramount and states sought to protect their vested interests in the product. This gave rise to issues of security of supply and the need to put in place agreements to secure ownership or oil rights. The first set of agreements for oil production took the form of oil concessions, which ceded rights to mineral development of large portions of land for long periods of time.[24] An example is William D'Arcy obtaining a concession from the

American Journal of International Law 846–851; A Grear and B H Weston, 'The Betrayal of Human Rights and the Urgency of Universal Corporate Accountability: Reflections in a Post-Kiobel Landscape' (2015) 15(1) *Human Rights Law Review* 21–44

19 <http://www.nnpcgroup.com/NNPCBusiness/BusinessInformation/OilGasinNigeria/IndustryHistory.aspx> (NNPC – Nigerian National Petroleum Corporation) accessed 30 April 2016

20 The Mineral Oil Ordinance of 1914 stipulated that oil licences and leases could only be granted to British Companies, see J Bamberg, *British Petroleum and Global Oil 1950–1975: The Challenge of Nationalism* (Cambridge University Press, Cambridge 2000) 109

21 Yergin (n. 4)

22 Howarth (n. 1)

23 Yergin (n. 4)

24 J S Dzienkowski, 'Concessions, Production Sharing and Participation Agreements for Developing a Country's Natural Resources' in E E Smith, J S Dzienkowski, O L Anderson, G B Conine, J S Lowe and B M Kramer, *International Petroleum Transactions* (Rocky Mountain Mineral Law Foundation (RMMLF), Denver, CO 2000) 392–478, 412; R O Anderson, *Fundamentals of the Petroleum Industry* (University of Oklahoma Press, Denver, CO 1984) 40; A Suleiman, 'The Oil Experience of the Middle East Emirates and Its Legal Framework' (1988) 6 *Journal of Energy and Natural Resources Law* 1, 3

Shah of Persia (modern-day Iran) in 1901 'for a $100,000 "bonus", another $100,000 in stock in his oil company and a 16% royalty and receiving exclusive oil rights to 500,000 square miles of Persia for the next 60 years'.[25] However, the host countries 'had no right to participate in managerial decisions', royalties were the main financial benefit and companies were free from taxation. Comparable agreements were reached in Saudi Arabia, Abu Dhabi and Kuwait for similar or an even greater number of years. These agreements were not in the best interest of the host countries as vast tracts of land were ceded to corporations for long periods of time. Inevitably, therefore, with the passage of time, the contractual agreements were renegotiated.

Shell itself was formed in 1897 through the initiative of Marcus Samuel, a trader in commodities including shells. Samuel perceived a business opportunity, which could be found in the counteraction of the dominance of the Rockefeller and Noble brothers.[26] His philosophy was simply that 'to outdo competition, the product must be at least good, cheaper if possible and somehow must provide added value to the customer'.[27] This is a philosophy that is discernible from Shell's company practices even today and may, in some regard, account for the foremost nature of its embrace of and approach to CSR and the desire to gain competitive advantage through some 'customer- perceived' added value. However, the current parent corporation is Royal Dutch Shell plc, a merger of Royal Dutch Petroleum Company and Shell Transport and Trading Company in 1907.[28]

For Nigeria, a major trigger for the renegotiation of the original licence was independence in 1960 and then joining OPEC in 1971. The formation of the Organisation of Petroleum Exporting Countries (OPEC) happened in 1960.[29] OPEC was formed by producing states as a reaction to a unilateral oil price slash

25 Ibid. William D'Arcy is in a sense the founder of modern BP. He was backed by Burmah Oil Company. The company was later reorganised as the Anglo-Persian Oil Company with him as director. Later it became Anglo-Iranian and, finally, BP

26 For the dominance of the Noble brothers in the Russian oil industry pre the revolution, see Howarth (n. 1) 29–30. For a detailed analysis of John D Rockfeller and the Standard oil empire, see Yergin (n. 4) 16–27. In 1911 Standard's oil monopoly was broken by the United States into 34 unrelated companies, with its anti-trust legislation through the Supreme Court judgment in the case of *Standard Oil Co of New Jersey v United States* 221 U.S 1 (1911). Some of the companies still survive today. Exxon, one of the largest oil MNCs, includes Standard Oil New Jersey (known as Esso). Later Exxon and Mobil, which was Standard Oil Company of New York (SOCONY), merged. Mobil merged with Exxon in 1999. Chevron, another large oil MNC, is an amalgamated form of the Standard Oil Company of California (SOCAL) and Gulf Oil Corporation. Texas Fuel Company (Texaco) merged with Chevron in 2001. In 1998 BP merged with Amoco, formerly Standard Oil of Indiana. It had also earlier acquired SOHIO (Standard Oil Ohio)

27 Howarth (n. 1) 37

28 See <http://www.shell.com/about-us/who-we-are/our-beginnings.html> accessed 30 April 2016

29 Dzienkowski (n. 24) 392–478, 418

by the oil companies.[30] The main oil companies at the time were Exxon (Esso), BP, Shell, Standard Oil of California, Mobil, Gulf and Texaco (referred to as 'the seven sisters'). OPEC, made up of the main producing countries – Iran, Iraq, Kuwait, Saudi Arabia and Venezuela, concluded that 'these seven multinationals were able to exercise tremendous control over production and prices of petroleum'[31] and decided to take a decisive role in the oil industry.

This led to a spate of nationalisations and the creation of new types of agreements such as the production sharing agreement and the joint venture.[32] While allowing for incentives and rewards for the risk-taking of oil multinationals, the contracts also enabled forms of state participation and reward. Production sharing contracts are contracts agreed between multinationals and the state to explore for oil, allowing the oil company to recover its cost and some profit before the commencement of production sharing between the multinational and the state. Joint ventures, on the other hand, involve partnerships formed either contractually or through the creation of an entity between the state and the oil multinational to develop and produce mineral resource in a specified area. The representative of the state in these arrangements is often a state-owned oil company. This accounts for the presence of state-owned oil companies in many developing oil-producing states. Examples include PDVSA (Petreoles de Venezuela S.A.), NNPC (Nigerian National Petroleum Corporation), PETROBRAS (Petroleo Brasileiro S/A), Saudi ARAMCO (Saudi Arabian Oil Company) and so on.

This coincided with a period of enthusiasm in developing countries for a New International Economic Order (NIEO) where a key factor for post-colonial countries was 'to regain effective control over their natural resources and economic activities'.[33] Yet ultimately this desire gave way in the 1980s and 90s to a fervour of neoliberal policies.[34]

30 Note, L Stoeher 'OPEC as a Legal Entity' (1979–1980) 3(1) *Fordham International Law Forum* 91–105, 92–93

31 Dzienkowski (n. 24)

32 Dzienkowski (n. 24) 419; R Fabrikant, 'Production Sharing Contracts in the Indonesian Petroleum Industry' (1975) 16(2) *Harvard International Law Journal* 303–351, 313; K Hossain, *Law and Policy in Petroleum Development* (Nichols Publishing Company, New York 1979)

33 The Declaration of the New International Economic Order (NIEO) UN General Assembly 1974 A/RES/S-6/3201 (1[h]); P Streeten, 'Approaches to a New International Economic Order' (1982) 10(1) *World Development* 1–17, 3

34 Sornarajah is of the view that 'though this was displaced by the fervour of neoliberalism, the ideas of the NIEO lived on and would be revived in the form of right to development, the Millennium Goals and recent declarations of the General Assembly requiring further study of the NIEO' – see M Sornarajah, *Resistance and Change in the International Law on Foreign Investment* (Cambridge University Press, Cambridge 2015) 329; see also Towards a New International Economic Order A/RES/64/209 <http://www.un.org/en/ga/search/view_doc.asp?symbol=A/RES/64/209> last accessed 30 April 2016

In Nigeria, Shell D'Arcy drilled the first successful well at Oloibiri in 1956 (they changed their name to Shell-BP Petroleum Development Company of Nigeria Ltd in the same year). Other oil MNCs were drawn to Nigeria because of the potential oil wealth and some joined the Nigerian oil industry in the early 1960s, after the end of British colonial rule. Frynas points out that 'the choice of exploration areas for newcomers was limited to areas previously abandoned by Shell-BP'.[35]

In Nigeria, post-independence of colonial rule, the period between the 1960s and the 1970s was a time of tremendous economic and political upheavals. Nigeria had the Biafra Civil War 1967–1970.[36] This involved the attempt of the south-eastern part of the country to secede. Some part of the drive to keep Nigeria as one can be traced to oil, because Nigeria, like most African post-colonial societies, is a conglomeration of diverse ethnic cultures.[37] There were some indigenisation attempts by the Nigerian government, which started in the 1970s,[38] but it can still be said that 'Shell has since maintained its head-start over the oil multinationals'.[39]

Shell in Nigeria is a domesticated corporation in line with Nigerian company law. Section 54 Companies and Allied Matters Act (CAMA) 1990 only permits a foreign company to carry out business in Nigeria if it incorporates a local subsidiary in the country.[40] Consequently Shell in Nigeria is the Shell Petroleum Development Company (SPDC) of Nigeria.[41] The SPDC operates in the upstream sector, which

35 Frynas (n. 15) 11. See also Shell Nigeria's SPDC website where it says 'SPDC is the pioneer and leader of the petroleum industry in Nigeria. It has the largest acreage in the country from which it produces some 39 per cent of the nation's oil'.' <http://www.shell.com.ng/aboutshell/our-business/bus-nigeria/e-and-p/spdc.html> last accessed 30 April 2016

36 F Forsyth, *The Biafra Story* (Pen & Sword, Barnsley 2015); 'Not being required to explain its policy at Question Time, big business has been able to keep much quieter over its true attitude towards the Nigeria-Biafra affair and participation in it than government'. p. 182

37 C Uche, 'Oil, British Interests and the Nigerian Civil War' (2008) 49(1) *The Journal of African History* 111–135. Uche argues that the British choice for 'one Nigeria' was partly prompted by British Investments in Shell-BP and the likelihood of a united Nigeria being a 'safer' bet for investment

38 This was predominantly the mood in developing countries at the time as indicated by the Declaration of the New Economic International Order UN General Assembly 1974 A/RES/S-6/3201. For Nigeria, see C Obi, 'Because of Oil: Understanding the Globalization of the Niger Delta and Its Consequences' in O Ukaga, U O Ukiwo and I S Ibaba, *Natural Resources, Conflict and Sustainable Development: Lessons from the Niger Delta* (Routledge, Abingdon 2014) 31; Frynas (n. 15) – Nigeria nationalised BP for political reasons, however Shell continued to run assets on its own

39 Obi ibid.

40 S. 56 allows certain exceptions

41 At least onshore. Shell Nigeria also has Shell Nigeria Exploration and Production Company (SNEPCO). It states that 'SNEPCO, 100% owned by Shell, was formed in 1993 to develop Nigeria's deep-water oil and gas resources offshore – the new frontier for the country's energy industry at the time. It signed a production-sharing contract with NNPC to operate two deep-water licences.' <http://www.shell.com.ng/aboutshell/our-business/bus-nigeria/e-and-p.html> accessed 30 April 2016

is the main earner for the country. The 2014 KPMG Oil and Gas Industry Brief states that:

> The upstream oil sector is the single most important sector in the economy, accounting for over 90% of the country's exports and about 80% of the Federal Government (FG's) revenue. Crude Oil is currently produced from three different basins: the onshore Anambra, the offshore Benin/Dahomey (deepwater and ultra-deepwater) and the Niger Delta (shallow and deep offshore basins). The Niger Delta and Benin basins are known to be the richest basins and hold the vast majority of reserves, and the source of a large portion of current production.[42]

Yet the Niger delta has become a crisis and conflict point for the oil industry predicated on a history of neglect, environmental pollution and local resistance. This is indicative of Santos' view of a major dichotomy within globalisation. On the one hand, the 'globalised localism', which is when a local phenomenon is globalised, for example, the worldwide spread of the MNC, and, on the other hand, 'localised globalism' which involves the altering of local conditions to respond to transnational imperatives, for example, depletion of resources to pay for debt.[43]

Nonetheless, some of the complexity of the conflicts cannot be reduced to simple dualisms because there are also ambiguities. These conflicts are primarily based on questions of oil pollution and violations of human rights and environmental rights but the 'local resistance' itself is not unproblematic. Obi identifies 'blurred boundaries, complexities, contradictions and ambiguities' in line with Gramsci's 'ambiguities of resistance'.[44] This covers questions of sabotage of oil installations and pipelines, oil theft and political conflict within resistance groups.[45]

CSR in this context is necessarily complex. Shell adopted its CSR policies as a 'defence' against accusations of inaction.[46] In such adoption they presented classic manifestations of power in trying to define the 'terms of engagement' but the

42 P. 5 (emphasis added)

43 B De Sousa Santos, *Towards a New Legal Common Sense* (2nd ed., Butterworths, London 2002) 179 (emphasis added)

44 Obi (n. 38) 27

45 A Etekpe, 'Non-governmental Organisations and Conflict Resolution in the Niger-Delta' in O Ukaga, U O Ukiwo and I S Ibaba, *Natural Resources, Conflict and Sustainable Development: Lessons from the Niger Delta* (Routledge, Abingdon 2014) 97–114, speaks in detail of the political problems which led to the loss of lives in Ogoni Kingdom and the divisions within the Movement for the Survival of the Ogoni People (MOSOP). C Katsouris and A Sayne, *Nigeria's Criminal Crude* (Chatham House, London September 2013). This focuses on oil theft often on an industrial scale:- <https://www.chathamhouse.org/sites/files/chathamhouse/. . ./0913pr_nigeriaoil_es.pdf> last accessed 30 April 2016

46 Frynas (n. 8) 6

local communities used the new-found publicity which globalisation now affords to attempt to transform their local issues into global demands for social responsibility with some limited success.[47] CSR in this context is clearly about legitimacy and accountability of power with issues of human rights, the environment, labour rights and corruption as 'triggers' and signs of the inadequate relationship between dominant oil companies and the local communities in which they operate.[48] This will also have implications for governmental responsibility although that is not the focus here.[49]

So, what can a law-jobs approach add to this context? Perhaps an opportunity to find out the role law has played and the roles that it could play in making a case for the reform of particular aspects of the society-corporation relationship. Thus, first a 'questing' aspect, that is, to discover the role of law in dispute resolution, channelling behaviour, net organisation, having the say and the methodology. This will lead to suggestions for a 'bettering' aspect, which will provide room for further research and legal action.

7.3 The quest[50]

There is significant legislation in Nigeria concerning the oil industry, although this does not address CSR directly.[51] The current legislation includes:[52] section 1 of the Nigerian Petroleum Act 1969, which vests the entire ownership and control of all petroleum in and under any lands in the state.[53] Section 1 Land Use Act 1978 also vests all land within the state in the state governor. Thus with the combination of both provisions, oil companies are able to achieve easy access to land and resources with the acquisition of licences. This is reinforced by a

47 This presents some interesting current research that I am involved in titled 'CSR from Below', an examination of counter-hegemonic uses of law in CSR

48 Manby (n. 14)

49 For the political role of corporations vis-à-vis states, especially with regard to development. see Frynas (n. 8) 170–171; see also U Idemudia, 'Corporate Social Responsibility and Development in Africa: Issues and Possibilities' (2014) 8(7) *Geography Compass* 421–435

50 'first of all the law-jobs is best interpreted as a heuristic device to look for legal or law-like phenomena . . . secondly Llewellyn makes room for judgements of variable achievement of the law jobs . . . finally in his broad approach he explicitly acknowledged that the law-job need not be performed by what is regarded as (official) law' S Taekema, 'The Point of Law: The Interdependent Functionality of State and Non-state Regulation' in H Van Schooten and J Verschuuren (eds), *International Governance and Law: State Regulation and Non-state Law* (Edward Elgar, Cheltenham 2008) 56–73, 57–58

51 Although a CSR bill was debated but not passed, see O Amao, *Corporate Social Responsibility, Human Rights and the Law* (Routledge, Abingdon 2011) 167

52 There are about 16 different pieces of relevant legislation. See KPMG Oil and Gas Industry Brief 2014 <https://www.kpmg.com/. . ./Nigerian%20oil%20and%20gas%20Industry%20 brief.pdf> last accessed 30 April 2016. See also Frynas (n. 15); Y Belgore, Problems with Oil Pollution Injury Litigation in the Nigerian Legal System: *Can Nigerian Litigants Gain Access to Courts in England and the USA?* PhD thesis, Dundee 2003 (unpublished)

53 Chapter 350 Laws of the Federation of Nigeria 1990

constitutional provision. Section 44(3) Constitution of the Federal Republic of Nigeria 1999 states that:

> (3) Notwithstanding the foregoing provisions of this section, the entire property in and control of all minerals, mineral oils and natural gas in under or upon any land in Nigeria or in, under or upon the territorial waters and the Exclusive Economic Zone of Nigeria shall vest in the Government of the Federation and shall be managed in such manner as may be prescribed by the National Assembly. [54]

There are significant protections for oil installations and licensee rights in the Oil Pipelines Act 1956 and the Petroleum Act 1969.

Nevertheless, there is also constitutional protection for a protected revenue allocation to the oil-producing states, which can be found in section 162(2):

> (2) The President, upon the receipt of advice from the Revenue Mobilisation Allocation and Fiscal Commission, shall table before the National Assembly proposals for revenue allocation from the Federation Account, and in determining the formula, the National Assembly shall take into account, the allocation principles especially those of population, equality of States, internal revenue generation, land mass, terrain as well as population density; Provided that the principle of derivation shall be constantly reflected in any approved formula *as being not less than thirteen per cent of the revenue* accruing to the Federation Account directly from any natural resources.[55]

The Supreme Court of Nigeria affirmed that this is only applicable to onshore resources.[56] There is also environmental legislation, which includes: the Federal Environmental Protection Act 1988 (as amended) with regulatory responsibility for the Nigerian Ministry of Environment to protect, develop and manage the environment; the Associated Gas Re-injection Act 1979 (as amended), which aims to stop the environmental polluting act of gas flaring; the Environmental Impact Assessment Act 1992,[57] which requires mandatory environmental impact assessment for oil and gas projects.

For the social development of the Niger delta, there is the Niger Delta Development Commission established in 2000 by the Niger Delta Development

54 This, however, allows the legislative assembly to pass laws from time to time which change the management structure and division of revenues

55 Constitution of the Federal Republic of Nigeria 1999 (emphasis added)

56 *Attorney-General of Nigeria v Attorney General of Abia & 35 others* 5 April 2002 (S.C. 28/2001). A copy of this judgment can be seen online <http://www.nigeria-law.org/LawReporting/2002/LawReporting2002.htm> accessed 30 April 2016

57 Originally a decree (made under military rule)

Commission Act which requires 'oil-producing companies operating in Nigeria to pay an annual contribution of 3 per cent of their total annual budget to the Commission'.[58] The Oil Pipelines Act also provides for compensation for disturbance of surface or other rights.[59] In addition, there is a right to adequate compensation for compulsory acquisition of land covered in section 44 of the Constitution of the Federal Republic of Nigeria 1999. This is reinforced by Nigeria's adoption of the Africa Charter of Human and People's Rights, Article 24, giving right to adequate compensation for environmental damage, although there is some uncertainty surrounding what is 'adequate compensation'.[60]

There is a renewed indigenisation effort through the Nigerian Oil Industry Content Development Act 2010 that aims to increase the level of Nigerian indigenous content in the oil industry[61] and the Nigerian Extractive Industries Transparency Initiative Act 2007, which enshrines the voluntary transparency and disclosure EITI standards in Nigerian law.

The overall picture emerging is not a lack of laws but rather a divergence between the laws and social realities on the ground. The oil industry is somewhat resistant to comprehensive reform. Wholesale reform is necessary because of the piecemeal nature in which legislation has developed in this area.[62] There has been a reform Petroleum Industry Bill since 2007 that has still not become an act. It has gone through many versions and the current one is the Petroleum Industry Governance Bill 2016.[63] The *Financial Times* estimates that the uncertainty and non-passage of the bill will cost Nigeria 'an estimated 470,000 in jobs and $100bn in lost investment by 2020'.[64]

The delay is partly linked to the opposition of oil companies to the wholesale reform of the industry, which would include tax and fiscal change, as well as a restructuring of the inefficient state oil company. However, the Petroleum Industry Bill (PIB) could also be a means of linking the oil revenues to contextual CSR demands.[65]

58 KPMG Oil and Gas Industry Brief 2014 (n. 52) 14. This is tax deductible. See also s. 14 (2)b Niger Delta Development Commission Act 2010 Laws of the Federation of Nigeria

59 S. 20

60 Belgore (n. 52) 85

61 For an overview of this regulatory framework, see L A Atsegbua, 'The Nigerian Oil and Gas Industry Content Development Act 2010: An Examination of Its Regulatory Framework' (2012) 36(4) *OPEC Energy Review* 479–494

62 This would include tax and fiscal legislation, see the KPMG Brief 2014 (n. 52)

63 See a dedicated website <http://www.petroleumindustrybill.com>

64 A Klassa, 'Nigeria's Oil Bill: Back to the Drawing Board' 9 July 2015, 'The controversial PIB aims to unify Nigeria's 16 petroleum laws in one document, while improving transparency at the NNPC. Stumbling blocks have included international oil companies' objections to royalty rate rises, disputes about revenue sharing from the federal oil account to each of Nigeria's 36 states, and the NNPC's resistance to increased oversight.'

65 A Okoye, 'Novel Linkages for Development: CSR, Law and Governance: Exploring the Nigerian Petroleum Industry Bill' (2012) 12(4) *Corporate Governance: International Journal of Business in Society* 460–471

Even with wholesale reforms, there is the palpable issue of the lack of enforcement of laws, which hints at some of the limitations of hard law: law's reliance on regulatory agencies, which can be bureaucratic, inefficient and sometimes corrupt, for enforcement. This is especially the case in the context of oil, where the oil rents provide some insulation for governments from taxable income and thus provide room for a distancing between the government and the governed.[66] For example, the limited impact of the Niger Delta Development Commission also hints at the wider governance issues in the area.[67]

Within Shell's own sphere of actions and influence are the conflicts over pollution. There have been significant oil pollution litigation and disputes. For a good summary of Nigerian cases see the work of Frynas.[68] Shell's position as joint-venture operator (operating the joint-venture form of oil production licence on behalf of the Nigerian government) has been pinpointed as the potential reason for often being the named party in disputes in this area.[69] However, it may also be that in its position as operator it has sometimes been found not to adopt best industry standards or even its own declared standards.[70]

There is significant evidence from the Frynas overview of cases of the additional use of torts law in Nigeria as legal bases in cases between local communities and oil companies such as Shell.[71] Victims of oil pollution have also utilised torts law on negligence, nuisance or strict liability following the principles of *Rylands v Fletcher.*[72] Having initially awarded low sums of compensation, Nigerian courts are now awarding significant sums as seen in *Shell Petroleum Development Company Nigeria Ltd v Farah*[73] and *Gbemre v Shell Petroleum Development Company Nigeria & Others.*[74]

Nigerian company law, similar to most common law systems, does not provide for company directors to take into account non-shareholder interests but it does

66 This rentier state effect can lead to a phenomenon known as the 'resource curse', where oil-rich states also manifest high levels of poverty and corruption (sometimes called the 'paradox of plenty'), see U Idemudia, 'Corporate Social Responsibility and the Rentier State: Rethinking the Role of Government and the Possibility of Corporate Social Development in the Niger Delta' (2010) 1–2 *Canadian Journal of Developmental Studies* 131–153; J D Sachs and A M Warner, 'The Curse of Natural Resources' (2001) 45(4–6) *European Economic Review* 827–838; R Auty, *Resource Abundance and Economic Development* (Oxford University Press, Oxford 2001). See also R Ako, 'Resource Exploitation and Environmental Justice: The Nigerian Experience' in F Botchway, *Natural Resouce Investment and Africa's Development* (Edward Elgar, Cheltenham 2011) 72–102

67 See Ako ibid.

68 Frynas (n. 15)

69 Belgore (n. 52) 76

70 UNEP Report (n. 2) calling for clean-up and remediation

71 Frynas (n. 15)

72 Frynas (n. 15), Belgore (n. 52)

73 (1995) 3 NWLR (Pt. 382)148

74 (2005) AHRLR 151 NgHC 2005. Gbemre in particular concerned the continued gas flaring pollution action carried out by Shell

provide for duties of the directors in section 279.[75] The overriding requirement is good faith: '279. (1) A director of a company stands in a fiduciary directors relationship towards the company and shall observe the utmost good faith towards the company in any transaction with it or on its behalf.' The lack of direct interest renders company law irrelevant to most litigation except as a shield for the corporation. In action by the Socio-Economic Rights and Accountability Project (SERAP) before the West African regional court (the Court of Justice of the Economic Community of West African States), the court held that it had no jurisdiction over corporations and so their names were struck off the suit.[76]

The lack of enforcement by regulatory agencies of environmental provisions complicates the situation.[77] There are also severe access to justice limitations, which include delay, cost and lack of enforcement of judgments.[78] This has prompted a move best attributed as 'globalisation from below', where NGOs and other non-state stakeholders have made attempts to use various legal instruments in resistance, that is, to sue MNCs such as Shell in their home countries. Shell has been taken to the US Supreme Court,[79] the English High Courts[80] and the Dutch courts with limited success.[81] The 'hard law' picture in the quest for law-jobs is one focused on judicial dispute resolution and overtly channelling conduct. The primary juristic method has been litigation.

In addition to this, other resources useful to CSR include codes, reports, tool kits and so on. In her study of documents on CSR, which guide behaviour, Leipziger highlighted the use of 'principles, codes of conduct, standards, norms, guidelines and framework agreements'.[82] Estimates place the number of such CSR resources that guide behaviour in the thousands.[83] The focus here is on codes

75 Companies and Allied Matters Act Laws of the Federation of Nigeria 1990

76 *SERAP v Federal Government of Nigeria* (2012) JUDGMENT N° ECW/CCJ/JUD/18/12 <http://www.courtecowas.org/site2012/pdf_files/decisions/judgements/2012/SERAP_V_FEDERAL_REPUBLIC_OF_NIGERIA.pdf> accessed 30 April 2016

77 R Ako, *Environmental Justice in African Countries* (Routledge, Abingdon 2013) 23–40

78 J G Frynas, 'Problems of Access to Courts in Nigeria: Results of a Survey of Legal Practitioners' (2001) 10 (3) *Social and Legal Studies* 397–419

79 *Kiobel v Royal Dutch Petroleum Co.* (2013) 133 S. Ct. 1659

80 Following *Chandler v Cape plc* the possibility of action against Shell in the UK opened up <https://www.leighday.co.uk/News/2015/January-2015/Shell-agrees-55m-compensation-deal-for-Nigeria-Del>, accessed 30 April 2016, and this led to action settled out of court and further action now being threatened <https://www.leighday.co.uk/News/News-2016/March-2016/Two-new-international-legal-actions-launched-again> accessed 30 April 2016

81 Cases propelled by Friends of the Earth Netherlands before the District Court of Hague: *Alfred Akpan v Shell, Oguru (Oguma) v Shell & Dooh (Goi) v Shell.* In December 2015, the Dutch court of appeal allowed Shell to provide access to documents <https://www.rechtspraak.nl/Organisatie-en-contact/Organisatie/Gerechtshoven/Gerechtshof-Den-Haag/Nieuws/Paginas/Dutch-Courts-have-jurisdiction-in-case-against-Shell-Nigeria-oil-spills.aspx> accessed 30 April 2016

82 D Leipziger, *The Corporate Responsibility Code Book* (2nd ed., Greenleaf, Sheffield 2010)

83 Ibid.

of conduct adopted by key oil industry multinationals such as Shell. CSR codes can be classed as 'soft law' and are subject to forms of regulation, albeit self-regulation.

The selection below is based on a review of the CSR codes and policies adopted by Shell as expressed on their websites and it attempts to cover a spectrum of codes of varying but representative types. It is also a reflection of Jenkins' general classification of codes into company codes, trade association codes, multi-stakeholder codes, model codes and intergovernmental codes[84] and the *Corporate Responsibility Code Book* list.[85] Within the industry each MNC has a CSR policy and code of conduct. In addition, some of the following CSR codes are widely cited:

- Extractive Industries Transparency Initiative (EITI) Statement of Principles and Agreed Actions
- The International Labour Organization (ILO) Declaration on Fundamental Principles and Rights at Work
- The Organisation for Economic Co-operation and Development Guidelines for Multinational Enterprises
- Transparency International Business Principles on Countering Bribery (2002)
- Principles for Countering Bribery (PACI)
- United Nations Declaration on Human Rights
- Voluntary Principles on Security and Human Rights
- UN Global Compact.

Each of these corporations produces CSR reports in accordance with the Global Reporting Initiative (GRI) and the International Petroleum Industry Environmental Conservation Association (IPIECA) guidelines, although the contents of the reports vary widely.

84 R Jenkins, 'Corporate Code of Conduct – Self-regulation in a Global Economy' UN Research Institute and Social Development Technology, Business and Society Programme, Paper No. 2 April 2001

85 Leipziger (n. 82)

The contents of these soft tools can be given the following law-jobs classification:

	Dispute resolution	*Channelling behaviour*	*The say: allocation of authority*	*Net organisation* **Specific areas*	*Juristic method*
Company code: (e.g. Shell Principles)	N	Y	Y	N *Company-related wide range of issues	Revisions & management systems
UN Global Compact	N	Y	N	N *HR, labour, environment & anti-corruption	Learning & dialogue reporting
EITI	N	Y	Y	N *Transparency & corruption	Incorporated in state law using reports & audits
Voluntary Principles on Security & HR	N	Y	Y	N *Security & human rights	Risk assessment & consultation
UDHR	N	Y	N	N *Human rights	None
ILO Fundamental Principles and Rights at Work	N	Y	Y	N *Labour	Tripartite structure & integration into state laws
OECD Guidelines for MNE	Y	Y	Y	N *Wide range of issues	Reports & national contact points
GRI	N	Y	Y	N *Reporting	Reporting framework
IPIECA/API Guidelines	N	Y	Y	N *Reporting & oil & gas	Reporting framework

From the foregoing analysis, it becomes evident that dispute resolution processes are omitted from most of these documents guiding behaviour. This corresponds with Leipziger's observation that few standards and codes contain formal written procedures for addressing complaints or resolving disputes.[86] Yet she admits that 'disputes will arise in most corporate responsibility systems, given different cultures and different interpretations . . .'.[87] The inclusion of dispute resolution procedures will serve as an indication of the utility of the codes in handling disputes that may arise as a result of deviance from the corporation's prescribed conduct. The UN Guiding Principles on Business and Human Rights 2011 through the third pillar, 'Access to Remedy', endorses this approach because it outlines that where people are harmed by business activities, there should be both adequate accountability and effective redress, judicial and non-judicial, including through effective operational-level grievance mechanisms.[88]

Whereas all the selected CSR resources are directed at channelling behaviour, their compliance can be deduced through the juristic method and the efficacy of its dispute resolution process. Very few codes are integrated into state law and there is predominance of reporting, system audits and other tools. With regard to net organisation, most tools deal with specific areas of focus that are classified by sector or by scope: such as human rights, labour, health, environment and anti-corruption. This points to a vacuum in the net organisation of CSR issues in the oil industry context: the involvement of key actors or stakeholders in the development of these resources is important and the allocation of responsibility will help with dispute resolution and further channelling of behaviour.

These roles are indicative of the legal aspects that further accountability and legitimacy processes for the use of power in the business-society relationship. It would perhaps be better to have all the relevant roles in a more comprehensive CSR document but CSR has not evolved in that fashion. It is a site of pluralisation of normative instruments. This plurality can make the net organisation somewhat difficult. Nevertheless when one examines CSR tools in a given context, it is important to deduce the doing of the roles, which go to accountability and legitimacy.

7.4 Conclusion – the 'bettering'

The law-jobs allow for an assessment of how the doing of dispute resolution, channelling conduct, allocation of authority, net organisation and juristic method is done. The brief quest into the context of Shell in Nigeria shows that the answer is simply 'not very well'. The assessment can be done in a more detailed fashion – this is just an example. The fuller assessment will serve as a basis for all stakeholders in corporations and society to interact and measure their interactive relationship in these key areas

86 Leipziger (n. 82) 49
87 Leipziger (n. 82) 49
88 <www.ohchr.org/Documents/Publications/GuidingPrinciplesBusinessHR_EN.pdf>

Werther and Chandler outline three kinds of stakeholder that affect corporations, corporate decisions and actions.[89] They are: organisational stakeholders, economic stakeholders and societal stakeholders.

- Organisational stakeholders exist within the organisation. They include shareholders, managers and even employees. These are the more traditional core groups which are within the scope of corporate models and corporate law.
- Economic stakeholders exist outside the organisation but have a direct effect on the organisation through finance and accountability. They are also contemplated within the traditional model of corporations and corporate law. This group includes creditors and consumers.
- Societal stakeholders exist outside the organisation and are often not recognised in the traditional model. Their effect is often external to the corporation but they are no less important because, as Dodd points out, business exists ultimately because society permits it to do so.[90]

CSR underscores this very issue that corporations must not lose sight of the point that ultimately they exist because society permits it. In a sense, actions taken in the credit crisis such as the bailing out of financial institutions demonstrate this point.[91] There is evidence to show that although investors remain vital stakeholders in the corporation, the societal stakeholders are no less important and, to a large extent, determine the business environment. This group includes the communities, government and NGOs. The situation in the Niger delta illustrates this point.

The contribution that a law-jobs approach would bring in this context is an opportunity to examine all the law-tools and their roles, highlighting both the vacuums and the opportunity for a 'bettering' aspect.

89 W B Werther Jr and D Chandler, *Strategic Corporate Social Responsibility: Stakeholders in a Global Environment* (Sage, Thousand Oaks, CA 2006) 4

90 E M Dodd, 'For Whom are Corporate Managers Trustees?' (1932) 45 *Harvard Law Review* 1145–1163

91 M Wolf, 'The Future of Capitalism: The Crisis is a Moment, but is It a Defining One?' *Financial Times* 19 May 2009

8 Conclusion

> What is emerging in the arena of CSR is a complex interaction between government, business, civil society, private, state regulation, at national and international levels, with social, legal, ethical and market pressures all being brought to bear in ways that cut across traditional pigeon-holes.[1]

8.1 Introduction

Traditional pigeonholes in law need not apply in deciphering a necessary and novel legal approach to CSR, especially in view of its core which is centred on the legitimacy of corporate power. The justification for this research can be found in the contestations about CSR's meaning and value as well as the contestations about the role of law within CSR. This must then be set against a background of critical incidents that have shown corporate irresponsibility and raised doubts about the value of an undefined concept. Horrigan points out that:

> A grand CSR is unfolding world-wide . . . this grand global CSR project remains a 21st century work-in-progress. Constructing tools for this grand CSR project at its highest levels of philosophical abstraction (e.g. theorising about corporate legitimacy) and collective effort (e.g. undertaking CSR-sensitive law reform across jurisdictions) is as important as discovering what works on the ground to embed CSR within individual companies and industry sectors (e.g. integrating CSR within standards business models).[2]

1 D McBarnet, 'Corporate Social Responsibility beyond Law, through Law, for Law: The New Corporate Accountability' in D McBarnet, A Voiculescu and T Campbell (eds), *The New Corporate Accountability: Corporate Social Responsibility and the Law* (Cambridge University Press, Cambridge 2007) 45–56, 55

2 B Horrigan, *Corporate Social Responsibility in the 21st Century: Debates, Models and Practices Across Government, Law and Business* (Edward Elgar, Cheltenham 2010) 339

The aspiration of this work is that it will have contributed to constructing tools that add to both theorising about corporate legitimacy and framing legal approaches that may shape future collective effort within CSR. The analysis within the research revealed the complexity within CSR.

By analysing from the perspective of an essentially contested concept, the book was able to identify a core for CSR which lies in the drive for legitimacy of corporate power in the face of the changing relationship between corporations and society in the context of globalisation. This globalised context is characterised by the emergence of various actors such as civil society, business groups and local communities. This pluralisation of actors within the CSR area appeared to be coupled with a de-emphasis on the role of law within CSR because of the fluidity of the concept. However, once CSR's core has been revealed the next question is, do law and legal approaches hold any potential for this core?

The research revealed that the meaning of CSR, centred on increasing corporate power and the consequential search for its legitimacy, would lead to an exploration for legal perspectives capable of addressing this core. The relevance of law to contemporary concepts such as this depends on law's ability to adapt to concepts which cut across 'traditional pigeon-holes'.[3]

The examination of legal approaches contrasted a traditional legal approach from corporate law with a non-traditional legal theoretical approach to law in 'law-jobs', to indicate that law can be viewed from both a traditional and a non-traditional approach. If the proposed law-jobs approach were adopted it would allow a broader overview of the role that law is capable of playing in the CSR relationship in order to legitimise power.

In the course of the examination it has been possible to gain novel insights into the relevant relationship between CSR and law. In this regard there are two underlying premises. First, that the extensions of law and its role are best conceived theoretically and, second, that this shift to a role-based pluralistic approach allows for the pluralisation of normative opportunities and the proper appreciation of the role of law under globalisation conditions. This book therefore suggests the law-jobs approach can provide a view of law that could help address CSR's core, which is the legitimacy of corporate power, by addressing the key areas of dispute resolution, channelling conduct, allocating authority and net organisation and the juristic method. This would provide scope for mapping, clearer identification of gaps and a basis for reform demands by relevant stakeholders. It is an approach that criss-crosses legal boundaries which are not recognised in globalised demands for social responsibility.

8.2 Contextual implications

The CSR law-jobs framework provides a systems-based analysis for anyone contemplating CSR law in context. It is inclusive of traditional legal approaches

3 McBarnet (n. 1) 55

but transforms the wider enquiry to a 'role-based' one. Therefore, it is possible to examine in a local context how these roles in the corporate-society relationship under CSR are being carried out and whether they could be done better. This is the sense in which Llewellyn comments that there is a questing aspect and a bettering aspect.[4] It responds to the need for a framework that is capable of giving structure to the role of law within CSR but it also gives flexibility because of the absence of its own content only allowing for roles which should be performed.

The substantive topics within CSR such as human rights, environment, labour and social issues can then be flexibly identified in each context towards adopted goals in that context so that even if more categories are identified the structure of law-jobs remains unaltered. This also does not detract from attempts to set universal standards for specific topics such as human rights because these rules will not affect the framework. They will only go to clarify the desired conduct for orientation.

When an analysis is carried out and it is discovered that in channelling conduct, the tools and instruments are weak or inadequate, the question of standards may be forced to come to the fore. The analysis may also reveal that where the standards (for example, codes of conduct) are not reorienting the conduct of corporations then perhaps other tools (such as regulation) can be explored. The juristic method allows for reform, re-evaluation and the potential for development of other law-tools that could do the law-jobs in a better way. Taekema points out

> first of all the law-jobs is best interpreted as a heuristic device to look for legal or law-like phenomena . . . secondly Llewellyn makes room for judgements of variable achievement of the law jobs . . . finally in his broad approach he explicitly acknowledged that the law-job need not be performed by what is regarded as (official) law.[5]

This approach provides a platform for a more contextual examination of CSR law. It allows a country, community or corporation to assess how the law-jobs in CSR are being done and to explore other law-tools that could be used to achieve a better doing of the law-jobs which then contributes to ensuring that such corporate power is exercised in an accountable and legitimate manner. This responds to ongoing issues of legitimacy and accountability by proposing a more nuanced role for law beyond the 'traditional legal' role. This inter-relational perspective allows room for stock-taking and review.

4 K Llewellyn, 'The Normative, the Legal and the Law Jobs: The Problem of the Juristic Method (1940) 49 *Yale Law Journal* 1355–1400

5 S Taekema, 'The Point of Law: The Interdependent Functionality of State and Non-state Regulation' in H Van Schooten and J Verschuuren (eds), *International Governance and Law: State Regulation and Non-state Law* (Edward Elgar, Cheltenham 2008) 56–73, 57–58

8.3 Conclusion and further research opportunities

This book establishes that CSR is centred on the legitimacy of corporate power and that this drive for legitimacy indicates the relevance of law. It examines the potential contribution of law from two perspectives: first, a traditional corporate law perspective because corporate law is seen as the home of laws for the corporations and reflects some universal legal notions about the corporate form. It discovers the important limitations of corporate theory that prevent corporate law from achieving the responsibility element of legitimacy. It then suggests a shift in focus within law from 'form' that is traditional substantive state law to a broader perspective that addresses questions of 'role'. The law-jobs perspective is suggested as a heuristic device that throws up fundamental question within CSR relevant to the responsibility and accountability element of legitimacy.

The analysis within the book represents a chosen approach to examining law's role in CSR. There are other approaches which could continue to explore the desirability of international or global laws, push for even more radical reform of corporate laws or even propose the irrelevance of law. This work does not detract from these other research aims which could be carried out in future. Rather, by redefining CSR and exploring the law-jobs it also provides a platform and wider framework for examining law within CSR.

This book, however, provides a useful framework for analysis in contextual circumstances, for example, exploring how these law-jobs are currently handled in the CSR sphere in specific countries or sectors. This type of research can be validly carried out from a legal approach applying the law-jobs framework. For example, there could be further detailed empirical research of how these law-jobs are currently handled in the CSR sphere of the Nigerian oil industry as justification for a push for reform on various levels. This approach highlights if and how the relationship is currently handling such jobs within CSR and can then go further to suggest a different or better way of handling the jobs.

Finally further research would attest to whether the law-jobs framework is a heuristic step that will ultimately lead to a body of CSR law that involves a mixture of state and non-state law linked through an enabling framework.

Index

For Product Safety Concerns and Information please contact our EU representative GPSR@taylorandfrancis.com Taylor & Francis Verlag GmbH, Kaufingerstraße 24, 80331 München, Germany